PENGUIN BOOKS

BROTHERS AND KEEPERS

Described by *The New York Times* as "one of America's pre-
mier writers of fiction," John Edgar Wideman published his
first novel, *A Glance Away,* in 1967 at the age of twenty-six.
His fifth novel, *Send for You Yesterday,* brought him the PEN/
Faulkner Award in 1984. His most recent novels are the
widely acclaimed *Philadelphia Fire* (1990) and *Reuben*
(1987), as well as *Fever* (1990), a collection of twelve short
stories. His other works of fiction include *Hurry Home*
(1969), *The Lynchers* (1973), *Damballah* (1981), and *Hiding
Place* (1981). Mr. Wideman lives in Amherst and teaches at
the University of Massachusetts.

SEP 1 5 1953

JOHN EDGAR WIDEMAN

BROTHERS AND KEEPERS

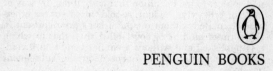

PENGUIN BOOKS

PENGUIN BOOKS
Published by the Penguin Group
Viking Penguin, a division of Penguin Books USA Inc.,
375 Hudson Street, New York, New York 10014, U.S.A.
Penguin Books Ltd, 27 Wrights Lane, London W8 5TZ, England
Penguin Books Australia Ltd, Ringwood, Victoria, Australia
Penguin Books Canada Ltd, 2801 John Street,
Markham, Ontario, Canada L3R 1B4
Penguin Books (N.Z.) Ltd, 182–190 Wairau Road, Auckland 10, New Zealand

Penguin Books Ltd, Registered Offices:
Harmondsworth, Middlesex, England

First published in the United States of America by
Holt, Rinehart and Winston 1984
Published in Penguin Books by arrangement with
Holt, Rinehart and Winston 1985

10 9 8

Copyright © John Edgar Wideman, 1984
All rights reserved

LIBRARY OF CONGRESS CATALOGING IN PUBLICATION DATA
Wideman, John Edgar.
  Brothers and keepers.
  Reprint. Originally published: New York: Holt,
Rinehart and Winston, 1984.
    1. Wideman, Robert Douglas, 1950–
2. Wideman, John Edgar.   3. Afro-American
criminals—Biography.   4. Brothers—United States—
Biography.   I. Title.
HV6245.W733   1985   364.3′092′4 [B]   85-9344
ISBN 0 14 00.8267 0

Grateful acknowledgment is made for permission to
quote from the song "Family Affair," by Sylvester Ste-
wart. Copyright © 1971 Warner-Tamerlane Publishing
Corp. and Stone Flower Music, Inc. All rights administered by Warner-Tamerlane Publishing Corp. All rights
reserved.

Printed in the United States of America
Set in Primer

Except in the United States of America, this book is
sold subject to the condition that it shall not, by way of
trade or otherwise, be lent, re-sold, hired out, or otherwise circulated without the publisher's prior consent in
any form of binding or cover other than that in which
it is published and without a similar condition including this condition being imposed on the subsequent
purchaser.

To Bette Wideman
Whose love, whose sweet dream of freedom blesses all her children

CONTENTS

AUTHOR'S NOTE

The style, the voices that speak this book, are an attempt to capture a process that began in earnest about four years ago: my brother and I talking about our lives.

To learn my brother's story I visited him in prison and listened to what he had to say. I'd take a few notes—names, dates, sequences of events—then, some time later, after I'd had an opportunity to absorb his words but while they were still fresh in my mind, I would reproduce on paper what I'd heard. Robby would read what I'd written and respond either when I visited him next or by letter. His suggestions and corrections usually concerned factual matters, although his sense of larger issues, of truth and correctness, his feeling for narrative tone and pace, as well as the invaluable quotes from his letters and poems, added immensely to the final result. As a novelist, I have had lots of practice creating written versions of speech, so I felt much more confident about borrowing narrative techniques learned from fiction than employing a tape recorder.

I read many books about prison and prisoners, talked long hours to family members, especially my mother, reviewed court transcripts, newspaper files, and police reports in order to document events and educate myself. I gratefully acknowledge these sources, but also take full responsibility for the final mix of memory, imagination, feeling and fact. Reconstructing the tragic chain of circumstances that caused one young man to die and sent three others to prison for life has been a harrowing experience. In the hope that there is something to learn from this account, something to salvage from the grief and waste, I've striven for accuracy and honesty. Some names have been changed to protect the privacy of people mentioned in the text.

—*John Edgar Wideman*

VISITS

When I was a very little child, oh, about six or seven, I had a habit of walking down Walnut and Copeland streets; you know those streets. As I walked I would look at the cars and in my mind I would buy them, but they only cost nickels or dimes. Big ones a dime, little ones a nickel, some that I liked a whole lot would cost a quarter. So as I got older this became a habit. For years I bought cars with the change that was in my pocket, which in those times wasn't very much.

Now this was a kind of wish, but more than that it was a way of looking at things—an unrealistic way—it's like I wanted things to be easy, and misguidedly tried to make everything that way, blinded then to the fact that nothing good or worthwhile comes without serious effort. What I'm trying to say is that while I was walking through life I had a distorted view of how I wanted things to be rather than how they really were or are. Always wanted things to be easy; so instead of dealing with things as they were, I didn't deal with them at all. I ducked hard things that took effort or work and tried to have fun, make a party, cause that was always easy.

I heard the news first in a phone call from my mother. My youngest brother, Robby, and two of his friends had killed a man during a holdup. Robby was a fugitive, wanted for armed robbery and murder. The police were hunting him, and his crime had given the cops license to kill. The distance I'd put between my brother's world and mine suddenly collapsed. The two thousand miles between Laramie, Wyoming, and Pittsburgh, Pennsylvania, my years of willed ignorance, of flight and hiding, had not changed a simple truth: I could never run fast enough or far enough. Robby was inside me. Wherever he was, running for his life, he carried part of me with him.

Nearly three months would pass between the day in November 1975 when I learned of my brother's crime and the February afternoon he appeared in Laramie. During that period no one in the family knew Robby's whereabouts. After the initial reaction of shock and disbelief subsided, people in Pittsburgh had settled into the inevitability of a long, tense wait. Prayers were said. As word passed along the network of family and friends, my people, who had long experience of waiting and praying, braced themselves for the next blow. A special watch was set upon those, like my mother, who would be hardest hit. The best was hoped for, but the worst expected; and no one could claim to know what the best might be. No news was good news. No news meant Robby hadn't been apprehended, that whatever else he'd lost, he still was free. But knowing nothing had its dark side, created a concern that sometimes caused my mother, in spite of herself, to pray for Robby's capture. Prison seemed safer than the streets. As long as he was free, there was a chance Robby could hurt someone or be killed. For my mother and the others who loved him, the price of my brother's freedom was a constant, gnawing fear that anytime the phone rang or a bulletin flashed across the TV screen, the villain, the victim might be Robert Wideman.

Because I was living in Laramie, Wyoming, I could shake loose from the sense of urgency, of impending disaster dogging my people in Pittsburgh. Never a question of forgetting Robby, more a matter of how I remembered him that distinguished my feelings from theirs. Sudden flashes of fear, rage, and remorse could spoil a class or a party, cause me to retreat into silence, lose whole days to gloominess and distance. But I had the luxury of dealing intermittently with my pain. As winter deepened and snow filled the mountains, I experienced a comforting certainty. The worst wouldn't happen. Robby wouldn't be cut down in a wild cops-and-robbers shootout, because I knew he was on his way to find me. Somehow, in spite of everything, we were going to get together. I was waiting for him to arrive. I knew he would. And this certainty guaranteed his safety.

Perhaps it was wishful thinking, a whistling away of the miles and years of silence between us, but I never doubted a reunion would occur.

On a Sunday early in February, huge, wet flakes of snow were falling continuously past the windows of the house on Harney Street—the kind of snow not driven by wolf winds howling in from the north, but soft, quiet, relentless snow, spring snow almost benign in the unhurried way it buried the town. The scale of the storm, the immense quantities of snow it dumped minute after minute, forced me to remember that Laramie was just one more skimpy circle of wagons huddling against the wilderness. I had closed the curtains to shut out that snow which seemed as if it might never stop.

That Sunday I wrote to my brother. Not a letter exactly. I seldom wrote letters and had no intention of sticking what I was scribbling in an envelope. Mailing it was impossible anyway, since I had no idea where my brother might be. Really it was more a conversation than a letter. I needed to talk to someone, and that Sunday Robby seemed the perfect someone.

So I talked to him about what I'd learned since coming west. Filled him in on the news. Shared everything from the metaphysics of the weather to the frightening circumstances surrounding the premature birth of Jamila, our new daughter. I explained how winter's outrageous harshness is less difficult to endure than its length. How after a tease of warm, springlike weather in late April the sight of a snowflake in May is enough to make a grown man cry. How Laramie old-timers brag about having seen snow fall every month of the year. How I'd almost killed my whole family on Interstate 80 near the summit of the Laramie range, at the beginning of our annual summer migration east to Maine, when I lost control of the Oldsmobile Custom Cruiser and it did a 360 on the icy road in the middle of June.

The letter rambled on and on for pages. Like good talk, it digressed and recycled itself and switched moods precipitously. Inevitably, one subject was home and family. After all, I was speaking to my brother. Whatever the new news happened to be, there was the old news, the deep roots of shared time and place and blood. When I touched on home, the distance between us melted. I could sense Robby's presence, just over my shoulder, a sensation so real I was sure I could have reached out and touched him if I had lifted my eyes from the page and swiveled my chair.

Writing that Sunday, I had no reason to believe my brother was on his way to Laramie. No one had heard from him in months. Yet he was on his way and I knew it. Two men, hundreds of miles apart, communicating through some mysterious process neither understood but both employed for a few minutes one Sunday afternoon as efficiently, effectively as dolphins talking underwater with the beeps and echoes of their sonar. Except that the medium into which we launched our signals was thin air. Thin, high mountain air spangled with wet snowflakes.

I can't explain how or why but it happened. Robby was in the study with me. He felt close because he was close, part of him outrunning the stolen car, outrunning the storm dogging him and his partners as they fled from Salt Lake City toward Laramie.

Reach out and touch. That's what the old songs could do. I'd begun that Sunday by reading a week-old *New York Times*. One of the beauties of living in Laramie. No point in frantically striving to keep abreast of the *Times*. The race was over before the paper arrived in town, Thursday after the Sunday it was published. The *Times* was stale news, all its urgency vitiated by the fact that I could miss it when it was fresh and the essential outline of my world, my retreat into willed ignorance and a private, leisurely pace would continue unchanged.

Five minutes of the paper had been enough; then I repacked the sections into their plastic sheath, let its weight pull it off the couch onto the rug. Reach out and touch. Sam Cooke and the Soul Stirrers, the Harmonizing Four, James Cleveland, the Davis Sisters, the Swan Silvertones. I dug out my favorite albums and lined them up against the stereo cabinet. A cut or two from each one would be my Sunday morning service. Deejaying the songs got me off my backside, forced me out of the chair where I'd been sitting staring at the ceiling. With good gospel tunes rocking the house I could open the curtains and face the snow. The sky was blue. Shafts of sunlight filtered through a deluge of white flakes. Snow, sunshine, blue sky, not a ripple of wind deflecting the heavy snow from its straight, downward path. An unlikely conjunction of elements perfectly harmonized. Like the pain and hope, despair and celebration of the black gospel music. Like the tiny body of the baby girl in her isolette, the minuscule, premature, two-pound-fourteen-ounce bundle of bone and sinew and nerve and will that had fought and continued to fight so desperately to live.

The songs had stirred me, flooded me with memories and sensations to the point of bursting. I had to talk to someone. Not anyone close, not anyone who had been living through what I'd been experiencing the past three years in the West. A stranger's ear would be better than a friend's, a stranger who wouldn't interrupt with questions, with alternate versions of events. I needed to do most of the talking. I wanted a listener, an intimate stranger, and summoned up Robby; and he joined me. I wrote something like a letter to wherever my brother might be, to whomever Robby had become.

Wrote the letter and of course never sent it, but got an answer anyway in just two days, the following Tuesday toward the end of the afternoon. I can pinpoint the hour because I was fixing a drink. Cocktail time is as much a state of mind as a particular hour, but during the week five o'clock is when I usually pour a stiff drink for myself and one for my lady if she's in the mood. At five on Tuesday, February 11, Robby phoned from a bowling alley down the street and around the corner to say he was in town.

Hey, Big Bruh.

Hey. How you doing? Where the hell are you?

We're in town. At some bowling alley. Me and Michael Dukes and Johnny-Boy.

In Laramie?

Yeah. Think that's where we's at, anyway. In a bowling alley.

Them nuts is bowling. Got to get them crazy dudes out here before they tear the man's place up.

Well, youall c'mon over here. Which bowling alley is it?

Just a bowling alley. Got some Chinese restaurant beside it.

Laramie Lanes. It's close to here. I can be there in a minute to get you.

Okay. That's cool. We be in the car outside. Old raggedy-ass Oldsmobile got Utah plates. Hey, man. Is this gon be alright?

What do you mean?

You know. Coming by your house and all. I know you heard about the mess.

Mom called and told me. I've been waiting for you to show up. Something told me you were close. You wait. I'll be right there.

In Pittsburgh, Pennsylvania, on November 15, 1975, approximately three months before arriving in Laramie, my youngest brother Robert (whom I had named), together with Michael Dukes and Cecil Rice, had robbed a fence. A rented truck allegedly loaded with brand-new Sony color TVs was the bait in a scam designed to catch the fence with a drawer full of money. The plan had seemed simple and foolproof. Dishonor among thieves. A closed circle, crooks stealing from crooks, with the law necessarily excluded. Except a man was killed. Dukes blew him away when the man reached for a gun Dukes believed he had concealed inside his jacket.

Stop. Stop, you stupid motherfucker.

But the fence broke and ran and kept running deaf and dumb to everything except the pounding of his heart, the burning in his lungs, as he dashed crouching like a halfback the fifty feet from the empty rental truck to an office at one corner of his used-car lot. He'd heard the gun pop and pop again as he stumbled and scrambled to his feet but he kept running, tearing open the fatal shoulder wound he wasn't even aware of yet. Kept running and kept pumping blood and pumping his arms and legs past the plate-glass windows of the office, past a boundary of plastic banners strung above one edge of the lot, out into the street, into traffic, waving his arms to get someone to stop. He made it two blocks up Greys Pond Road, dripping a trail of blood, staggering, stumbling, weaving up the median strip between four lanes of cars. No one wanted anything to do with a guy drunk or crazy enough to be playing in the middle of a busy highway. Only when he pitched face first and lay crumpled on the curb did a motorist pull over and come to his aid.

Meanwhile, at the rear of the rental truck, a handful of money, coins, and wadded bills the dying man had flung down before he ran, lay on the asphalt between two groups of angry, frightened men. Black men. White men. No one in control. That little handful of chump change on the ground, not enough to buy two new Sonys at K Mart, a measure of the fence's deception, proof of the game he intended to run on the black men, just as they'd planned their trick for him. There had to be more money somewhere, and somebody would have to pay for this mess, this bloody double double-cross; and the men stared across the money at each other too choked with rage and fear to speak.

By Tuesday when Robby called, the chinook wind that had melted Sunday's snow no longer warmed and softened the air. "Chinook" means "snow-eater," and in the high plains country—Laramie sits on a plateau seven thousand feet above sea level—wind and sun can gobble up a foot of fresh snow from the ground in a matter of hours. The chinook had brought spring for a day, but just as rapidly as it appeared, the mellow wind had swept away, drawing in its wake arctic breezes and thick low-lying clouds. The clouds which had darkened the sky above the row of tacky, temporary-looking storefronts at the dying end of Third Street where Laramie Lanes hunkered.

Hey, Big Bruh.

Years since we'd spoken on the phone, but I had recognized Robby's voice immediately. He'd been with me when I was writing Sunday, so my brother's voice was both a shock and no surprise at all.

Big Brother was not something Robby usually called me. But he'd chimed the words as if they went way back, as if they were a touchstone, a talisman, a tongue-in-cheek greeting we'd been exchanging for ages. The way Robby said "Big Bruh" didn't sound phony, but it didn't strike me as natural either. What I'd felt was regret, an instant, devastating sadness because the greeting possessed no magic. If there'd ever been a special language we shared, I'd forgotten it. Robby had been pretending. Making up a magic formula on the spot. *Big Bruh.* But that had been okay. I was grateful. Anything was better than dwelling on the sadness, the absence, better than allowing the distance between us to stretch further. . . .

On my way to the bowling alley I began to ask questions I hadn't considered till the phone rang. I tried to anticipate what I'd see outside Laramie Lanes. Would I recognize anyone? Would they look like killers? What had caused them to kill? If they were killers, were they dangerous? Had crime changed my brother into someone I shouldn't bring near my house? I recalled Robby and his friends playing records, loud talking, giggling and signifying in the living room of the house on Marchand Street in Pittsburgh. Rob's buddies had names like Poochie, Dulamite, Hanky, and Bubba. Just kids messing around, but already secretive, suspicious of strangers. And I had been a stranger, a student, foreign to the rhythms of their lives, their talk as I sat, home from college, in the kitchen talking to Robby's mother. I'd have to yell into the living room sometimes. Ask them to keep the noise down so I could hear myself think. If I walked through the room, they'd fall suddenly silent. Squirm and look at each other and avoid my eyes. Stare at their own hands and feet mute as little speak-no-evil monkeys. Any question might get at best a nod or grunt in reply. If five or six kids were hanging out in the little living room they made it seem dark. *Do wop, do wop* forty-fives on the record player, the boys' silence and lowered eyes conjuring up night no matter what time of the day I passed through the room.

My father had called them thugs. Robby and his little thugs. The same word he'd used for me and my cut buddies when we were coming up, loafing around the house on Copeland Street, into playing records and bullshucking about girls, and saying nothing to nobody not part of our gang. Calling Rob's friends thugs was my father's private joke. Thugs not because they were incipient criminals or particularly bad kids, but because in their hip walks and stylized speech and caps pulled down on their foreheads they were declaring themselves on the lam, underground, in flight from the daylight world of nice, respectable adults.

My father liked to read the Sunday funnies. In the "Nancy" comic strip was a character named Sluggo, and I believe that's who my father had in mind when he called them thugs. That self-proclaimed little tough guy, snub-nosed, bristle-haired, knuckleheaded Sluggo. Funny, because like Sluggo they were dead serious about the role they were playing. Dead serious and fooling nobody. So my father had relegated them to the funny papers.

Road grime caked the windows of the battered sedan parked outside the bowling alley. I couldn't tell if anyone was inside. I let my motor run, talked to the ghost of my brother the way I'd talked that Sunday, waiting for a flesh-and-blood version to appear.

Robby was a fugitive. My little brother was wanted for murder. For three months Robby had been running and hiding from the police. Now he was in Laramie, on my doorstep. Robbery. Murder. Flight. I had pushed them out of my mind. I hadn't allowed myself to dwell on my brother's predicament. I had been angry, hurt and afraid, but I'd had plenty of practice cutting myself off from those sorts of feelings. Denying disruptive emotions was a survival mechanism I'd been forced to learn early in life. Robby's troubles could drive me crazy if I let them. It had been better to keep my feelings at a distance. Let the miles and years protect me. Robby was my brother, but that was once upon a time, in another country. My life was relatively comfortable, pleasant, safe. I'd come west to escape the demons Robby personified. I didn't need outlaw brothers reminding me how much had been lost, how much compromised, how terribly the world still raged beyond the charmed circle of my life on the Laramie plains.

In my Volvo, peering across the street, searching for a sign of life in the filthy car or the doorway of Laramie Lanes, pieces of my life rushed at me, as fleeting, as unpredictable as the clusters of cloud scudding across the darkening sky.

Rob: Hey, Rob. Do you remember the time we were living on the third floor of Grandma's house on Copeland Street and we were playing and Daddy came scooting in from behind the curtain where he and Mommy slept, dropping a trail of farts, blip, blip, blip, and flew out the door and down the steps faster than anybody'd ever made it before? I don't know what he was doing or what we were doing before he came farting through the room, but I do remember the stunned silence afterward, the five of us kids looking at one another like we'd seen the Lone Ranger and wondering what the hell was that. Was that really Daddy? Were those sounds actual blipping farts from the actual behind of our actual father? Well, we sat on the floor, staring at each other, a couple seconds; then Tish laughed or I laughed. Somebody had to start it. A choked-back, closed-mouth, almost-swallowed, one-syllable laugh. And then another and another. As irresistible then as the farts blipping in a train from Daddy's pursed behind. The first laugh sneaks out then it's all hell bursting loose, it's one pop after another, and mize well let it all hang out. We crack up and start to dance. Each one of us takes a turn being Edgar Wideman, big daddy, scooting like he did across the floor, fast but sneakylike till the first blip escapes and blows him into overdrive. Bip. Blap. Bippidy-bip. And every change and permutation of fart we can manufacture with our mouths, or our wet lips on the back of our hands, or a hand cupped in armpit with elbow pumping. A Babel of squeaky farts and bass farts and treble and juicy and atom-bomb and trip-hammer, machine-gun, suede, firecracker, slithery, bubble-gum-cracking, knuckle-popping, gone-with-the-wind menagerie of every kind of fart we can imagine. Till Mommy pokes her head from behind the curtain and says, That's enough youall. But she can't help grinning her ownself cause she had to hear it too. Daddy trailing that wedding-car tin-can tail of farts and skidding down the steps to the bathroom on the second floor where he slammed the door behind himself before the door on the third floor had time to swing shut. Mom's smiling so we sputter one last fusillade and grin and giggle at each other one more time while she says again, That's enough now, that's enough youall.

Robby crossed Third Street alone, leaving his friends behind in the muddy car. I remember how glad I was to see him. How ordinary it seemed to be meeting him in this place he'd never been before. Here was my brother miraculously appearing from God-knows-where, a slim, bedraggled figure, looking very much like a man who's been on the road for days, nothing like an outlaw or killer, my brother striding across the street to greet me. What was alien, unreal was not the man but the town, the circumstances that had brought him to this juncture. By the time Robby had reached my car and leaned down smiling into the open window, Laramie, robbery, murder, flight, my litany of misgivings had all disappeared.

Rob rode with me from the bowling alley to the Harney Street house. Dukes and Johnny-Boy followed in the Olds. Rob told me Cecil Rice had split back to Pittsburgh to face the music. Johnny-Boy was somebody Robby and Mike had picked up in Utah.

Robby and his two companions stayed overnight. There was eating, drinking, a lot of talk. Next day I taught my classes at the university and before I returned home in the afternoon, Robby and his crew had headed for Denver. My brother's last free night was spent in Laramie, Wyoming. February 11, 1976, the day following their visit, Robby, Mike, and Johnny were arrested in Fort Collins, Colorado. The Oldsmobile they'd been driving had stolen plates. Car they'd borrowed in Utah turned out to be stolen too, bringing the FBI into the case because the vehicle and plates had been transported across state lines. The Colorado cops didn't know the size of the fish in their net until they checked the FBI wire and suddenly realized they had some "bad dudes" in their lockup. "Niggers wanted for Murder One back East" was how one detective described the captives to a group of curious bystanders later, when Robby and Michael were being led, manacled, draped with chains, through the gleaming corridor of a Colorado courthouse.

I can recall only a few details about Robby's last night of freedom. Kentucky Fried Chicken for dinner. Nobody as hungry as I thought they should be. Michael narrating a tale about a basketball scholarship he won to NYU, his homesickness, his ambivalence about the Apple, a coach he didn't like whose name he couldn't remember.

Johnny-Boy wasn't from Pittsburgh. Small, dark, greasy, he was an outsider who knew he didn't fit, ill at ease in a middle-class house, the meandering conversations that had nothing to do with anyplace he'd been, anything he understood or cared to learn. Johnny-Boy had trouble talking, trouble staying awake. When he spoke at all, he stuttered riffs of barely comprehensible ghetto slang. While the rest of us were talking, he'd nod off. I didn't like the way his heavy-lidded, bubble eyes blinked open and searched the room when he thought no one was watching him. Perhaps sleeping with one eye open was a habit forced upon him by the violent circumstances of his life, but what I saw when he peered from "sleep," taking the measure of his surroundings, of my wife, my kids, me, were a stranger's eyes, a stranger's eyes with nothing in them I could trust.

I should have understood why the evening was fragmentary, why I have difficulty recalling it now. Why Mike's story was full of inconsistencies, nearly incoherent. Why Robby was shakier than I'd ever seen him. Why he was tense, weary, confused about what his next move should be. I'm tired, man, he kept saying. I'm tired. . . . You don't know what it's like, man. Running . . . running. Never no peace. Certain signs were clear at the time but they passed right by me. I thought I was giving my guests a few hours' rest from danger, but they knew I was turning my house into a dangerous place. I believed I was providing a respite from pursuit. They knew they were leaving a trail, complicating the chase by stopping with me and my family. A few "safe" hours in my house weren't long enough to come down from the booze, dope, and adrenaline high that fueled their flight. At any moment my front door could be smashed down. A gunfire fight begin. I thought they had stopped, but they were still on the road. I hadn't begun to explore the depths of my naïveté, my bewilderment.

Only after two Laramie Police Department detectives arrived at dawn on February 12, a day too late to catch my brother, and treated me like a criminal, did I know I'd been one. Aiding and abetting a fugitive. Accessory after the fact to the crime of first-degree murder. The detectives hauled me down to the station. Demanded that I produce an alibi for the night a convenience store had been robbed in Utah. Four black men had been involved. Three had been tentatively identified, which left one unaccounted for. I was black. My brother was a suspect. So perhaps I was the fourth perpetrator. No matter that I lived four hundred miles from the scene of the crime. No matter that I wrote books and taught literature and creative writing at the university. I was black. Robby was my brother. Those unalterable facts would always incriminate me.

Robby passed through Laramie briefly and continued on his way. That's about it. I wished for more, then and now. Most of what I can recall makes the evening of his visit seem bland, uneventful, though an incident in Jamila's room, beside her crib, is an exception. That and the moment I watched Robby's shoulders disappear down the hallway stairs to the kids' playroom, where a roll-away cot and some extra mattresses had been set out for sleeping. Those moments imprinted. I'll carry the sounds and sights to my grave.

I'd been alone with my brother a few minutes in the kitchen, then in the hall outside Jamila's room. I advised him to stay in Laramie a few days, catch his breath, unwind. Warned him about the shoot-em-up mentality of Western cops, the subtle and not-so-subtle racism of the region. How three black men in a car would arouse suspicion anytime, anywhere they stopped.

Little else to say. I started a thousand conversations inside my head. None was appropriate, none addressed Robby's anguish, his raw nerves. He was running, he was afraid, and nothing anyone said could bring the dead man in Pittsburgh back to life. I needed to hear Robby's version of what had happened. Had there been a robbery, a shooting? Why? Why?

In our first private moment since I'd picked him up at Laramie Lanes, as we stood outside the baby's room, my questions never got asked. Too many whys. Why did I want to know? Why was I asking? Why had this moment been so long in coming? Why was there a murdered man between us, another life to account for, now when we had just a few moments alone together? Perhaps Robby did volunteer a version of the crime. Perhaps I listened and buried what I heard. What I remember is telling him about the new baby. In the hall, then in her room, when we peeked in and discovered her wide awake in her crib, I recounted the events surrounding her birth.

Jamila. Her name means "beautiful" in Arabic. Not so much outer good looks as inner peace, harmony. At least that's what I've been told. Neither Judy nor I knew the significance of the name when we chose it. We just liked the sound. It turns out to fit perfectly.

Your new niece is something else. Beautiful inside and out. Hard to believe how friendly and calm she is after all she's been through. You're the first one from home to see her.

I didn't tell my brother the entire story. We'd need more time. Anyway, Judy should fill in the gory details. In a way it's her story. I'd almost lost them both, wife and daughter. Judy had earned the right to tell the story. Done the bleeding. She was the one who nearly died giving birth.

Besides, on that night eight years ago I wasn't ready to say what I felt. The incidents were too close, too raw. The nightmare ride behind an ambulance, following it seventy miles from Fort Collins to Denver. Not knowing, the whole time, what was happening inside the box of flashing lights that held my wife. Judy's water had broken just after a visit to a specialist in Fort Collins. Emergency procedures were necessary because she had developed placenta previa, a condition that could cause severe hemorrhaging in the mother and fatal prematurity for her baby. I had only half listened to the doctor's technical explanation of the problem. Enough to know it could be life-threatening to mother and infant. Enough to picture the unborn child trapped in its watery cell. Enough to get tight-jawed at the irony of nature working against itself, the shell of flesh and blood my woman's body had wrapped round our child to protect and feed it also blocking the exit from her womb. Placenta previa meant a child's only chance for life was cesarian section, with all the usual attendant risks extremely heightened.

Were the technicians in the back of the ambulance giving blood, taking blood? Were they administering oxygen to my wife? To our child? Needles, tubes, a siren wailing, the crackle of static as the paramedics communicated with doctors in Denver. Had the fetus already been rushed into the world, flopping helpless as a fish because its lungs were still too much like gills to draw breath from the air?

A long, bloody birth in Denver. Judy on the table three and a half hours. Eight pints of blood fed into her body as eight pints seeped out into a calibrated glass container beside the operating table. I had watched it happening. Tough throughout the cutting, the suturing, the flurries of frantic activity, the appearance of the slick, red fetus, the snipping of the umbilical, the discarding of the wet, liverish-looking, offending bag, tough until near the end when the steady ping, ping, ping of blood dripping into the jar loosened the knot of my detachment and my stomach flip-flopped once uncontrollably, heaving up bile to the brim of my throat. Had to get up off the stool then, step back from the center of the operating room, gulp fresh air.

With Judy recovered and Jamila home, relatively safe after a two-month ordeal in the hospital, I still couldn't talk about how I had felt during my first visit to the preemie ward at Colorado General. I was shocked by the room full of tiny, naked, wrinkled infants, each enclosed in a glass cage. Festooned with tubes and needles, they looked less like babies than like ancient, shrunken little men and women, prisoners gathered for some bizarre reason to die together under the sizzling lights.

Jamila's arms and legs were thinner than my thinnest finger. Her threadlike veins were always breaking down from the pressure of I.V.'s. Since I.V.'s were keeping her alive, the nurses would have to search for new places to stick the needles. Each time she received an injection or had her veins probed for an I.V., Jamila would holler as if she'd received the final insult, as if after all the willpower she'd expended enduring the pain and discomfort of birth, no one had anything better to do than jab her one more time. What made her cries even harder to bear was their tininess. In my mind her cries rocked the foundations of the universe; they were bellows anything, anywhere with ears and a soul could hear. In fact, the high-pitched squeaks were barely audible a few feet from her glass cage. You could see them better than hear them because the effort of producing each cry wracked her body.

My reactions to the preemie ward had embarrassed me. I couldn't help thinking of the newborns as diseased or unnatural, as creatures from another planet, miniature junkies feeding in transparent kennels. I had to get over the shame of acknowledging my daughter was one of them. Sooner than I expected, the shame, the sense of failure disintegrated and was replaced by fear, a fear I had yet to shake. Would probably never completely get over. The traumas attending her birth, the long trial in the premature ward, her continuous touch-and-go flirtation with death had enforced the reality of Jamila's mortality. My fear had been morbid at first but gradually it turned around. Each breath she drew, each step she negotiated became cause for celebration. I loved all my children, but this girl child was precious in a special way that had brought me closer to all three. Life and death. Pain and joy. Having and losing. You couldn't experience one without the other. Background and foreground. The presence of my daughter would always remind me that things didn't have to be the way they were. We could have lost her. Could lose her today. And that was the way it would always be. Ebb and flow. Touch and go. Her arrival shattered complacency. When I looked in her eyes I was reminded to love her and treasure her and all the people I loved because nothing could be taken for granted.

I had solemnly introduced the new baby to my brother.

This is your Uncle Robby.

Robby's first reaction had been to say, grinning from ear to ear, She looks just like Mommy. . . . My God, she's a little picture of Mom.

As soon as Robby made the connection, its rightness, its uncontestability, its uncanny truth hit me. Of course. My mother's face rose from the crib. I remembered a sepia, tattered-edged, oval portrait of Mom as a baby. And another snapshot of Bette French in Freeda

French's lap on the steps of the house on Cassina Way. The fifty-year-old images hovered, opaque, halfway between the crib and my eyes, then faded, dissolving slowly, blending into the baby's face, alive inside the new skin, part of the new life, linked forever by my brother's words.

Robby took the baby in his arms. Coochy-cooed and gently rocked her, still marveling at the resemblance.

Lookit those big, pretty brown eyes. Don't you see Mommy's eyes?

Time continues to loosen my grasp on the events of Robby's last free night. I've attempted to write about my brother's visit numerous times since. One version was called "Running"; I conceived of it as fiction and submitted it to a magazine. The interplay between fiction and fact in the piece was too intense, too impacted, finally too obscure to control. Reading it must have been like sitting down at a bar beside a stranger deeply involved in an intimate conversation with himself. That version I'd thought of as a story was shortened and sent to Robby in prison. Though it didn't quite make it as a story, the letter was filled with stories on which I would subsequently draw for two novels and a book of short fiction.

Even as I manufactured fiction from the events of my brother's life, from the history of the family that had nurtured us both, I knew something of a different order remained to be extricated. The fiction writer was also a man with a real brother behind real bars. I continued to feel caged by my bewilderment, by my inability to see clearly, accurately, not only the last visit with my brother, but the whole long skein of our lives together and apart. So this book. This attempt to break out, to knock down the walls.

At a hearing in Colorado Johnny-Boy testified that Robby had recounted to him a plot to rob a fence, a killing, the flight from Pittsburgh. After his performance as a cooperative witness for the state, a performance he would repeat in Pittsburgh at Robby's trial, Johnny-Boy was carted away to Michigan, where he was wanted for murder. Robby and Michael were extradited to Pittsburgh, charged with armed robbery and murder, and held for trial. In separate trials both were convicted and given the mandatory sentence for felony murder: life imprisonment without possibility of probation or parole. The only way either man will ever be released is through commutation of his sentence. Pennsylvania's governor is empowered to commute prison sentences, and a state board of commutations exists to make recommendations to him; but since the current governor almost never grants commutations, men in Pennsylvania's prisons must face their life sentences with minimal hope of being set free.

Robby remained in custody six months before going on trial. Not until July 1978, after a two-year lockup in a county jail with no facilities for long-term prisoners, was Robby sentenced. Though his constitutional rights to a speedy trial and speedy sentencing had clearly been violated, neither those wrongs nor any others—including a prejudiced charge to the jury by the trial judge—which were brought to the attention of the Pennsylvania Supreme Court, moved that august body to intercede on Robert Wideman's behalf. The last legal action in Robby's case, the denial of his appeal by the Supreme Court of Pennsylvania, did not occur until September 1981. By that time Robby had already been remanded to Western State Penitentiary to begin serving a life sentence.

You never know exactly when something begins. The more you delve and backtrack and think, the more clear it becomes that nothing has a discrete, independent history; people and events take shape not in orderly, chronological sequence but in relation to other forces and events, tangled skeins of necessity and interdependence and chance that after all could have produced only one result: what is. The intertwining strands of DNA that determine a creature's genetic predispositions might serve as a model for this complexity, but the double helix, bristling with myriad possibilities, is not mysterious enough. The usual notion of time, of one thing happening first and opening the way for another and another, becomes useless pretty quickly when I try to isolate the shape of your life from the rest of us, when I try to retrace your steps and discover precisely where and when you started to go bad.

When you were a chubby-cheeked baby and I stood you upright, supporting most of your weight with my hands but freeing you just enough to let you feel the spring and bounce of strength in your new, rubbery thighs, when you toddled those first few bowlegged, pigeon-toed steps across the kitchen, did the trouble start then? Twenty-odd years later, when you shuffled through the polished corridor of the Fort Collins, Colorado, courthouse dragging the weight of iron chains and fetters, I wanted to give you my hands again, help you make it across the floor again; I shot out a clenched fist, a black power sign, which caught your eye and made you smile in that citadel of whiteness. You made me realize I was tottering on the edge, leaning on you. You, in your baggy jumpsuit, three days' scraggly growth on your face because they didn't trust you with a razor, manacled hand and foot so you were theatrically displayed as their pawn, absolutely under their domination; you were the one clinging fast, taking the weight, and your dignity held me up. I was reaching for your strength.

Always there. The bad seed, the good seed. Mommy's been saying for as long as I can remember: That Robby . . . he wakes up in the morning looking for the party. She's right, ain't she? Mom's nearly always right in her way, the special way she has of putting words together to take things apart. Every day God sends here Robby thinks is a party. Still up there on the third floor under his covers and he's thinking, Where's it at today? What's it gonna be today? Where's the fun? And that's how he's been since the day the Good Lord put him on this earth. That's your brother, Robert Douglas Wideman.

The Hindu god Venpadigedera returned to earth and sang to the people: Behold, the light shineth in all things. Birds, trees, the eyes of men, all giveth forth the light. Behold and be glad. Gifts wait for any who choose to see. Cover the earth with flowers. Shower flowers to the four corners. Rejoice in the bounty of the light.

The last time we were all together, cousin Kip took a family portrait. Mom and Daddy in a line with their children. The third generation of kids, a nappy-headed row in front. Five of us grown-up brothers and sisters hanging on one another's shoulders. Our first picture together since I don't remember when. We're all standing on Mom's about-to-buckle porch with cousin Kip down in the weeds of the little front yard pointing his camera up at us. I was half-scared those rickety boards would crack and we'd sink, arms still entwined, like some brown *Titanic*, beneath the rippling porch floor.

Before I saw the picture I had guessed how we'd look frozen in shades of black and white. I wasn't too far off. Tish is grinning ear to ear—the proud girl child in the middle who's survived the teasing and protections of her four brothers. Even though he isn't, Gene seems the tallest because of the way he holds that narrow, perfect head of his bal-

anced high and dignified on his long neck. Dave's eyes challenge the
camera, meet it halfway and dare it to come any closer, and the camera
understands and keeps its distance from the smoldering eyes. No matter what Dave's face seems to be saying—the curl of the lip that could
be read as smile or sneer, as warning or invitation—his face also projects another level of ambiguity, the underground history of interracial
love, sex, and hate, what a light-eyed, brown-skinned man like David
embodies when he confronts other people. I'm grinning too (it's obvious
Tish is my sister) because our momentary togetherness was a reprieve,
a possibility I believed I'd forfeited by my selfishness and hunger for
more. Giddy almost, I felt like a rescued prince ringed by his strong,
handsome people, my royal brothers and sister who'd paid my ransom.
Tickled even by the swell and pitch of the rotting porch boards under
my sandals.

You. You are mugging. Your best side dramatically displayed. The
profile shot you'd have demanded on your first album, the platinum
million seller you'd never cut but knew you could because you had talent and brains and you could sing and mimic anybody and that long
body of yours and those huge hands were instruments more flexible
and expressive than most people's faces. You knew what you were capable of doing and knew you'd never get a chance to do it, but none of
that defeat for the camera, no, only the star's three-quarter profile. Billy
Eckstineing your eyes, the Duke of Earl tilting the slim oval of your face
forward to emphasize the pout of your full lips, the clean lines of your
temples and cheekbones tapering down from the Afro's soft explosion.
Your stage would be the poolroom, the Saturday-night basement social,
the hangout corner, the next chick's pad you swept into with all the el-
egance of Smokey Robinson and the Count of Monte Cristo, slowly un-
buttoning your cape, inching off your kid gloves, everything
pantomimed with gesture and eye flutters till your rap begins and your
words sing that much sweeter, purer for the quiet cradling them.
You're like that in the picture. Stylized, outrageous under your big
country straw hat pushed back off your head. Acting. And Tish, holding
up the picture to study it, will say something like, Look at you, boy. You
ought to be 'shamed. And your mask will drop and you'll grin cause Tish
is like Mom, and ain't no getting round her. So you'll just grin back and
you are Robby again at about age seven, cute and everybody's pet, grin
at Sis and say, "G'wan, girl."

Daddy's father, our grandfather, Harry Wideman, migrated from Greenwood, South Carolina, to Pittsburgh, Pennsylvania, in 1906. He found a raw, dirty, double-dealing city. He learned its hills and rivers, the strange names of Dagos and Hunkies and Polacks who'd been drawn, as he had, by steel mills and coal mines, by the smoke and heat and dangerous work that meant any strong-backed, stubborn young man, even a black one, could earn pocketfuls of money. Grandpa's personal quest connected him with hordes of other displaced black men seeking a new day in the promised land of the North. Like so many others, he boarded in an overcrowded rooming house, working hard by day, partying hard at night against the keen edge of exhaustion. When his head finally hit the pillow, he didn't care that the sheets were still warm from the body of the man working nights who rented the bed ten hours a day while Harry pulled his shift at the mill.

Harry Wideman was a short, thick, dark man whose mahogany color passed on to Daddy, blended with the light, bright skin of John and Freeda French's daughter Bette to produce the brown we wear. Do you remember anything about him, or were you too young? Have you ever wondered how the city appeared through his eyes, the eyes of a rural black boy far from home, a stranger in a strange land? Have you ever been curious? Grandpa took giant steps forward in time. As a boy not quite old enough to be much help in the fields, his job was looking out for Charley Rackett, his ancient, crippled grandfather, an African, a former slave. Grandpa listened to Charley Rackett's African stories and African words, then lived to see white men on the moon. I think of Grandpa high up on Bruston Hill looking over the broad vista spreading out below him. He's young and alone; he sees things with his loins as much as his eyes. Hills rolling to the horizon, toward the invisible rivers, are breasts and buttocks. Shadowed spaces, nestling between the rounded hills, summon him. Whatever happens to him in this city, whatever he accomplishes will be an answer to the soft, insinuating challenge thrown up at him as he stares over the teeming land. This city will measure his manhood. *Our Father Who art* . . . I hear prayer words interrupting his dreaming, disturbing the woman shapes his glance fashions from the landscape. The earth turns. He plants his seed. In the blink of an eye he's an old man, close to death. He has watched the children of his children's children born in this city. Some of his children's children dead already. He ponders the wrinkled tar paper on the backs of his hands. Our Father. A challenge still rises from the streets and rooftops the way it once floated up from long-gone, empty fields. And the old man's no nearer now to knowing, to understanding why the call digs so deeply at his heart.

Wagons once upon a time in the streets of Pittsburgh. Delivering ice and milk and coal. Sinking in the mud, trundling over cobblestones, echoing in the sleep of a man who works all day in the mouth of a fiery furnace, who dreams of green fish gliding along the clear, stony bottom of a creek in South Carolina. In the twenty years between 1910 and 1930, the black population of Pittsburgh increased by nearly fifty thousand. Black music, blues and jazz, came to town in places like the Pythian Temple, the Ritz, the Savoy, the Showboat. In the bars on the North Side, Homewood, and the Hill you could get whatever you thought you wanted. Gambling, women, a good pork chop. Hundreds of families took in boarders to earn a little extra change. A cot in a closet in somebody's real home seemed nicer, better than the dormitories with their barracks-style rows of beds, no privacy, one toilet for twenty men. Snores and funk, eternal coming and going because nobody wanted to remain in those kennels one second longer than he had to. Fights, thieves, people dragged in stinking drunk or bloody from the streets, people going straight to work after hanging out all night with some whore and you got to smell him and smell her beside you while you trying to pull your shift in all that heat. Lawd. Lawdy. Got no money in the bank. Joints was rowdy and mean and like I'm telling you if some slickster don't hustle your money in the street or a party-time gal empty your pockets while you sleep and you don't nod off and fall in the fire, then maybe you earn you a few quarters to send home for that wife and them babies waiting down yonder for you if she's still waiting and you still sending. If you ain't got no woman to send for then maybe them few quarters buy you a new shirt and a bottle of whiskey so you can find you some trifling body give all your money to.

The strong survive. The ones who are strong and *lucky*. You can take that back as far as you want to go. Everybody needs one father, two grandfathers, four great-grandfathers, eight great-great-grandfathers, sixteen great-great-great-grandfathers, then thirty-two, then sixty-four, and that's only eight generations backward in time, eight generations linked directly, intimately with what you are. Less than 150 years ago, 128 men made love to 128 women, not all in the same hotel or on the same day but within a relatively short expanse of time, say twenty years, in places as distant as Igboland, New Amsterdam, and South Carolina. Unknown to each other, probably never even coming face to face in their lifetimes, each of these couples was part of the grand conspiracy to produce you. Think of a pyramid balanced on one of its points, a vast cone of light whose sides flare outward, vectors of force like the slanted lines kids draw to show a star's shining. You once were a pinprick of light, a spark whose radiance momentarily upheld the design, stabilized the ever-expanding V that opens to infinity. At some inconceivable distance the light bends, curves back on itself like a ram's horn or conch shell, spiraling toward its greatest compass but simultaneously narrowing to that needle's eye it must enter in order to flow forth bounteously again. You hovered at that nexus, took your turn through that open door.

The old people die. Our grandfathers, Harry Wideman and John French, are both gone now. The greatest space and no space at all separates us from them. I see them staring, dreaming this ravaged city; and we are in the dream, it's our dream, enclosed, enclosing. We could walk down into that valley they saw from atop Bruston Hill and scoop up the houses, dismantle the bridges and tall buildings, pull cars and trucks off the streets, roll up roads and highways and stuff them all like toys into the cotton-picking sacks draped over our shoulders. We are that much larger than the things that happen to us. Accidents like the city poised at the meeting of three rivers, the city strewn like litter over precipitous hills.

Did our grandfathers run away from the South? Black Harry from Greenwood, South Carolina, mulatto white John from Culpepper, Virginia. How would they answer that question? Were they running from something or running to something? What did you figure you were doing when you started running? When did your flight begin? Was escape the reason or was there a destination, a promised land exerting its pull? Is freedom inextricably linked with both, running *from* and running *to*? Is freedom the motive and means and end and everything in between?

I wonder if the irony of a river beside the prison is intentional. The river was brown last time I saw it, mud-brown and sluggish in its broad channel. Nothing pretty about it, a working river, a place to dump things, to empty sewers. The Ohio's thick and filthy, stinking of coal, chemicals, offal, bitter with rust from the flaking hulls of iron-ore barges inching grayly to and from the steel mills. But viewed from barred windows, from tiered cages, the river must call to the prisoners' hearts, a natural symbol of flight and freedom. The river is a path, a gateway to the West, the frontier. Somewhere it meets the sea. Is it somebody's cruel joke, an architect's way of giving the knife a final twist, hanging this sign outside the walls, this river always visible but a million miles away beyond the spiked steel fence guarding its banks?

When I think of the distance between us in terms of miles or the height and thickness of walls or the length of your sentence or the deadly prison regimen, you're closer to me, more accessible than when I'm next to you in the prison visiting room trying to speak and find myself at the edge of a silence vaster than oceans. I turned forty-three in June and you'll be thirty-three in December. Not kids any longer by any stretch of the imagination. You're my little brother and maybe it's generally true that people never allow their little brothers and sisters to grow up, but something more seems at work here, something more damaging than vanity, than wishful thinking that inclines us to keep our pasts frozen, intact, keeps us calling our forty-year-old cronies "the boys" and a grown man "little brother." I think of you as little brother because I have no other handle. At a certain point a wall goes up and easy memories stop.

When I think back, I have plenty of recollections of you as a kid. How you looked. The funny things you said. Till about the time you turned a gangly, stilt-legged, stringbean thirteen, we're still family. Our lives connect in typical, family ways: holidays, picnics, births, deaths, the joking and teasing, the time you were a baby just home from the hospital and Daddy John French died and I was supposed to be watching you while the grown-ups cleaned and cooked, readying the house on Finance Street for visitors, for Daddy John to return and lie in his coffin downstairs. Baby-sitting you in Aunt Geraldine's room while death hovered in there with us and no way I could have stayed in that room alone. Needing you much more than you needed me. You just zzz'ed away in your baby sleep, your baby ignorance. You couldn't have cared less whether death or King Kong or a whole flock of those loose-feathered, giant birds haunting my sleep had gathered round your crib. If the folks downstairs were too quiet, my nerves would get jumpy and I'd snatch you up and walk the floor. Hold you pressed in my arms against my heart like a shield. Or if the night cracks and groans of the house got too loud, I'd poke you awake, worry you so your crying would keep me company.

After you turned thirteen, after you grew a mustache and fuzz on your chin and a voluminous Afro so nobody could call you "Beanhead" anymore, after girls and the move from Shadyside to Marchand Street so you started Westinghouse High instead of Peabody where the rest of us had done our time, you begin to get separate. I have to struggle to recall anything about you till you're real again in prison. It's as if I was asleep for fifteen years and when I awakened you were gone. I was out of the country for three years then lived in places like Iowa City and Philly and Laramie, so at best I couldn't have seen much of you, but the sense of distance I'm trying to describe had more to do with the way I related to you than with the amount of time we spent together. We had chances to talk, opportunities to grow beyond the childhood bonds linking us. The problem was that in order to be the person I thought I wanted to be, I believed I had to seal myself off from you, construct a wall between us.

Your hands, your face became a man's. You accumulated scars, a deeper voice, lovers, but the changes taking place in you might as well have been occurring on a different planet. The scattered images I retain of you from the sixties through the middle seventies form no discernible pattern, are rooted in no vital substance like childhood or family. Your words and gestures belonged to a language I was teaching myself to unlearn. When we spoke, I was conscious of a third party short-circuiting our conversations. What I'd say to you came from the mouth of a translator who always talked down or up or around you, who didn't know you or me but pretended he knew everything.

Was I as much a stranger to you as you seemed to me? Because we were brothers, holidays, family celebrations, and troubles drew us to the same rooms at the same time, but I felt uncomfortable around you. Most of what I felt was guilt. I'd made my choices. I was running away from Pittsburgh, from poverty, from blackness. To get ahead, to make something of myself, college had seemed a logical, necessary step; my exile, my flight from home began with good grades, with good English, with setting myself apart long before I'd earned a scholarship and a train ticket over the mountains to Philadelphia. With that willed alienation behind me, between us, guilt was predictable. One measure of my success was the distance I'd put between us. Coming home was a kind of bragging, like the suntans people bring back from Hawaii in the middle of winter. It's sure fucked up around here, ain't it? But look at me, I got away. I got mine. I didn't want to be caught looking back. I needed home to reassure myself of how far I'd come. If I ever doubted how good I had it away at school in that world of books, exams, pretty, rich white girls, a roommate from Long Island who unpacked more pairs of brand-new jockey shorts and T-shirts than they had in Kaufmann's department store, if I ever had any hesitations or reconsiderations about the path I'd chosen, youall were back home in the ghetto to remind me how lucky I was.

Fear marched along beside guilt. Fear of acknowledging in myself any traces of the poverty, ignorance, and danger I'd find surrounding me when I returned to Pittsburgh. Fear that I was contaminated and would carry the poison wherever I ran. Fear that the evil would be discovered in me and I'd be shunned like a leper.

I was scared stiff but at the same time I needed to prove I hadn't lost my roots. Needed to boogie and drink wine and chase pussy, needed to prove I could still do it all. Fight, talk trash, hoop with the best playground players at Mellon Park. Claim the turf, wear it like a badge, yet keep my distance, be in the street but not of it.

Your world. The blackness that incriminated me. Easier to change the way I talked and walked, easier to be two people than to expose in either world the awkward mix of school and home I'd become. When in Rome. Different strokes for different folks. Nobody had pulled my coat and whispered the news about Third Worlds. Just two choices as far as I could tell: either/or. Rich or poor. White or black. Win or lose. I figured which side I wanted to be on when the Saints came marching in. Who the Saints, the rulers of the earth were, was clear. My mind was split by oppositions, by mutually exclusive categories. Manichaeism, as Frantz Fanon would say. To succeed in the man's world you must become like the man and the man sure didn't claim no bunch of nigger relatives in Pittsburgh.

Who, me? You must be kidding. You must be thinking of those other guys. They're the ones listen to the Midnighters, the Miracles, the Turbans, Louis Berry, the Spaniels, the Flamingos. My radio stays set on WFLN. They play that nigger stuff way down the dial, at the end, on WDAS, down where WAMO is at home.

Some of that mess so dumb, so unbelievable I can laugh now. Like when I was driving you up to Maine to work as a waiter in summer camp. Just you and me and Judy in the car for the long haul from Pittsburgh to Takajo on Long Lake. Nervous the whole time because you kept finding black music on the radio. Not only did you find it. You played it loud and sang along. Do wah diddy and ow bop she bop, having a good ole nigger ball like you'd seen me having with my cut buddies when we were the Commodores chirping tunes on the corner and in Mom's living room. The music we'd both grown up hearing and loving and learning to sing, but you were doing it in my new 1966 Dodge Dart, on the way to Martha's Vineyard and Maine with my new white wife in the backseat. Didn't you know we'd left Pittsburgh, didn't you understand that classical music volume moderate was preferred in these circumstances? Papa's got a brand-new bag. And you were gon act a nigger and let the cat out.

Of course I was steady enjoying the music, too. James Brown. Baby Ray and the Raylettes. The Drifters. Missed it on the barren stretches of turnpike between cities. Having it both ways. Listening my ass off and patting my foot but in between times wondering how Judy was reacting, thinking about how I'd complain later about your monolithic fondness for rhythm and blues, your habit of turning the volume up full blast. In case she was annoyed, confused, or doubting me in any way, I'd reassure her by disassociating myself from your tastes, your style. Yeah, when I was a kid. Yes. Once upon a time I was like that but now . . .

Laughing now to keep from crying when I think back to those days.

My first year at college when I was living in the dorms a white boy asked me if I liked the blues. Since I figured I *was* the blues I answered, Yeah, sure. We were in Darryl Dawson's room. Darryl and I comprised approximately one-third of the total number of black males in our class. About ten of the seventeen hundred men and women who entered the University of Pennsylvania as freshmen in 1959 were black. After a period of wariness and fencing, mutual embarrassment and resisting the inevitable, I'd buddied up with Darryl, even though he'd attended Putney Prep School in Vermont and spoke with an accent I considered phony. Since the fat white boy in work shirt, motorcycle boots, and dirty jeans was in Darryl's room, I figured maybe the guy was alright in spite of the fact he asked dumb questions. I'd gotten used to answering or ignoring plenty of those in two months on campus. "Yeah, sure," should have closed the topic but the white boy wasn't finished. He said he had a big collection of blues records and that I ought to come by his room sometime with Darryl and dig, man.

Who do you like? Got everybody, man. Leadbelly and Big Bill Broonzy. Lightning and Lemon and Sonny Boy. You dig Broonzy? Just copped a new side of his.

None of the names meant a thing to me. Maybe I'd heard Leadbelly at a party at a white girl's house in Shadyside but the other names were a mystery. What was this sloppy-looking white boy talking about? His blond hair, long and greasy, was combed back James Dean style. Skin pale and puffy like a Gerber baby. He wore a smartass, whole-lot-hipper-than-you expression on his face. His mouth is what did it. Pudgy, soft lips with just a hint of blond fuzz above them, pursed into a permanent sneer.

He stared at me, waiting for an answer. At home we didn't get in other people's faces like that. You talked toward a space and the other person had a choice of entering or not entering, but this guy's blue eyes bored directly into mine. Waiting, challenging, prepared to send a message to that sneering mouth. I wanted no part of him, his records, or his questions.

Blues. Well, that's all I listen to. I like different songs at different times. Midnighters. Drifters got one I like out now.

Not that R-and-B crap on the radio, man. Like the real blues. Down home country blues. The old guys picking and singing.

Ray Charles. I like Ray Charles.

Hey, that ain't blues. Tell him, Darryl.

Darryl don't need to tell me anything. Been listening to blues all my life. Ray Charles is great. He's the best there is. How you gon tell me what's good and not good? It's my music. I've been hearing it all my life.

You're still talking about rock 'n' roll. Rhythm and blues. Most of it's junk. Here today and gone tomorrow crap. I'm talking about authentic blues. Big Bill Broonzy. The Classics.

When he talked, he twisted his mouth so the words slithered out of one corner of his face, like garbage dumped off one end of a cafeteria tray. He pulled a cigarette from a pack in his shirt pocket. Lit it without disturbing the sneer.

Bet you've never even heard Bill Broonzy.

Don't need to hear no Broonzy or Toonsy or whoever the fuck he is. I don't give a shit about him nor any of them other old-timey dudes you're talking about, man. I know what I like and you can call it rhythm and blues or rock 'n' roll, it's still the best music. It's what I like and don't need nobody telling me what's good.

What are you getting mad about, man? How can you put down something you know nothing about? Bill Broonzy is the greatest twelve-string guitar player who ever lived. Everybody knows that. You've never heard a note he's played but you're setting yourself up as an expert. This is silly. You obviously can't back up what you're saying. You have a lot to learn about music, my friend.

He's wagging his big head and looking over at Darryl like Darryl's supposed to back his action. You can imagine what's going through my mind. How many times I've already gone upside his fat jaw. Biff. Bam. My fists were burning. I could see blood running out both his nostrils. The sneer split at the seams, smeared all over his chin. Here's this white boy in this white world bad-mouthing me to one of the few black faces I get to see, messing with the little bit of understanding I'm beginning to have with Darryl. And worse, trespassing on the private turf of my music, the black sounds from home I carry round in my head as a saving grace against the pressures of the university.

Talk about uptight. I don't believe that pompous ass could have known, because even I didn't know at that moment, how much he was hurting me. What hurt most was the truth of what he was saying. His whiteness, his arrogance made me mad, but it was truth putting the real hurt on me.

I didn't hit him. I should have but never did. A nice forget-me-knot upside his jaw. I should have but didn't. Not that time. Not him.

Smashing his mouth would have been too easy, so I hated him instead. Let anger and shame and humiliation fill me to overflowing so the hate is still there, today, over twenty years later. The dormitory room had pale green walls, a bare wooden floor, contained the skimpy desk and sagging cot allotted to each cubicle in the hall. Darryl's things scattered everywhere. A self-portrait he'd painted stared down from one dirt-speckled wall. The skin of the face in the portrait was wildly mottled, violent bruises of color surrounding haunted jade eyes. Darryl's eyes were green like my brother David's, but I hadn't noticed their color until I dropped by his room one afternoon between classes and Darryl wasn't there and I didn't have anything better to do than sit and wait and study the eyes in his painting. Darryl's room had been a sanctuary but when the white boy started preaching there was no place to hide. Even before he spoke the room had begun to shrink. He sprawled, lounged, an exaggerated casualness announcing how comfortable he felt, how much he belonged, Lord of the manor wherever he happened to plant his boots.

Darryl cooled it. His green eyes didn't choose either of us when we looked toward him for approval. Dawson had to see what a miserable corner I was in. He had to feel that room clamped tight around my neck and the sneer tugging the noose tighter.

A black motorcycle jacket, carved from a lump of coal, studded with silver and rhinestones, was draped over the desk chair. I wanted to stomp it, chop it into little pieces.

Hey, you guys, knock it off. Let's talk about something else. Obviously you have different tastes in music.

Darryl knew damn well that wasn't the problem. Together we might have been able to say the right things. Put the white boy in his place. Recapture some breathing space. But Darryl had his own ghosts to battle. His longing for his blonde, blue-eyed Putney girl friend whose parents had rushed her off to Europe when they learned of her romance with the colored boy who was Putney school president. His ambivalence toward his blackness that would explode one day and hurtle him into the quixotic campaign of the Black Revolutionary Army to secede from the United States. So Darryl cooled it that afternoon in his room and the choked feeling never left my throat. I can feel it now as I write.

Why did that smartass white son of a bitch have so much power over me? Why could he confuse me, turn me inside out, make me doubt myself? Waving just a tiny fragment of truth, he could back me into a corner. Who was I? What was I? Did I really fear the truth about myself that much? Four hundred years of oppression, of lies had empowered him to use the music of my people as a weapon against me. Twenty years ago I hadn't begun to comprehend the larger forces, the ironies, the obscenities that permitted such a reversal to occur. All I had sensed was his power, the raw, crude force mocking me, diminishing me. I should have smacked him. I should have affirmed another piece of the truth he knew about me, the nigger violence.

Darryl and I would ride buses across Philly searching for places like home. Like the corner of Frankstown and Bruston in Homewood. A poolroom, barbershop, rib joint, record store strip with bloods in peacock colors strolling up and down and hanging out on the corner. After a number of long, unsuccessful expeditions (how could you ask directions? Who in the island of University would know what you were asking, let alone be able to tell you how to get there?), we found South Street. Just over the bridge, walking distance if you weren't in a hurry, but as far from school, as close to home as we could get. Another country.

Coming home from the university, from people and situations that continually set me against them and against myself, I was a dangerous person. If I wanted to stay in one piece and stay in school, I was forced to pull my punches. To maintain any semblance of dignity and confidence I had to learn to construct a shell around myself. Be cool. Work on appearing dignified, confident. Fool people with appearances, surfaces, live my real life underground in a region where no one could touch me. The trouble with this survival mechanism was the time and energy expended on upkeep of the shell. The brighter, harder, more convincing and impenetrable the shell became, the more I lost touch with the inner sanctuary where I was supposed to be hiding. It was no more accessible to me than it was to the people I intended to keep out. Inside was a breeding ground for rage, hate, dreams of vengeance.

Nothing original in my tactics. I'd adopted the strategy of slaves, the oppressed, the powerless. I thought I was running but I was fashioning a cage. Working hand in hand with my enemies. Knowledge of my racial past, of the worldwide struggle of people of color against the domination of Europeans would have been invaluable. History could have been a tool, a support in the day-to-day confrontations I experienced in the alien university environment. History could have taught me I was not alone, my situation was not unique. Believing I was alone made me dangerous, to myself and others.

College was a time of precipitous ups and downs. I was losing contact with the truth of my own feelings. Not trusting, not confiding in anyone else, learning to mistrust and deny my own responses left me no solid ground, nowhere to turn. I was an expert at going with the flow, protecting myself by taking on the emotional or intellectual coloring of whatever circumstance I found myself in. All of this would have been bad enough if I'd simply been camouflaging my feelings. Yet it was far worse. I had no feelings apart from the series of roles and masquerades I found myself playing. And my greatest concern at the time had nothing to do with reestablishing an authentic core. What I feared most and spent most of my energy avoiding, was being unmasked.

Away from school I worked hard at being the same old home boy everybody remembered, not because I identified with that mask but because I didn't want youall to discover I was a traitor. Even at home a part of me stood outside, watching me perform. Even within the family. The watching part was unnamable. I hated it and depended on it. It was fear and cunning and anger and alienation; it was chaos, a yawning emptiness at the center of my being.

Once, in Wyoming, I saw a gut-shot antelope. A bullet had dropped the animal abruptly to its knees. It waggled to its feet again, tipsy, dazed. Then it seemed to hear death, like a prairie fire crackling through the sagebrush at its heels. The antelope bolted, a flat-out, bounding sprint, trailing guts like streamers from its low-slung potbelly. I was running that hard, that fast, but without the antelope's blessed ignorance. I knew I was coming apart.

I could get ugly, vicious with people real quick. They'd think they knew the person they were dealing with, then I'd turn on them. Get drunk or fed up or just perverse for perversity's sake. Exercise the dark side of my power. Become a stranger, a different person. I'd scare people, hurt them. What I did to others, I was doing to myself. I wasn't sure I cried real tears, bled real blood. Didn't know whose eyes stared back at me from the mirror.

Problem is, I'm not talking about ancient history. I've changed. We've all changed. A lot's happened in the last twenty years. But what I was, I still am. You have to know this. My motives remain suspect. A potential for treachery remains deep inside the core. I can blend with my surroundings, become invisible. An opaque curtain slides down between me and others, between the part of me that judges and weighs and is accountable for my actions and that part that acts. Then, as always, I'm capable of profound irresponsibility. No way of being accountable because there's no one, no place to turn to.

I try harder these days. Love, marriage, children, a degree of success in the world, leisure to reconsider, to reason with myself, to read and write have increased my insight and altered my perspective. But words like "insight" and "altered perspective" are bullshit. They don't tell you what you need to know. Am I willing to go all the way? Be with you? Share the weight? Go down with you wherever you have to go? No way to know beforehand. Words can't do that. Words may help me find you. Then we'll have to see. . . .

You've seen Jamila almost yearly. Since she was a baby she's accompanied us on our visits to the prison. One of the family. I date your time in prison by her age. She used to cry coming and going. Now she asks questions, the hard kind I can't answer. The kinds of questions few in this society bother to pose about the meaning, the intent, the utility of locking people behind bars.

How long will Robby be in cage?

In a book about the evolution of imprisonment during the Middle Ages I discovered the word "jail" does in fact derive from "cage." Prisons in medieval England were basically custodial *cages* where convicted felons awaited punishment or the accused were held till traveling magistrates arrived to pass judgment. At specified towns or villages within the circuit of his jurisdiction a justice would *sit* (old French *assise*, hence the modern "assizes"), and prisoners would be transported from gaol to have their fate determined. Jamila knew what she was talking about. We said "jail" and she heard "cage," heard steel doors clanking, iron locks rattling, remembered animals penned in the zoo. Kids use words in ways that release hidden meanings, reveal the history buried in sounds. They haven't forgotten that words can be more than signs, that words have magic, the power to be things, to point to themselves and materialize. With their back-formations, archaisms, their tendency to play the music in words—rhythm, rhyme, alliteration, repetition—children peel the skin from language. Words become incantatory. Open Sesame. Abracadabra. Perhaps a child will remember the word and will bring the walls tumbling down.

Maybe Jamila's a yardstick for you too. Years registering in terms of pounds and inches. The changes in her body are the reality of time passing, the reality less observable in your outward appearance. People ask, How's Robby? and I don't know what to answer. If I say he's okay, people take that to mean he's the same. He's still the person we knew when he was free. I don't want to give anyone that impression of you. I know you're changing, growing as fast as Jamila. No one does time outside of time.

A narrow sense of time as a material entity, as a commodity like money that can be spent, earned, lost, owed, or stolen is at the bottom of the twisted logic of incarceration. When a person is convicted of a crime, the state dispossesses that *criminal* of a given number of days, months, years. Time pays for crime. By surrendering a certain portion of his allotment of time on earth the malefactor pays his debt to society.

But how does anyone *do* time outside of time? Since a person can't be removed from time unless you kill him, what prison does to its inmates is make time as miserable, as unpleasant, as possible. Prison time must be hard time, a metaphorical death, a sustained, twilight condition of death-in-life. The prisoner's life is violently interrupted, enclosed within a parenthesis. The point is to create the fiction that he doesn't exist. Prison is an experience of death by inches, minutes, hours, days.

Yet the little death of a prison sentence doesn't quite kill the prisoner, because prisons, in spite of their ability to make the inmate's life unbearable, can't kill time. Incarceration as punishment always achieves less and more than its intent. No matter how drastically you deprive a prisoner of the benefits of society, abridge his civil and legal rights, unman and torture him, unless you take his life, you can't take away his time. Many inmates die violently in prisons, almost all suffer in ways beyond an outsider's comprehension, but life goes on and since it does, miracles occur. Bodies languish, spirits are broken, yet in some rare cases the prison cell becomes the monk's cell, exile a spiritual retreat, isolation the blessed solitude necessary for self-examination, self-discipline.

In spite of all the measures Western society employs to secularize time, time transcends the conventional social order. Prisoners can be snatched from that order but not from time. Time imprisons us all. When the prisoner returns to society after serving his time, in an important sense he's never been away. Prisoners cannot step into the same river twice—prison may have rendered them unfit to live in *free* society, prison may have radically altered the prisoner's sense of self, his relation to his family and friends—but the river never goes away; it breaches the walls, washes them, washes us. We only pretend the prisoner has gone away.

We visit you in prison. Here we come. The whole family. Judy, Dan, Jake, Jamila. Our nuclear unit and Mom and whoever else we can fit into the Volvo station wagon. We try to arrive at the prison as early as possible, but with five in our crew competing for time and space in Mom's tiny bathroom in the house on Tokay, and slow-as-molasses nieces Monique and Tameka to pick up in East Liberty after we're all ready, we're lucky if we set off before noon. But here we come. Getting ready as we'd get ready for any family outing. Baths, teeth brushed, feeding, coaxing, the moment somewhere at the height of the bustle, frustration, and confusion when I say to myself, Shit. Is it worth all this hassle? Let's just call it off. Let's muzzle these little beasts and go back to bed and forget the whole thing. But we persevere. We're on our way.

Jamila is the youngest visitor. Five and a half years old, my only daughter, your niece, approximately three feet tall, at the time of this visit, this visit which can stand for all visits. She has very large eyes. *Mom's eyes*, you christened them in Laramie; she is petite but built strong, taut like her mother. It's summer so her skin is tanned a golden-toned beige. As a consequence of prematurity and having her head shaved so feeding tubes could be inserted in the veins crisscrossing her skull, for a long while Jamila was bald. Now her hair is coming in nicely, tending to blond at the wispy edges where it curls loose from whatever style her mother chooses to bind it in. She is a beautiful child, I think. She moves with an athletic grace and economy. Jamila chatters incessantly and makes friends easily. A blithe, fey quality attracts people to her. Already she's aware of the seductive power of her enormous, curly eyelashes, the deep, brown pools of her eyes. She's remarkably sophisticated in conversation, in her capacity to listen and concentrate on what other people are saying. She grasps abstract ideas quickly, intuitively. Her early flirtation with death has without a doubt stamped her personality. She's curious about graveyards. Keeps track of them when we make trips. *When we go to the beach, Mom, there's three.* Like her brother, Jake, whom she resembles in skin tone and features, she possesses the gift of feeling. One of her good friends, Vass, resides in the Laramie cemetery. Jamila picked up this buddy by reading his name on a large headstone visible from the road and greets him cheerily whenever we drive past the clutter of tombstones abutting the fence on Fifteenth Street.

Jamila, tell me about going to see Robby. What do you remember about going to visit him?

Usually when we go there, when we go there . . . the visiting place . . . he eats an apple. And he wears braids. Or sometimes he would . . . got that? . . . get Doritos instead.

Yes, I *got that*, smartass. I'll write it down. You just try to remember what you think when we visit.

Looks like Stevie Wonder.

What else?

I remember him being sort of happy . . . happy to see us.

Why *sort of*?

Well, because he was sort of happy to see us and not happy he was in jail.

Anything else?

I think about him getting out of cage.

Should they let him out?

Yes. Because he wants to see people and be around other people and have life outside of him and jail.

Do you remember anything he said?

It's nice to see you. I remember Robby saying that. And the activity place. Crayons and stuff. Telling the names of characters up on the wall.

Do you talk to people about Robby?

No. It's sort of like a secret. It's a secret because other people . . .

why would they be interested in it, because they don't see him and they don't know him and it's not none of their business.

Would you talk to anyone about him?

Maybe one of my special friends like Jens. He would know what I'm talking about. Even though he's the youngest of all of us in Open School. I know Jens would understand more than anybody else because he would understand more. Like if I told Claire she would just say, *Oh*. She wouldn't know what I was talking about, but Jens he would tell me a different story and I would know he would understand.

Anything else you can remember?

One time when we went there and we were finding out we couldn't see him that day, I heard him call and say come back another time.

Why's he in jail?

So that he doesn't go out and do the same thing again. They're keeping him there till they think that he won't do the same thing again.

When everybody's finally ready and in, I back the Volvo station wagon down the steep, cobblestone street to the intersection of Tokay and Seagirt. There I can turn around, ease the wagon's rear end into Seagirt, point us toward Bennett Street, and we're on our way. Backing down Tokay can be a real trick at busy traffic times of day. It's a chore anytime, fighting the high, broken curb, the blind corners where cars from Seagirt and Bricelyn pop into Tokay. Cars come at you shuddering down the hill, cars behind your back gun their engines for a running start up Tokay. In Homewood you still get points for laying rubber, for flying full blast down the precipitous, potholed slopes of streets like Tokay and Seagirt. People enjoy tearing up big, shiny cars. But early in the morning, at the hour we shoot for when we visit you in prison, the streets are relatively quiet.

Down Tokay, left on Bennett, seven blocks over to Braddock till it crosses Penn Avenue, and Homewood's behind us. That quick. That little snatch of Bennett, then Braddock till it crosses Penn carry us past the heart of the ghetto. Or where the heart once was. Since 1860 black people have lived in a pocket of streets, dirt paths before they were paved, between Homewood Avenue and Dunfermline Street. Kelly, Hamilton, Tioga, Cassina, Susquehanna, Finance—Braddock Avenue touches them all before passing under a concrete bridge that launches trains into the sky of Homewood. The railroad tracks linking this bridge on Braddock with the one over Homewood Avenue separate Homewood from the once predominantly white neighborhoods along its southern edge. When we lived on Finance Street those tracks marked one border of my world. Across Finance the pavement ended. A steep, weed-covered embankment rose to the railroad tracks. Before you were born, my sleep was couched in the rhythm of trains. Some nights I'd lie awake waiting for the crash of steel wheels, for the iron fist to grab me and shake me, for the long, echoing silence afterward to carry me away. Homewood was a valley between the thunder of the tracks and the quiet hills to the east, hills like Bruston, up whose flanks narrow streets meandered or, like Tokay, shot straight to the sky.

Homewood's always been the wrong side of the tracks from the perspective of its white neighbors south of Penn Avenue. On the wrong side of the tracks—*under* the tracks, if the truth be told—in a deep hollow between Penn and the abrupt rise of Bruston Hill. When we leave for the prison the five minutes we spend negotiating an edge of this valley seem to take forever. Traffic lights on every corner attempt to slow down people for whom driving is not so much a means of moving from one place to another as a display of aggression, fearlessness, and style. When you drive an automobile in Homewood you commit yourself to a serious game of chicken. On narrow, two-way streets like Finance you automatically whip down the center, claiming it, daring anyone to buck your play. Inside your car with WAMO cooking on the radio, you are lord and master and anyplace your tires kiss becomes your domain. Jesus have mercy on the chump who doesn't get out your way.

The trip to visit you in prison begins with me behind the wheel, backing down Tokay then trying to run a string of green lights to get us quickly out of Homewood. No matter how skillfully I cheat on yellow, one or two red lights catch us and that's part of the reason it seems to take so long to cover a short distance. But being stalled by a red light does not slow us down as much as the weight of the Homewood streets in my imagination. The streets had been my stomping ground, my briar patch. The place I'd fled from with all my might, the place always snatching me back.

Memories of the streets are dense, impacted. Threads of guilt bind each tapestry of associations. Guilt bright red as the black blood sealed beneath Homewood's sidewalks. Someone had stripped Homewood bare, mounted it, and ridden it till it collapsed and lay dying, sprawled beneath the rider, who still spurred it and bounced up and down and screamed, Giddyup. I knew someone had done that to Homewood, to its people, to me. The evidence plain as day through the windshield of my car: an atrocious crime had been committed and I had witnessed it, continued to witness it during those short visits home each summer or for the Christmas holidays, yet I did nothing about what I saw. Not the crime, not the damage that had been wrought. I knew too much but most of the time counted myself lucky because I had escaped and wasn't required to act on what I knew. Today, this morning on the way to visit you in Western Penitentiary, the rape of Homewood was being consummated, was flourishing in broad daylight, and nobody, including me, was uttering a mumbling word.

A need to go slowly, to register each detail of violated terrain competes with an urge to get the hell out before some doped-up fool without insurance or a pot to piss in comes barreling out of a side street and totals my new Volvo wagon. Cords at the back of my neck ache. Street names trigger flashbacks. Uncle Ote's laughing voice, the blue-flowered china bowl in my grandmother's closet, Aunt Geraldine sneaking me a hot sausage smothered in peppers and onions from DiLeo's late on Saturday night, hiding in the stiff weeds on the hillside, riding on Big Melvin's shoulders. Melvin was a giant and twenty years old but played with us kids and was dumber than a stone and died under the wheels of a bread truck because he was too dumb to cross Tioga Street. Fragments. A blues verse fading in and out. *Got two minds to leave here. Just one telling me stay.*

The parkway parallels the Monongahela River. Below us, across the water, on the South Side are some of the steel mills that gave Pittsburgh its claim to fame. The smokestacks of Jones & Laughlin and United States Steel. People say better steel is manufactured now across the ocean in Japan and Scandinavia. Better steel produced more efficiently by modern, computerized mills. I don't doubt it. J & L's huge blast furnaces appear antique. Old, rusty guts that the ghost of Fred Willis, the junkman, will rip off one night and cart away. From the colonial period onward, steel determined the economic health of Pittsburgh and it continues to color the city's image of itself. Steeltown, U.S.A. Home of the

Iron Dukes and NFL Champion Steelers. Home of Iron City Beer. But for decades Pittsburgh's steel industry has been suffering from foreign competition. Miles of deserted sheds, part of J & L's original mill stretch below the highway. Too many layoffs and cutbacks and strikes. Too much greed and too little imagination in the managerial class, too much alienation among workers. Almost any adult male in Pittsburgh, black or white, can tell you a story about how these hulking, rusty skeletons lining the riverfront haunted his working life.

To get to the North Side of the city from the parkway, I exit at Fort Duquesne Bridge. After the bridge the car winds around Three Rivers Stadium. It's a dumb way to go but I don't get lost. Inside the concrete bowl tiers of orange, blue, and gold seats are visible. Danny and Jake always have something to say here. Danny is a diehard Steelers fan and Jake roots for the team closest to home, the Denver Broncos. One brother will remind the other of a play, a game in the series between the two AFC rivals. Then it's put down and shout down till one silences the other or an adult short-circuits impending mayhem and silences both. I still live and die with the Steelers but I stay out of the bickering, unless they need a fact confirmed, which they need me for less and less each year as their grasp of stats and personalities begins to exceed mine. Even if I'm not consulted (and it hurts a little when I'm not), I welcome the diversion. I listen to them squabble and I pick my way through confusing signs and detours and blind turns that, if I'm lucky, get us off the merry-go-round ramps circling Three Rivers and down onto Ohio River Boulevard.

Again we parallel a river, this time the brown Ohio. To an outsider Pittsburgh must seem all bridges, tunnels, rivers, and hills. If you're not climbing into the sky or burrowing into the bowels of the earth, you're suspended, crossing water or looking down on a hodgepodge scramble of houses strewn up and down the sides of a ravine. You'd wonder how people live clinging to terraced hillsides. Why they trust ancient, doddering bridges to ferry them over the void. Why they truck along at seventy miles an hour on a narrow shelf chiseled in the stone shoulders of a mountain. A funicular railway erected in 1875 inches up Mount Washington, connecting the lower South Side to Duquesne Heights. Pittsburghers call it the Incline. Ride the rickety cars up the mountain's sheer face for fun now, since tunnels and expressways and bridges have made the Incline's service obsolete.

After Fort Duquesne Bridge and the Stadium, we're on the North Side, an adjoining city called Allegheny until it was incorporated into Pittsburgh proper in 1907. Urban renewal has destroyed nearly all the original residential buildings. We skirt the high rises, low rises, condos, malls, the shopping centers, singles bars, and discos that replaced the stolid, foursquare architecture of Old Allegheny. Twin relics, two ugly, ornate, boxish buildings squat deserted on Ohio River Boulevard. When I see these unusual structures, I know I've lucked out, that I've negotiated the maze of dead ends, one-ways, and anonymous streets and all that's left is a straight shot out the boulevard to the prison.

Western Penitentiary sprouts like a giant wart from the bare, flat stretches of concrete surrounding it. The prison should be dark and forbidding, but either its stone walls have been sand-blasted or they've somehow escaped the decades of industrial soot raining from the sky.

Western is a direct descendant of the world's first penitentiary, Philadelphia's Quaker-inspired Walnut Street Jail, chartered in 1773. The good intentions built into the Walnut Street Jail—the attempt to substitute an enforced regime of solitary confinement, labor, and moral rehabilitation, for the whipping post, pillory, fines, and executions of the British penal code—did not exempt that humane experiment from the ills that beset all societies of caged men. Walnut Street Jail became a cesspool, overcrowded, impossible to maintain, wracked by violence, disease, and corruption. By the second decade of the nineteenth century it was clear that the reforms instituted in the jail had not procured the results its zealous supporters had envisioned, and two new prisons, one for the east, one for the western half of the state, were mandated by the Commonwealth of Pennsylvania. From the ashes of the Walnut Street experiment rose the first Western penitentiary. The architect, a William Strickland known for revivals of classic Greek models and his engineering skill, created a classic of a different sort on a plain just west of Allegheny City. With massive, forbidding bulwarks, crenellated parapets, watchtowers buttressing the corners of the walls, his notion of a prison recapitulated the forms of medieval fear and paranoia.

The immediate successor of Strickland's Norman castle was constructed sporadically over a period of seventeen years. This new Western, grandson of the world's first penitentiary, received its first contingent of prisoners in 1886, and predictably black men made up a disproportionate percentage of these pioneers, who were marched in singing. Today, nearly a hundred years later, having survived floods, riots, scandals, fires, and blue-ribboned panels of inquiry, Western remains in working order.

Approaching the prison from Ohio River Boulevard, you can see coils of barbed wire and armed guards atop the ramparts. The steepled towers that, like dunce caps, once graced its forty-foot walls have been lopped off. There's a visitors' parking lot below the wall facing the boulevard. I ignore it and pull into the fenced lot beside the river, the one marked Official Business Only. I save everybody a quarter-mile walk by parking in the inner lot. Whether it's summer or winter, that last quarter mile can be brutal. Sun blazing down on your head or icy wind off the river, or snow or rain or damp fog creeping off the water, and nothing but one high, gritty wall that you don't want to hug no matter how much protection it might afford. I drive through the tall gate into the official business lot because even if the weather's summery pleasant, I want to start the visit with a small victory, be one up on the keepers. Because that's the name of the game and chances are I won't score again. I'll be playing on their turf, with their ball and their rules, which are nothing if not one-sided, capricious, cruel, and corrupting. What's written says one thing. But that's not really the way things are. Always a catch. Always an angle so the published rules don't literally apply. What counts are the unwritten rules. The now-you-see-it-now-you-don't-sleight-of-hand rules whose function is to humiliate visitors and preserve the absolute, arbitrary power of the keepers.

Onto whose lot we trespass. Pulling as close to the visitors' building as possible. Not too close because the guard on duty in the kiosk adjacent to the stairs of the visitors' annex might feel compelled to turn us back if we break into the narrow compass of his alertness. Close but far enough away so he'd have to poke out his head and shout to get our attention.

I find a space and the kids scoot out of their seats. Tish's girls are with us so we used the *way back* of the station wagon. For safety the rear hatch unlocks only from outside, so I insert the key and lift the lid and Danny and Jake and Tameka scramble out to join the others.

"We're in a parking lot, so watch for cars!" I shout after them as they race down the broad center lane of the parking area. What else can I say? Cramped in the car for the past half hour, they're doing now what they need to do. Long-legged, snake-hipped, brown children. They had tried to walk in an orderly fashion, smallest one grabbing largest one's hand, lock step, slowly, circumspectly, progressing in that fashion for approximately three steps before one tore away and another followed and they're all skipping and scampering now, polished by the sun. Nobody sprints toward the prison full tilt, they know better than that, but they get loose, flinging limbs and noise every which way. They crunch over a patch of gravel. Shorts and T-shirts make their bodies appear vulnerable, older and younger at the same time. Their high-pitched cries bounce off the looming wall. I keep my eyes on them as I lock the car. No real danger here but lessons, lessons everywhere, all the time. Every step and the way you take it here on enemy ground is a lesson.

Mom and Judy walk side by side, a black woman and a white woman, the white one tanned darker than the black. They add their two cents' worth of admonitions to the kids. Walk, don't run. Get Jamila's hand. Be careful. Slow down, youall. I fall in behind them. Far enough away to be alone. To be separate from the women and separate from the children. I need to say to whoever's watching—guards, prisoners invisible behind the barred three-story windows partitioning the walls, These are my people. They're with me. I'm responsible. I need to say that, to hang back and preside, to stroll, almost saunter, aware of the weight, the necessity of vigilance because here I am, on alien turf, a black man, and I'm in charge. For a moment at least these women, these children have me to turn to. And I'm one hundred percent behind them, prepared to make anyone who threatens them answer to me. And that posture, that prerogative remains rare for a black man in American society. Rare *today*, over 120 years after slavery and second-class citizenship have been abolished by law. The guards know that. The prisoners know. It's for their benefit as well as my own and my family's that I must carry myself in a certain way, make certain rules clear even though we are entering a hostile world, even though the bars exist to cut off the possibility of the prisoners seeing themselves as I must see myself, striding free, in charge of women and children, across the official lot.

Grass grows in the margin between the spiked fence paralleling the river and the asphalt lot. Grass clipped harshly, uniformly as the bristle heads of convicts in old movies about prison. Plots of manicured green define a path leading to steps we must climb to enter the visitors' building. Prisoner trustees in ill-fitting blue uniforms—loose tunics, baggy, string-tied trousers a shade darker—putter at various make-work jobs near the visitors' entrance. Another prisoner, farther away, near the river edge of the parking lot sidles into a slate-gray Mercedes sedan. A pudgy, bull-necked white guy. When he plops into the driver's seat the car shudders. First thing he does is lower the driver's side window and hang out his ham arm. Then full throttle he races the Mercedes engine, obviously relishing the roar, as pleased with himself as he'd been when the precise, solid slam of the door sealed him in. If the driver is hot shit, big shot for a few seconds behind the wheel, he'll pay for the privilege soon enough when he adds the Mercedes to the row of Cadillacs, Oldsmobiles, and Buicks he must scrub and spit shine for the bosses.

Another prisoner leans on a push broom. The asphalt walks are spotless, but every minute or so he advances the broom another foot, punching its bristles into the gray surface as if his job is not to keep the path clean but punish it for unmentionable crimes against humanity. Others sweep, rake, and supervise. Two or three trustees have no apparent duties. They are at their ease, talking and smoking. A lethargy, a stilted slow-motion heaviness stylizes their gestures. It's as if they inhabit a different element, as if their bodies are enfolded in a dreamy ether or trapped at the bottom of the sea. I watch the prisoners watch the kids mount the steps. No outward signs betray what the men are thinking but I can feel them appraising, measuring. Through the prisoners' eyes I see the kids as sexual objects. Clean, sleek bodies. Young, smooth, and supple. The coltish legs and high, muscley butts of my nieces. The boys' long legs and slim hips. They are handsome children, a provocative banner waved in front of men who must make do with their own bodies or the bodies of other men. From the vantage point of the blue-uniformed trustees on the ground, the double staircase and the landing above are a stage free-world people must ascend. An auction block, an inspection stand where the prisoners can sample with their hungry eyes the meat moving in and out of prison.

But I don't have their eyes. Perhaps what they see when the kids climb the steps are their own lost children, their sons and daughters, their younger brothers and sisters left behind in the treacherous streets. Not even inside the walls yet and I can sense the paranoia, the curtain of mistrust and suspicion settling over my eyes. Except for the car jockey and a runner outside the guards' kiosk, all the trustees in the yard are black, black men like me, like you. In spite of knowing better, I can't shake the feeling that these men are different. Not just different. Bad. People who are dangerous. I can identify with them only to the extent that I own up to the evil in myself. Yeah. If I was shut away from the company of women, I'd get freaky. Little kids, alley cats, anything got legs and something between them start to looking good to me. Yeah. It's a free show when wives and mamas tippy-tap up them steps. And I'd be right there leaning on my broom taking it all in. I don't want to feel angry or hostile toward the prisoners but I close up the space between myself and my two women, glad they're both looking good and glad they're both wearing slacks.

It's crazy. It's typical of the frame of mind visiting prison forces on me. I have trouble granting the prisoners a life independent of mine, I impose my terms on them, yet I want to meet their eyes. Plunge into the depths of their eyes to learn what's hidden there, what reservoirs of patience and pain they draw from, what sustains them in this impossible place. I want to learn from their eyes, identify with their plight, but I don't want anyone to forget I'm an outsider, that these cages and walls are not my home. I want to greet the prisoners civilly as I would if we passed each other outside, on Homewood Avenue. But locks, bars, and uniforms frustrate the simplest attempts at communication; the circumstances under which we meet inform me unambiguously that I am not on Homewood Avenue, not speaking to a fellow citizen. Whether or not I acknowledge that fact I'm ensnared by it. Damned if I do, damned if I don't. I'm not wearing funny blue clothes. I walked into this zoo because I chose to; I can return home and play with these children, make love to my woman. These privileges, which in my day-to-day blindness I often don't even count as privileges, are as embarrassing to me, as galling in this prison context as the inmates' state of drastic deprivation must be to them. Without speaking a word, without having ever seen each other before, we know too much about each other. Our rawest, most intimate secrets are exposed, there's no room for small talk. We can't take our time and proceed in the gradual give-and-take, willed unveiling natural to human interaction. This place where we meet one another is called the slammer and sure as shit it slams us together.

People don't so much meet as explode in each other's faces. I say "Hi" to a tall guy who looks like somebody I might have played ball with once. He wasn't anybody I knew but he could have been. One ballplayer knows every other ballplayer anyway, so I said "Hi." Got back no hint of recognition. Nothing saying yes or no or maybe in his black face. The basketball courts where I sweated and he sweated, the close scores, the impossible shots, the chances to fly, to be perfect a second or two, to rise above the hard ground and float so time stands still and you make just the right move before your sneakers touch down again. None of that. No past or future we might have shared. Nothing at all. A dull, hooded "Hey, man" in reply and I backed off quickly.

Are the steps up to the porch landing iron or wood or concrete? I can't recall. I'll check next time. I feel them now, narrow, metal, curving like a ship's spiral ladder. My feet ring against latticed rungs. I can peer through the winding staircase to the ground. People can look up between the rungs at me. The first violation of privacy. Arranged so that the prisoners are party to it. One privilege conferred on the trustees is this opportunity to greet free-world people first. Form a casual gauntlet of eyes outsiders must endure. Behind the prisoners' eyes may be nothing more than curiosity, perhaps even gratitude toward anybody willing to share a few hours with a man inside. Envy. Concern. Indifference. Any or all of these; but my ignorance, the insecurity bred by the towering walls incite me to resent the eyes.

I don't enjoy being seen entering or leaving the prison. Enormous stores of willpower must be expended pretending it doesn't exist. For the hour or so of the visit I want to forget what surrounds us, want to free myself and free you from the oppressive reality of walls, bars, and guards. And other prisoners. I resent them. And need them. Without them it wouldn't be a prison. In the back of my mind I rely on the other prisoners to verify the mistake committed in your case. Some of these guys are bad, very bad. They must be. That's why prisons exist. That's why you shouldn't be here. You're not like these others. You're my brother, you're like me. Different.

A brother behind bars, my own flesh and blood, raised in the same

houses by the same mother and father; a brother confined in prison has
to be a mistake, a malfunctioning of the system. Any other explanation
is too incriminating. The fact that a few twists and turns of fate could
land you here with the bad guys becomes a stark message about my
own vulnerability. It could easily be me behind bars instead of you. But
that wouldn't make sense because I'm not bad like the bad guys for
whom prisons are built. The evil in others defines your goodness, frees
me. If it's luck or circumstance, some arbitrary decision that determines who winds up behind prison bars, then good and evil are super-
fluous. Nobody's safe. Except the keepers, the ones empowered to say
You go to the right. You go to the left. And they're only safe as long as
they're keepers. If prisons don't segregate good from evil, then what
we've created are zoos for human beings. And we've given license to the
keepers to stock the cages.

Once, on a previous visit, waiting an hour through a lock-in and count-
down for you to be released to the visitors' lounge, I was killing time on
the porch of the visitors' annex, resting my elbows on the stone railing,
daydreaming at the river through the iron spears of the fence. An inmate called up to me. "You Faruq's brother, ain't you?" The man speaking was tall and broad-shouldered, a few years younger than you. His
scarred head was shaved clean. He carried extra weight in soft pads on
his hips, his belly, his cheeks. Like a woman, but also like the over-
weight lions in Highland Park Zoo.

I thought, Yes. Robby Wideman's my brother. Then I said, "Faruq
is my brother," and expected more from the prisoner, but he'd turned
back to the prisoners beside him, smoking, staring at nothing I could
see.

A few minutes before, I'd noticed two men jogging along the river.
I recognized their bright orange running shorts later as they hustled
past me up the steps into the prison. Both greeted me, smiling broadly,
the sort of unself-conscious, innocuous smiles worn by Mormon mis-
sionaries who periodically appear at our door in Laramie. Young, clean-
cut, all-American white faces. I figured they had to be guards out
for exercise. A new breed. Keepers staying in shape. Their friendly
smiles said we'd be delighted to stay and chat with you awhile if we wer-
en't needed elsewhere. I thought of the bland, empty stare of the man

who had recognized me as Faruq's brother. Somebody had extinguished the light in his eyes, made him furtive, scared him into erecting a wall around his brown skin, trained him to walk and talk like a zombie. The healthy, clean sweat sheen on the runners' suntanned brows and lean muscled shoulders made me hate them. I wanted to rush after them. Smash them out of their dream of righteousness.

Up the steps, across the porch, through an outer lobby opening out on both sides to alcoves with benches and vending machines where trustees can visit with their families in a less noisy, less crowded setting than the general visitors' lounge. A short passageway next, ending at a floor-to-ceiling guards' cage. To the right of the guards' enclosure a steel-screened staircase. To the left a narrow corridor lined with lockers leads into the waiting room. I sign us in with the guard in the cage. Give him your name and number. He duly registers the information in his book. He's the one who initiates your release to the visiting room. He also holds the key to the rest room, keys to the lockers where visitors must store items not permitted inside the prison. It's a job and the guard treats it like most people treat theirs. Bored, numbed by routine. He wants things to run smoothly, to avoid hassles, and he's learned the best way to accomplish this is not to concern himself with matters beyond his immediate, assigned tasks. The larger scheme in which he participates is really not his problem. Like most of us he gets paid to do a job and the job's basically a pain in the ass and the pay is shitty so why ask for more trouble when you're underpaid for the trouble you got already. He resents having to explain why some people sit for hours and others get shuttled from waiting room to visitors' room in five minutes. He just relays through a loudspeaker the names and numbers another guard inside the prison phones to him.

P3468, Robert Wideman.

He knows it's not his fault some visits last three hours and others thirty minutes. Some days are busier than others. For him too. Fridays are bad. Attorneys always a pain. He wears a dull gray uniform and sits in a cage all day and has nobody to talk to except the con runner who lounges beside the cage or squats in the sunshine on the porch, freer than him, he thinks.

The guard in the cage doesn't run the prison. He just works there.

He didn't rob nobody or stab nobody. He didn't pack his kids in a station wagon and drag them at dawn to this lousy place, so just have a seat, buddy. When they find Wideman I'll call you.

Once I counted the walls, the tall windows, estimated the height of the waiting-room ceiling. Eight walls, a ceiling twice as high as an ordinary room, four perverse, fly-speckled, curtainless windows admitting neither light nor air. I couldn't account for the room's odd shape and dimensions. Had no idea what its original purpose might have been or if it had been designed with any particular function in mind. The room made me feel like a bug in the bottom of a jar. I remembered all the butterflies, grasshoppers, praying mantises, and beetles I had captured on the hillside below the tracks. At least the insects could see through the glass walls, at least they could flutter or hop or fly, and they always had enough air until I unscrewed the perforated top and dumped them out.

The waiting room was uglier and dirtier the first few years we visited you. The same directive that ordered beautification of the grounds must have included the annex interior in its plan. A paint job—brown woodwork, baby-blue walls; new furniture—chrome tubing with pastel, vinyl cushions; a good hard scrubbing of the rest room to remove most of the graffiti—these rehabilitated what was most immediately insulting about the area where we waited for a phone to ring in the guard's cage and for him to call the name we wanted to hear over the loudspeaker. But the paint's peeling again already, flaking from pipes and radiators, drooping in clots from the ceiling. The vinyl cushions are faded, stained. In the *Ladies and/or Gents* the toilet seats are pocked by cigarette burns, graffiti has blossomed again. Wall art of a different sort decorates the main room. Murals tattoo the walls—a Chinese junk, a ship's wheel circling a clock. The most ambitious painting is above a bricked-in fireplace. A full-masted sailing ship plowing through marcelled waves. I wonder why it's only three-quarters complete. Was the artist released, the art program suspended because of lack of funds? Or did prison mayhem cause the picture to be left unfinished? A man beaten or raped or dead or consigned to the hole? A personality change, a soul too crushed even to fantasize anymore a proud clipper ship shouldering its way against sea and wind?

Our group occupies half the seats along one wall of the waiting room.

The kids clearly don't belong here. Summer color glows in their faces. They are bright, alert kids somebody scrubs and cares about and dresses neatly. Both my boys sport shiny, digital watches on their wrists. But whose kids belong here? Who fits the image this room imposes on anybody who must use it? You said the prisoners complained about the state of the visitors' facilities and were granted, after much bullshit and red tape, the privilege of sprucing them up. But when it came down to supplies or time to work on the project, the administration backed off. Yes, you can fix up the place. No, we won't provide decent materials or time to do it. Typical rat-ass harassment. Giving with one hand, taking away with the other. If the waiting room's less squalid than it was three years ago, it's still far short of decent and it's turning nasty again. The room thus becomes one more proof of the convicts' inability to do anything right. We said you fellows could fix it up and look what a crummy job you did. We gave you a chance and you fucked up again. Like you fuck up probation and fuck up parole. Like you fucked up when you were in the street. And that's why you're here. That's why keepers are set over you.

I can hear the bickering, the frustration, the messages encoded in the tacky walls. It's a buzzing in my ears that never goes away inside the prison. Like the flies in the rest room waiting for the kids to start trooping in. Like the guard waiting to run his hand down in my mother's purse. Like the machine waiting to peek under everybody's clothes. Like all the locks and steel doors and bars we must pass through when they finally announce your number and name.

I drew the room once but I can't find the sketch. The picture was to serve as a jog for my memory. Documentation of the systematic abuse visitors must undergo from start to finish when they enter a prison. I knew that one day I'd write about visiting you and I'd need a careful blueprint of physical details, the things that bear so heavily on the soul. But it's not the number of doors or their thickness or composition or the specific route from the visitors' annex to the prison, not the clangorous steps and drafty, dank passageways and nightmare-size locks and keys, or the number of guards frisking me with their eyes or the crash of steel on steel ringing in my ears. It's the idea, the image of myself these things conspire to produce and plant in my head. That image, that idea is what defines the special power of the prison over those who enter it.

The process of implanting the idea is too efficient to be accidental. The visitor is forced to become an inmate. Subjected to the same sorts of humiliation and depersonalization. Made to feel powerless, intimidated by the might of the state. Visitors are treated like both children and ancient, incorrigible sinners. We experience a crash course that teaches us in a dramatic, unforgettable fashion just how low a prisoner is in the institution's estimation. We also learn how rapidly we can descend to the same depth. Our pretensions to dignity, to difference are quickly dispelled. We are on the keepers' turf. We must play their game, their way. We sit where they tell us to sit. Surrender the personal possessions they order us to surrender. Wait as long as it pleases them to keep us waiting in the dismal anteroom. We come (and are grateful for the summons) whenever we are called. We allow them to pass us through six-inch steel doors and don't protest when the doors slam shut behind us. We suffer the keepers' prying eyes, prying machines, prying hands. We let them lock us in without any guarantee the doors will open when we wish to leave. We are in fact their prisoners until they release us.

That was the idea. To transform the visitor into something he despised and feared. A prisoner. Until I understood what was being done, the first few moments at the threshold of the visiting lounge always confused me. There was an instant of pure hatred. Hatred lashing out at what I'd been forced to become, at them, even at you. The humiliation I'd undergone for the sake of seeing you poisoned the air, made me rigid, angry. I felt guilty for feeling put upon, guilty for allowing the small stuff to get inside me, guilty for turning on you.

That to get over first. And it's no simple matter in a noisy room crowded with strangers, in the short space of an hour or so, after a separation of months or years, to convince you and convince myself that yes, yes, we are people and yes, we have something to say to each other, something that will rise above the shouting, the fear, the chaos around us. Something that, though whispered, can be heard. Can connect us again.

You seem taller than you are. Long hands and feet where Mom used to say all your food went because you ate like a horse and stayed skinny. Long legs and arms. In prison your shoulders have thickened. Your arms are tautly muscled from the thousand push-ups each day in your cell. Like Dave and Daddy and Grandpa you're losing your hair. The early thirties, but already your hair thinning, receding from your forehead. On top, toward the back, a circle of bare skull sneaks through if you don't comb your naps just right. Dave calls that balding patch we all sport our toilet seat. Other than that inherited sparse spot you're doing much better than I am in the keeping-your-hair department. More than most women, when you comb it out. When you plait it into braids and decorate each one with a colored rubber band, it gives you a modified dreadlocks look that emphasizes your high forehead and long, gaunt cheekbones. Bob Marley, or Stevie Wonder on his *Talking Book* album, or Albrecht Dürer's marcelled Christ. Faruq, the Muslim name you've chosen, is perfectly suited to your eyes. Burning. The terrible Turk declaring holy war on the infidels.

When you appear, I'm glad the kids are along. Happy that Judy insisted upon bringing them the first time we visited. You scoop them all into your long arms. All five squeezed in one hungry embrace. They squirm but endure the hug for your sake, then for their own as you press them to your need, to your strength, to each other. I'm grateful for the kids, cling to them as tightly as you do. Those are my children, your sister's children. We've brought the best of us into this godforsaken place. As you touch them, pick them up, and hug each one separately, the air is easier to breathe. You are their uncle, you are loving them, and for the moment that's all they need to know. Loving them because they're here, and loving the ones not here through them. That's all they need. All they ask. Jamila, the youngest, who's been here at least once every year of her life, hops up and down and squeals for another turn in your arms. Monique towers a foot above the others, a teenager suddenly remembering to be shy, awkward when you gather her last to your chest.

Look at my big girl. Look at her.

You grasp both Monique's shoulders and lean her back arm's length so you can get a good look too.

Ain't she growing. Look at this big thing. My little sweetheart's getting grown.

Her feet's bigger than Gammy's.

Hush up, Tameka.

Monique glowers at her younger sister. You better shut up, girl. A look full of the anger she can't quite summon up for you even though you're the one teasing and laughing louder than anybody. She turns back to you and a smile cracks the death-threat mask she'd flashed at her sister.

A bear hug and nuzzle for Judy. The same thing for Mom. Then we smack together, chest to chest. Hard the first time like testing shoulder pads before a football game. We grip each other's forearms.

We've made it. The visit's beginning. The room roars behind our backs.

OUR TIME

You remember what we were saying about young black men in the street-world life. And trying to understand why the "square world" becomes completely unattractive to them. It has to do with the fact that their world is the GHETTO and in that world all the glamour, all the praise and attention is given to the slick guy, the gangster especially, the ones that get over in the "life." And it's because we can't help but feel some satisfaction seeing a brother, a black man, get over on these people, on their system without playing by their rules. No matter how much we have incorporated these rules as our own, we know that they were forced on us by people who did not have our best interests at heart. So this hip guy, this gangster or player or whatever label you give these brothers that we like to shun because of the poison that they spread, we, black people, still look at them with some sense of pride and admiration, our children openly, us adults somewhere deep inside. We know they represent rebellion—what little is left in us. Well, having lived in the "life," it becomes very hard—almost impossible—to find any contentment in joining the status quo. Too hard to go back to being nobody in a world that hates you. Even if I had struck it rich in the life, I would have managed to throw it down the fast lane. Or have lost it on a revolutionary whim. Hopefully the latter.

I have always burned up in my fervent passions of desire and want. My senses at times tingle and itch with my romantic, idealistic outlook on life, which has always made me keep my distance from reality, reality that was a constant insult to my world, to my dream of happiness and peace, to my people-for-people kind of world, my easy-cars-for-a-nickel-or-a-dime sorta world. And these driving passions, this sensitivity to the love and good in people, also turned on me because I used it to play on people and their feelings. These aspirations of love and desire turned on me when I wasn't able to live up to this sweet-self morality, so I began to self-destruct, burning up in my sensitivity, losing direction, because nowhere could I find this world of truth and love and harmony.

In the real world, the world left for me, it was unacceptable to be "good," it was square to be smart in school, it was jive to show respect to people outside the street world, it was cool to be cold to your woman and the people that loved you. The things we liked we called "bad." "Man, that was a bad girl." The world of the angry black kid growing up in the sixties was a world in which to be in was to be out—out of touch with the square world and all of its rules on what's right and wrong. The thing was to make your own rules, do your own thing, but make sure it's contrary to what society says or is.

I SHALL ALWAYS PRAY

I

Garth looked bad. Real bad. Ichabod Crane anyway, but now he was a skeleton. Lying there in the bed with his bones poking through his skin, it made you want to cry. Garth's barely able to talk, his smooth, medium-brown skin yellow as pee. Ichabod legs and long hands and long feet, Garth could make you laugh just walking down the street. On the set you'd see him coming a far way off. Three-quarters leg so you knew it had to be Garth the way he was split up higher in the crotch than anybody else. Wilt the Stilt with a lean bird body perched on top his high waist. Size-fifteen shoes. Hands could palm a basketball easy as holding a pool cue. Fingers long enough to wrap round a basketball, but Garth couldn't play a lick. Never could get all that lankiness together on the court. You'd look at him sometimes as he was trucking down Homewood Avenue and think that nigger ain't walking, he's trying to remember how to walk. Awkward as a pigeon on roller skates. Knobby joints out of whack, arms and legs flailing, going their separate ways, his body jerking to keep them from going too far. Moving down the street like that wouldn't work, didn't make sense if you stood back and watched, if you pretended you hadn't seen Garth get where he was going a million times before. Nothing funny now, though. White hospital sheets pulled to his chest. Garth's head always looked small as a tennis ball way up there on his shoulders. Now it's a yellow, shrunken skull.

Ever since Robby had entered the ward, he'd wanted to reach over and hide his friend's arm under the covers. For two weeks Gar had been wasting away in the bed. Bad enough knowing Gar was dying. Didn't need that pitiful stick arm reminding him how close to nothing his main man had fallen. So fast. It could happen so fast. If Robby tried to raise that arm it would come off in his hand. As gentle as he could would not be gentle enough. The arm would disintegrate, like a long ash off the end of a cigarette.

Time to leave. No sense in sitting any longer. Garth not talking, no way of telling whether he was listening either. And Robby has nothing more to say. Choked up the way he gets inside hospitals. Hospital smell and quiet, the bare halls and bare floors, the echoes, something about all that he can't name, wouldn't try to name, rises in him and chills him. Like his teeth are chattering the whole time he's inside a hospital. Like his entire body is trembling uncontrollably, only nobody can see it or hear it but him. Shaking because he can't breathe the stuffy air. Hot and cold at the same time. He's been aching to leave since he entered the ward. Aching to get up and bust through the big glass front doors. Aching to pounce on that spidery arm flung back behind Gar's head. The arm too wasted to belong to his friend. He wants to grab it and hurl it away.

Robby pulls on tight white gloves the undertaker had dealt out to him and the rest of the pallbearers. His brown skin shows through the thin material, turns the white dingy. He's remembering that last time in Garth's ward. The hospital stink. Hot, chilly air. A bare arm protruding from the sleeve of the hospital gown, more dried-up toothpick than arm, a withered twig, with Garth's fingers like a bunch of skinny brown bananas drooping from the knobby tip.

Robby had studied the metal guts of the hospital bed, the black scuff marks swirling round the chair's legs. When he'd finally risen to go, his chair scraping against the vinyl floor broke a long silence. The noise must have roused Garth's attention. He'd spoken again.

You're good, man. Don't ever forget, Rob. You're the best.

Garth's first words since the little banter back and forth when Robby had entered the ward and dragged a chair to the side of Gar's bed. A whisper scarcely audible now that Robby was standing. Garth had tried to grin. The best he could manage was a pained adjustment of the bones of his face, no more than a shadow scudding across the yellow skull, but Robby had seen the famous smile. He hesitated, stopped rushing toward the door long enough to smile back. Because that was Gar. That was the way Gar was. He always had a smile and a good word for his cut buddies. Garth's grin was money in the bank. You could count on it like you could count on a good word from him. Something in his face would tell you you were alright, better than alright, that he believed in you, that you were, as he'd just whispered, "the best." You could depend on Garth to say something to make you feel good, even though you knew he was lying. With that grin greasing the lie you had to believe it, even though you knew better. Garth was the gang's dreamer. When he talked, you could see his dreams. That's why Robby had believed it, seen the grin, the bright shadow lighting Garth's face an instant. Out of nothing, out of pain, fear, the certainty of death gripping them both, Garth's voice had manufactured the grin.

Now they had to bury Garth. A few days after the visit to the hospital the phone rang and it was Garth's mother with the news of her son's death. Not really news. Robby had known it was just a matter of time. Of waiting for the moment when somebody else's voice would pronounce the words he'd said to himself a hundred times. *He's gone. Gar's dead.* Long gone before the telephone rang. Gar was gone when they stuck him up in the hospital bed. By the time they'd figured out what ailed him and admitted him to the hospital, it was too late. The disease had turned him to a skeleton. Nothing left of Garth to treat. They hid his messy death under white sheets, perfumed it with disinfectant, pumped him full of drugs so he wouldn't disturb his neighbors.

The others had squeezed into their pallbearers' gloves. Cheap white cotton gloves so you could use them once and throw them away like the rubber ones doctors wear when they stick their fingers up your ass. Michael, Cecil, and Sowell were pallbearers, too. With Robby and two men from Garth's family they would carry the coffin from Gaines Funeral Parlor to the hearse. Garth had been the dreamer for the gang. Robby counted four black fingers in the white glove. Garth was the thumb. The hand would be clumsy, wouldn't work right without him. Garth was different. But everybody else was different, too. Mike, the ice man, supercool. Cecil indifferent, ready to do most anything or nothing and couldn't care less which it was. Sowell wasn't really part of the gang; he didn't hang with them, didn't like to take the risks that were part of the "life." Sowell kept a good job. The "life" for him was just a way to make quick money. He didn't shoot up; he thought of himself as a businessman, an investor not a partner in their schemes. They knew Sowell mostly through Garth. Perhaps things would change now. The four survivors closer after they shared the burden of Gar's coffin, after they hoisted it and slid it on steel rollers into the back of Gaines's Cadillac hearse.

Robby was grateful for the gloves. He'd never been able to touch anything dead. He'd taken a beating once from his father rather than touch the bloody mousetrap his mother had nudged to the back door with her toe and ordered him to empty. The brass handle of the coffin felt damp through the glove. He gripped tighter to stop the flow of blood or sweat, whatever it was leaking from him or seeping from the metal. Garth had melted down to nothing by the end so it couldn't be him nearly yanking off Robby's shoulder when the box shifted and its weight shot forward. Felt like the coffin full of bricks. Robby stared across at Mike but Mike was a soldier, eyes front, riveted to the yawning rear door of the hearse. Mike's eyes wouldn't admit it, but they'd almost lost the coffin. They were rookie pallbearers and maneuvering down the carpeted front steps of Gaines Funeral Parlor they'd almost let Garth fly out their hands. They needed somebody who knew what he was doing. An old, steady head to show them the way. They needed Garth. But Garth was long gone. Ashes inside the steel box.

They began drinking later that afternoon in Garth's people's house. Women and food in one room, men hitting the whiskey hard in another. It was a typical project apartment. The kind everybody had stayed in or visited one time or another. Small, shabby, featureless. Not a place to live. No matter what you did to it, how clean you kept it or what kind of furniture you loaded it with, the walls and ceilings were not meant to be home for anybody. A place you passed through. Not yours, because the people who'd been there before you left their indelible marks everywhere and you couldn't help adding your bruises and knots for the next tenants. You could rent a kitchen and bedroom and a bathroom and a living room, the project flats were laid out so you had a room for each of the things people did in houses. Problem was, every corner was cut. Living cramped is one thing and people can get cozy in the closest quarters. It's another thing to live in a place designed to be just a little less than adequate. No slack, no space to personalize, to stamp the flat with what's peculiar to your style. Like a man sitting on a toilet seat that's too small and the toilet too close to the bathtub so his knees shove against the enamel edge. He can move his bowels that way and plenty of people in the world have a lot less but he'll never enjoy sitting there, never feel the deep down comfort of belonging where he must squat.

Anyway, the whiskey started flowing in that little project apartment. Robby listened, for Garth's sake, as long as he could to old people reminiscing about funerals they'd attended, about all the friends and relatives they'd escorted to the edge of Jordan, old folks sipping good whiskey and moaning and groaning till it seemed a sin to be left behind on this side of the river after so many saints had crossed over. He listened to people express their grief, tell sad, familiar stories. As he got high he listened less closely to the words. Faces and gestures revealed more than enough. When he split with Mike and Cecil and their ladies, Sowell tagged along. By then the tacky, low-ceilinged rooms of the flat were packed. Loud talk, laughter, storytellers competing for audiences. Robby half expected the door he pushed shut behind himself to pop open again, waited for bottled-up noise to explode into the funky hallway.

Nobody thinking about cemeteries now. Nobody else needs to be buried today, so it was time to get it on. Some people had been getting close to rowdy. Some people had been getting mad. Mad at one of the guests in the apartment, mad at doctors and hospitals and whites in general who had the whole world in their hands but didn't have the slightest idea what to do with it. A short, dark man, bubble-eyed, immaculately dressed in a three-piece, wool, herringbone suit, had railed about the callousness, the ignorance of white witch doctors who, by misdiagnosing Garth's illness, had sealed his doom. His harangue had drawn a crowd. He wasn't just talking, he was testifying, and a hush had fallen over half the room as he dissected the dirty tricks of white folks. If somebody ran to the hospital and snatched a white-coated doctor and threw him into the circle surrounding the little fish-eyed man, the mourners would tear the pale-faced devil apart. Robby wished he could feed them one. Remembered Garth weak and helpless in the bed and the doctors and nurses flitting around in the halls, jiving the other patients, ignoring Gar like he wasn't there. Garth was dead because he had believed them. Dead because he had nowhere else to turn when the pain in his gut and the headaches grew worse and worse. Not that he trusted the doctors or believed they gave a flying fuck about him. He'd just run out of choices and had to put himself in their hands. They told him jaundice was his problem, and while his liver rotted away and pain cooked him dizzy Garth assured anyone who asked that it was just a matter of giving the medicine time to work. To kill the pain he blew weed as long as he had strength to hold a joint between his lips. Take a whole bunch of smoke to cool me out these days. Puffing like a chimney till he lost it and fell back and Robby scrambling to grab the joint before Garth torched hisself.

When you thought about it, Garth's dying made no sense. And the more you thought the more you dug that nothing else did neither. The world's a stone bitch. Nothing true if that's not true. The man had you coming and going. He owned everything worth owning and all you'd ever get was what he didn't want anymore, what he'd chewed and spit out and left in the gutter for niggers to fight over. Garth had pointed to the street and said, If we ever make it, it got to come from there, from the curb. We got to melt that rock till we get us some money. He grinned then, Ain't no big thing. We'll make it, brother man. We got what it takes. It's our time.

Something had crawled in Garth's belly. The man said it wasn't nothing. Sold him some aspirins and said he'd be alright in no time. The man killed Garth. Couldn't kill him no deader with a .357 magnum slug, but ain't no crime been committed. Just one those things. You know, everybody makes mistakes. And a dead nigger ain't really such a big mistake when you think about it. Matter of fact you mize well forget the whole thing. Nigger wasn't going nowhere, nohow. I mean he wasn't no brain surgeon or astronaut, no movie star or big-time athlete. Probably a dope fiend or gangster. Wind up killing some innocent person or wasting another nigger. Shucks. That doctor ought to get a medal.

Hey, man. Robby caught Mike's eye. Then Cecil and Sowell turned to him. They knew he was speaking to everybody. Late now. Ten, eleven, because it had been dark outside for hours. Quiet now. Too quiet in his pad. And too much smoke and drink since the funeral. From a bare bulb in the kitchen ceiling light seeped down the hallway and hovered dimly in the doorway of the room where they sat. Robby wondered if the others felt as bad as he did. If the cemetery clothes itched their skin. If they could smell grave dust on their shoes. He hoped they'd finish this last jug of wine and let the day be over. He needed sleep, downtime to get the terrible weight of Garth's death off his mind. He'd been grateful for the darkness. For the company of his cut buddies after the funeral. For the Sun Ra tape until it ended and plunged them into a deeper silence than any he'd ever known. Garth was gone. In a few days people would stop talking about him. He was in the ground. Stone-cold dead. Robby had held a chunk of crumbly ground in his white-gloved fingers and mashed it and dropped the dust into the hole. Now the ground had closed over Garth and what did it mean? Here one day and gone the next and that was that. They'd bury somebody else out of Gaines tomorrow. People would dress up and cry and get drunk and tell lies and next day it'd be somebody else's turn to die. Which one of the shadows in this black room would go first? What did it matter? Who cared? Who would remember their names; they were ghosts already. Dead as Garth already. Only difference was, Garth didn't have it to worry about no more. Garth didn't have to pretend he was going anywhere cause he was there. He'd made it to the place they all were headed fast as their legs could carry them. Every step was a step closer to the stone-cold ground, the pitch-black hole where they'd dropped Garth's body.

Hey, youall. We got to drink to Garth one last time.

They clinked glasses in the darkness. Robby searched for something to say. The right words wouldn't come. He knew there was something proper and precise that needed to be said. Because the exact words eluded him, because only the right words would do, he swallowed his gulp of heavy, sweet wine in silence.

He knew he'd let Garth down. If it had been one of the others dead, Michael or Cecil or Sowell or him, Garth wouldn't let it slide by like this, wouldn't let it end like so many other nights had ended, the fellows nodding off one by one, stupefied by smoke and drink, each one beginning to shop around in his mind, trying to figure whether or not he should turn in or if there was a lady somewhere who'd welcome him in her bed. No. Garth would have figured a way to make it special. They wouldn't be hiding in the bushes. They'd be knights in shining armor around a big table. They'd raise their giant, silver cups to honor the fallen comrade. Like in the olden days. Clean, brave dudes with gold rings and gold chains. They'd draw their blades. Razor-edged swords that gleam in the light with jewels sparkling in the handles. They'd make a roof over the table when they stood and raised their swords and the points touched in the sky. A silver dagger on a satin pillow in the middle of the table. Everybody roll up their sleeves and prick a vein and go round, each one touching everybody else so the blood runs together and we're brothers forever, brothers as long as blood flows in anybody's arm. We'd ride off and do unbelievable shit. The dead one always with us cause we'd do it all for him. Swear we'd never let him down.

It's our time now. We can't let Garth down. Let's drink this last one for him and promise him we'll do what he said we could. We'll be the best. We'll make it the top for him. We'll do it for Garth.

Glasses rattle together again. Robby empties his and thinks about smashing it against a wall. He'd seen it done that way in movies but it was late at night and these crazy niggers might not know when to stop throwing things. A battlefield of broken glass for him to creep through when he gets out of bed in the morning. He doesn't toss the empty glass. Can't see a solid place anyway where it would strike clean and shatter to a million points of light.

My brother had said something about a guy named Garth during one of my visits to the prison. Just a name mentioned in passing. *Garth* or *Gar*. I'd asked Robby to spell it for me. Garth had been a friend of Robby's, about Robby's age, who died one summer of a mysterious disease. Later when Robby chose to begin the story of the robbery and killing by saying, "It all started with Gar dying," I remembered that first casual mention and remembered a conversation with my mother. My mom and I were in the kitchen of the house on Tokay Street. My recollection of details was vague at first but something about the conversation had made a lasting impression because, six years later, hearing Robby say the name *Garth* brought back my mother's words.

My mother worried about Robby all the time. Whenever I visited home, sooner or later I'd find myself alone with Mom and she'd pour out her fears about Robby's *wildness*, the deep trouble he was bound for, the web of entanglements and intrigues and bad company he was weaving around himself with a maddening disregard for the inevitable consequences.

I don't know. I just don't know how to reach him. He won't listen. He's doing wrong and he knows it but nothing I say makes any difference. He's not like the rest of youall. You'd misbehave but I could talk to you or smack you if I had to and you'd straighten up. With Robby it's like talking to a wall.

I'd listen and get angry at my brother because I registered not so much the danger he was bringing on himself, but the effect of his escapades on the woman who'd brought us both into the world. After all, Robby was no baby. If he wanted to mess up, nobody could stop him. Also Robby was my brother, meaning that his wildness was just a stage, a chaotic phase of his life that would only last till he got his head together and decided to start doing right. Doing as the rest of us did. He was my brother. He couldn't fall too far. His brushes with the law (I'd had some, too), the time he'd spent in jail, were serious but temporary setbacks. I viewed his troubles, when I thought about them at all, as a form of protracted juvenile delinquency, and fully expected Robby would learn his lesson sooner or later and return to the fold, the prodigal son, chastened, perhaps a better person for the experience. In the meantime the most serious consequence of his wildness was Mom's devastating unhappiness. She couldn't sustain the detachment, the laissez-faire optimism I had talked myself into. Because I was two thousand miles away, in Wyoming, I didn't have to deal with the day-to-day evidence of Robby's trouble. The syringe Mom found under his bed. The twenty-dollar bill missing from her purse. The times he'd cruise in higher than a kite, his pupils reduced to pinpricks, with his crew and they'd raid the refrigerator and make a loud, sloppy feast, all of them feeling so good they couldn't imagine anybody not up there on cloud nine with them enjoying the time of their lives. Cruising in, then disappearing just as abruptly, leaving their dishes and pans and mess behind. Robby covering Mom with kisses and smiles and drowning her in baby-talk hootchey-coo as he staggers through the front door. Her alone in the ravaged, silent kitchen, listening as doors slam and a car squeals off on the cobblestones of Tokay, wondering where they're headed next, wishing, praying Robby will return and eat and eat and eat till he falls asleep at the table so she can carry him upstairs and tuck him in and kiss his forehead and shut the door gently on his sleep.

I wasn't around for all that. Didn't want to know how bad things were for him. Worrying about my mother was tough enough. I could identify with her grief, I could blame my brother. An awful situation, but simple too. My role, my responsibilities and loyalties were clear. The *wildness* was to blame, and it was a passing thing, so I just had to help my mother survive the worst of it, then everything would be alright. I'd steel myself for the moments alone with her when she'd tell me the worst. In the kitchen, usually, over a cup of coffee with the radio playing. When my mother was alone in the house on Tokay, either the TV or a radio or both were always on. Atop the kitchen table a small clock radio turned to WAMO, one of Pittsburgh's soul stations, would background with scratchy gospel music whatever we said in the morning in the kitchen. On a morning like that in 1975, while I drank a cup of coffee and part of me, still half-sleep, hidden, swayed to the soft beat of gospel, my mother had explained how upset Robby was over the death of his friend, Garth.

It was a terrible thing. I've known Garth's mother for years. He was a good boy. No saint for sure, but deep down a good boy. Like your brother. Not a mean bone in his body. Out there in the street doing wrong, but that's where most of them are. What else can they do, John? Sometimes I can't blame them. No jobs, no money in their pockets. How they supposed to feel like men? Garth did better than most. Whatever else he was into, he kept that little job over at Westinghouse and helped out his mother. A big, playful kid. Always smiling. I think that's why him and Robby were so tight. Neither one had good sense. Giggled and acted like fools. Garth no wider than my finger. Straight up and down. A stringbean if I ever saw one. When Robby lived here in the house with me, Garth was always around. I know how bad Robby feels. He hasn't said a word but I know. When Robby's quiet, you know something's wrong. Soon as his eyes pop open in the morning he's looking for the party. First thing in the morning he's chipper and chattering. Looking for the party. That's your brother. He had a match in Garth.

Shame the way they did that boy. He'd been down to the clinic two or three times but they sent him home. Said he had an infection and it would take care of itself. Something like that anyway. You know how they are down there. Have to be spitting blood to get attention. Then all they give you is a Band-Aid. He went back two times, but they kept telling him the same dumb thing. Anybody who knew Garth could see something awful was wrong. Circles under his eyes. Sallow look to his skin. Losing weight. And the poor thing didn't have any weight to lose. Last time I saw him I was shocked. Just about shocked out my shoes. Wasn't Garth standing in front of me. Not the boy I knew.

Well, to make a long story short, they finally took him in the hospital but it was too late. They let him walk the streets till he was dead. It was wrong. Worse than wrong how they did him, but that's how those dogs do us every day God sends here. Garth's gone, so nothing nobody can say will do any good. I feel so sorry for his mother. She lived for that boy. I called her and tried to talk but what can you say? I prayed for her and prayed for Garth and prayed for Robby. A thing like that tears people up. It's worse if you keep it inside. And that's your brother's way. He'll let it eat him up and then go out and do something crazy.

Until she told me Garth's story I guess I hadn't realized how much my mother had begun to change. She had always seemed to me to exemplify the tolerance, the patience, the long view epitomized in her father. John French's favorite saying was, Give 'em the benefit of the doubt. She could get as ruffled, as evil as the rest of us, cry and scream or tear around the house fit to be tied. She had her grudges and quarrels. Mom could let it all hang out, yet most of the time she radiated a deep calm. She reacted strongly to things but at the same time held judgment in abeyance. Events, personalities always deserved a second, slower appraisal, an evaluation outside the sphere of everyday hassles and vexations. You gave people the benefit of the doubt. You attempted to remove your ego, acknowledge the limitations of your individual view of things. You consulted as far as you were equipped by temperament and intelligence a broader, more abiding set of relationships and connections.

You tried on the other person's point of view. You sought the other, better person in yourself who might talk you into relinquishing for a moment your selfish interest in whatever was at issue. You stopped and considered the long view, possibilities other than the one that momentarily was leading you by the nose. You gave yourself and other people the benefit of the doubt.

My mother had that capacity. I'd admired, envied, and benefited infinitely from its presence. As she related the story of Garth's death and my brother's anger and remorse, her tone was uncompromisingly bitter. No slack, no margin of doubt was being granted to the forces that destroyed Garth and still pursued her son. She had exhausted her reserves of understanding and compassion. The long view supplied the same ugly picture as the short. She had an enemy now. It was that revealed truth that had given the conversation its edge, its impact. *They* had killed Garth, and his dying had killed part of her son; so the battle lines were drawn. Irreconcilably. Absolutely. The backside of John French's motto had come into play. Giving someone the benefit of the doubt was also giving him enough rope to hang himself. If a person takes advantage of the benefit of the doubt and keeps on taking and taking, one day the rope plays out. The piper must be paid. If you've been the one giving, it becomes incumbent on you to grip your end tight and take away. You turn the other cheek, but slowly, cautiously, and keep your fist balled up at your side. If your antagonist decides to smack rather than kiss you or leave you alone, you make sure you get in the first blow. And make sure it's hard enough to knock him down.

Before she told Garth's story, my mother had already changed, but it took years for me to realize how profoundly she hated what had been done to Garth and then Robby. The gentleness of my grandfather, like his fair skin and good French hair, had been passed down to my mother. Gentleness styled the way she thought, spoke, and moved in the world. Her easy disposition and sociability masked the intensity of her feelings. Her attitude to authority of any kind, doctors, clerks, police, bill collectors, newscasters, whites in general partook of her constitutional gentleness. She wasn't docile or cowed. The power other people possessed or believed they possessed didn't frighten her; she accommodated herself, offered something they could accept as deference but that was in fact the same resigned, alert attention she paid to roaches or weather or poverty, any of the givens outside herself that she couldn't do much about. She never engaged in public tests of will, never pushed herself or her point of view on people she didn't know. Social awkwardness embarrassed her. Like most Americans she didn't like paying taxes, was suspicious of politicians, resented the disparity between big and little people in our society and the double standard that allowed big shots to get away with murder. She paid particular attention to news stories that reinforced her basic political assumption that power corrupts. On the other hand she knew the world was a vale of tears and one's strength, granted by God to deal with life's inevitable calamities, should not be squandered on small stuff.

In spite of all her temperamental and philosophic resistance to extremes, my mother would be radicalized. What the demonstrations, protest marches, and slogans of the sixties had not effected would be accomplished by Garth's death and my brother's troubles. She would become an aggressive, acid critic of the status quo in all its forms: from the President ("If it wasn't for that rat I'd have a storm door to go with the storm windows but he cut the program") on down to bank tellers

("I go there every Friday and I'm one of the few black faces she sees all day and she knows me as well as she knows that wart on her cheek but she'll still make me show my license before she'll cash my check"). A son she loved would be pursued, captured, tried, and imprisoned by the forces of law and order. Throughout the ordeal her love for him wouldn't change, couldn't change. His crime tested her love and also tested the nature, the intent of the forces arrayed against her son. She had to make a choice. On one side were the stark facts of his crime: robbery, murder, flight; her son an outlaw, a fugitive; then a prisoner. On the other side the guardians of society, the laws, courts, police, judges, and keepers who were responsible for punishing her son's transgression.

She didn't invent the two sides and initially didn't believe there couldn't be a middle ground. She extended the benefit of the doubt. Tried to situate herself somewhere in between, acknowledging the evil of her son's crime while simultaneously holding on to the fact that he existed as a human being before, after, and during the crime he'd committed. He'd done wrong but he was still Robby and she'd always be his mother. Strangely, on the dark side, the side of the crime and its terrible consequences, she would find room to exercise her love. As negative as the elements were, a life taken, the grief of the survivors, suffering, waste, guilt, remorse, the scale was human; she could apply her sense of right and wrong. Her life to that point had equipped her with values, with tools for sorting out and coping with disaster. So she would choose to make her fight there, on treacherous yet familiar ground—familiar since her son was there—and she could place herself, a woman, a mother, a grieving, bereaved human being, there beside him.

Nothing like that was possible on the other side. The legitimacy of the other side was grounded not in her experience of life, but in a set of rules seemingly framed to sidestep, ignore, or replace her sense of reality. Accepting the version of reality encoded in *their* rules would be like stepping into a cage and locking herself in. Definitions of her son, herself, of need and frailty and mercy, of blackness and redemption and justice had all been neatly formulated. No need here for her questions, her uncertainty, her fear, her love. Everything was clean and clear. No room for her sense that things like good and evil, right and wrong bleed into each other and create a dreadful margin of ambiguity no one could name but could only enter, enter at the risk of everything because everything is at stake and no one on earth knows what it means to enter or what will happen if and when the testing of the margin is over.

She could love her son, accept his guilt, accept the necessity of punishment, suffer with him, grow with him past the stage of blaming everyone but himself for his troubles, grieve with him when true penitence began to exact its toll. Though she might wish penance and absolution could be achieved in private, without the intervention of a prison sentence, she understood dues must be paid. He was her son but he was also a man who had committed a robbery in the course of which another woman's son had been killed. What would appall her and what finally turned her against the forces of law and order was the incapacity of the legal system to grant her son's humanity. "Fair" was the word she used—a John French word. She expected them to treat Robby fair. Fairness was what made her willing to give him up to punishment even though her love screamed no and her hands clung to his shoulders. Fairness was what she expected from the other side in their dealings with her and her son.

She could see their side, but they steadfastly refused to see hers. And when she realized fairness was not forthcoming, she began to hate. In the lack of reciprocity, in the failure to grant that Robby was first a man, then a man who had done wrong, the institutions and individuals who took over control of his life denied not only his humanity but the very existence of the world that had nurtured him and nurtured her—the world of touching, laughing, suffering black people that established Robby's claim to something more than a number.

Mom expects the worst now. She's peeped their hole card. She understands they have a master plan that leaves little to accident, that most of the ugliest things happening to black people are not accidental but the predictable results of the working of the plan. What she learned about authority, about law and order didn't make sense at first. It went against her instincts, what she wanted to believe, against the generosity she'd observed in her father's interactions with other Homewood people. He was fair. He'd pick up the egg rolls he loved from the back kitchen door of Mr. Wong's restaurant and not blame Wong, his old talking buddy and card-playing crony, for not serving black people in his restaurant. Wong had a family and depended on white folks to feed them, so Wong didn't have any choice and neither did John French if he wanted those incredible egg rolls. He treated everyone, high and low, the same. He said what he meant and meant what he said. John French expected no more from other people than he expected from himself. And he'd been known to mess up many a time, but that was him, that was John French, no better, no worse than any man who pulls on his britches one leg at a time. He needed a little slack, needed the benefit of that blind eye people who love, or people who want to get along with other people, must learn to cast. John French was grateful for the slack, so was quick to extend it to others. Till they crossed him.

My mother had been raised in Homewood. The old Homewood. Her relations with people in that close-knit, homogeneous community were based on trust, mutual respect, common spiritual and material concerns. Face-to-face contact, shared language and values, a large fund of communal experience rendered individual lives extremely visible in Homewood. Both a person's self-identity ("You know who you are") and accountability ("Other people know who you are") were firmly established.

If one of the Homewood people said, "That's the French girl" or, "There goes John French's daughter," a portrait with subtle shading and complex resonance was painted by the words. If the listener addressed was also a Homewood resident, the speaker's voice located the young woman passing innocently down Tioga Street in a world invisible to outsiders. A French girl was somebody who lived in Cassina Way, somebody you didn't fool with or talk nasty to. Didn't speak to at all except in certain places or on certain occasions. French girls were church girls, Homewood African Methodist Episcopal Zion Sunday-school-picnic and social-event young ladies. You wouldn't find them hanging around anywhere without escorts or chaperones. French girls had that fair, light, bright, almost white red-bone complexion and fine blow hair and nice big legs but all that was to be appreciated from a distance because they were nice girls and because they had this crazy daddy who wore a big brown country hat and gambled and drank wine and once ran a man out of town, ran him away without ever laying a hand on him or making a bad-mouthed threat, just cut his eyes a certain way when he said the man's name and the word went out and the man who had cheated a drunk John French with loaded dice was gone. Just like that. And there was the time Elias Brown was cleaning his shotgun in his backyard. Brown had his double-barreled shotgun across his knees and a jug of Dago Red on the ground beside him and it was a Saturday and hot and Brown was sweating through his BVD undershirt and paying more attention to the wine than he was to the gun. Next thing you know, *Boom!* Off it goes and buckshot sprayed down Cassina Way, and it's Saturday and summer like I said, so chillens playing everywhere but God watches over fools and babies so nobody hit bad. Nobody hit at all except the little French girl, Geraldine, playing out there in the alley and she got nicked in her knee. Barely drew blood. A sliver of that buckshot musta ricocheted off the cobblestones and cut her knee. Thank Jesus she the only one hit and she ain't hit bad. Poor Elias Brown don't quite know what done happened till some the mens run over in his yard and snatch the gun and shake the wine out his head. What you doing, fool? Don't you know no better all those children running round here? Coulda killed one these babies. Elias stone drunk and don't hear nothing, see nothing till one the men say French girl. Nicked the little French girl, Geraldine. Then Elias woke up real quick. His knees, his dusty butt, everything he got starts to trembling and his eyes get big as dinner plates. Then he's gone like a turkey through the corn. Nobody seen Elias for a week. He's in Ohio at his sister's next time anybody hear anything about Elias. He's cross there in Ohio and still shaking till he git word John French ain't after him. It took three men gon over there telling the same story to get Elias back to Homewood. John French ain't mad. He *was* mad but he ain't mad now. Little girl just nicked is all and French ain't studying you, Brown.

You heard things like that in Homewood names. Rules of etiquette, thumbnail character sketches, a history of the community. A dire warning to get back could be coded into the saying of a person's name, and a further inflection of the speaker's voice could tell you to ignore the facts, forget what he's just reminded you to remember and go on. Try your luck.

Because Homewood was self-contained and possessed such a strong personality, because its people depended less on outsiders than they did on each other for so many of their most basic satisfactions, they didn't notice the net settling over their community until it was already firmly in place. Even though the strands of the net—racial discrimination, economic exploitation, white hate and fear—had existed time out of mind, what people didn't notice or chose not to notice was that the net was being drawn tighter, that ruthless people outside the community had the power to choke the life out of Homewood, and as soon as it served their interests would do just that. During the final stages, as the net closed like a fist around Homewood, my mother couldn't pretend it wasn't there. But instead of setting her free, the truth trapped her in a cage as tangible as the iron bars of Robby's cell.

Some signs were subtle, gradual. The A & P started to die. Nobody mopped filth from the floors. Nobody bothered to restock empty shelves. Fewer and fewer white faces among the shoppers. A plate-glass display window gets broken and stays broken. When they finally close the store, they paste the going-out-of-business notice over the jagged, taped crack. Other signs as blatant, as sudden as fire engines and patrol cars breaking your sleep, screaming through the dark Homewood streets. First Garth's death, then Robby's troubles brought it all home. My mother realized her personal unhappiness and grief were inseparable from what was happening *out there*. Out there had never been further away than the thousand insults and humiliations she had disciplined herself to ignore. What she had deemed petty, not worth bothering about, were strings of the net just as necessary, as effective as the most dramatic intrusions into her life. She decided to stop letting things go by. No more benefit of the doubt. Doubt had been cruelly excised. She decided to train herself to be as wary, as unforgiving as she'd once been ready to live and let live. My mother wouldn't become paranoid, not even overtly prickly or bristling. That would have been too contrary to her style, to what her blood and upbringing had instilled. The change was inside. What she thought of people. How she judged situations. Things she'd say or do startled me, set me back on my heels because I didn't recognize my mother in them. I couldn't account for the stare of pure unadulterated hatred she directed at the prison guard when he turned away from her to answer the phone before handing her the rest-room key she'd requested, the vehemence with which she had cussed Richard Nixon for paying no taxes when she, scraping by on an income of less than four thousand dollars a year, owed the IRS three hundred dollars.

Garth's death and Robby's troubles were at the center of her new vision. Like a prism, they caught the light, transformed it so she could trace the seemingly random inconveniences and impositions coloring her life to their source in a master plan.

I first heard Garth's story in the summer of 1975, the summer my wife carried our daughter Jamila in her belly, the summer before the robbery and killing. The story contained all the clues I'm trying to decipher now. Sitting in the kitchen vaguely distracted by gospel music from the little clock radio atop the table, listening as my mother expressed her sorrow, her indignation at the way Garth was treated, her fears for my brother, I was hearing a new voice. Something about the voice struck me then, but I missed what was novel and crucial. I'd lost my Homewood ear. Missed all the things unsaid that invested her words with special urgency. People in Homewood often ask: You said that to say what? The impacted quality of an utterance either buries a point too obscurely or insists on a point so strongly that the listener wants the meat of the message repeated, wants it restated clearly so it stands alone on its own two feet. If I'd been alert enough to ask that question, to dig down to the root and core of Garth's story after my mother told it, I might have understood sooner how desperate and dangerous Homewood had become. Six years later my brother was in prison, and when he began the story of his troubles with Garth's death, a circle completed itself; Robby was talking to me, but I was still on the outside, looking in.

That day six years later, I talked with Robby three hours, the maximum allotted for weekday visits with a prisoner. It was the first time in life we'd ever talked that long. Probably two and a half hours longer than the longest, unbroken, private conversation we'd ever had. And it had taken guards, locks, and bars to bring us together. The ironies of the situation, the irony of that fact, escaped neither of us.

I listened mostly, interrupting my brother's story a few times to clarify dates or names. Much of what he related was familiar. The people, the places. Even the voice, the words he chose were mine in a way. We're so alike, I kept thinking, anticipating what he would say next, how he would say it, filling in naturally, easily with my words what he left unsaid. Trouble was our minds weren't interchangeable. No more than our bodies. The guards wouldn't have allowed me to stay in my brother's place. He was the criminal. I was the visitor from outside. Different as night and day. As Robby talked I let myself forget that difference. Paid too much attention to myself listening and lost some of what he was saying. What I missed would have helped define the difference. But I missed it. It was easy to half listen. For both of us to pretend to be closer than we were. We needed the closeness. We were brothers. In the prison visiting lounge I acted toward my brother the way I'd been acting toward him all my life, heard what I wanted to hear, rejected the rest.

When Robby talked, the similarity of his Homewood and mine was a trap. I could believe I knew exactly what he was describing. I could relax into his story, walk down Dunfermline or Tioga, see my crippled grandmother sitting on the porch of the house on Finance, all the color her pale face had lost blooming in the rosebush beneath her in the yard, see Robby in the downstairs hall of the house on Marchand, rapping with his girl on the phone, which sat on a three-legged stand just inside the front door. I'd slip unaware out of his story into one of my own. I'd be following him, an obedient shadow, then a cloud would blot the sun and I'd be gone, unchained, a dark form still skulking behind him but no longer in tow.

The hardest habit to break, since it was the habit of a lifetime, would be listening to myself listen to him. That habit would destroy any chance of seeing my brother on his terms; and seeing him in his terms, learning his terms, seemed the whole point of learning his story. However numerous and comforting the similarities, we were different. The world had seized on the difference, allowed me room to thrive, while he'd been forced into a cage. Why did it work out that way? What was the nature of the difference? Why did it haunt me? Temporarily at least, to answer these questions, I had to root my fiction-writing self out of our exchanges. I had to teach myself to listen. Start fresh, clear the pipes, resist too facile an identification, tame the urge to take off with Robby's story and make it my own.

I understood all that, but could I break the habit? And even if I did learn to listen, wouldn't there be a point at which I'd have to take over the telling? Wasn't there something fundamental in my writing, in my capacity to function, that depended on flight, on escape? Wasn't another person's skin a hiding place, a place to work out anxiety, to face threats too intimidating to handle in any other fashion? Wasn't writing about people a way of exploiting them?

A stranger's gait, or eyes, or a piece of clothing can rivet my attention. Then it's like falling down to the center of the earth. Not exactly fear or panic but an uneasy, uncontrollable momentum, a sense of being swallowed, engulfed in blackness that has no dimensions, no fixed points. That boundless, incarcerating black hole is another person. The detail grabbing me functions as a door and it swings open and I'm drawn, sucked, pulled in head over heels till suddenly I'm righted again, on track again and the peculiarity, the ordinariness of the detail that usurped my attention becomes a window, a way of seeing out of another person's eyes, just as for a second it had been my way in. I'm scooting along on short, stubby legs and the legs are not anybody else's and certainly not mine, but I feel for a second what it's like to motor through the world atop those peculiar duck thighs and foreshortened calves and I know how wobbly the earth feels under those run-over-at-the-heel, split-seamed penny loafers. Then just as suddenly I'm back. I'm me again, slightly embarrassed, guilty because I've been trespassing and don't know how long I've been gone or if anybody noticed me violating somebody else's turf.

Do I write to escape, to make a fiction of my life? If I can't be trusted with the story of my own life, how could I ask my brother to trust me with his?

The business of making a book together was new for both of us. Difficult. Awkward. Another book could be constructed about a writer who goes to a prison to interview his brother but comes away with his own story. The conversations with his brother would provide a stage for dramatizing the writer's tortured relationship to other people, himself, his craft. The writer's motives, the issue of exploitation, the inevitable conflict between his role as detached observer and his responsibility as a brother would be at the center of such a book. When I stopped hearing Robby and listened to myself listening, that kind of book shouldered its way into my consciousness. I didn't like the feeling. That book compromised the intimacy I wanted to achieve with my brother. It was as obtrusive as the Wearever pen in my hand, the little yellow sheets of Yard Count paper begged from the pad of the guard in charge of overseeing the visiting lounge. The borrowed pen and paper (I was not permitted into the lounge with my own) were necessary props. I couldn't rely on memory to get my brother's story down and the keepers had refused my request to use a tape recorder, so there I was. Jimmy Olson, cub reporter, poised on the edge of my seat, pen and paper at ready, asking to be treated as a brother.

We were both rookies. Neither of us had learned very much about sharing our feelings with other family members. At home it had been assumed that each family member possessed deep, powerful feelings and that very little or nothing at all needed to be said about these feelings because we all were stuck with them and talk wouldn't change them. Your particular feelings were a private matter and family was a protective fence around everybody's privacy. Inside the perimeter of the fence each family member resided in his or her own quarters. What transpired in each dwelling was mainly the business of its inhabitant as long as nothing generated within an individual unit threatened the peace or safety of the whole. None of us knew how traditional West African families were organized or what values the circular shape of their villages embodied, but the living arrangements we had worked out among ourselves resembled the ancient African patterns. You were granted emotional privacy, independence, and space to commune with your feelings. You were encouraged to deal with as much as you could on your own, yet you never felt alone. The high wall of the family, the collective, communal reality of other souls, other huts like yours eliminated some of the dread, the isolation experienced when you turned inside and tried to make sense out of the chaos of your individual feelings. No matter how grown you thought you were or how far you believed you'd strayed, you knew you could cry *Mama* in the depths of the night and somebody would tend to you. Arms would wrap round you, a soft soothing voice lend its support. If not a flesh-and-blood mother then a mother in the form of song or story or a surrogate, Aunt Geral, Aunt Martha, drawn from the network of family numbers.

Privacy was a bridge between you and the rest of the family. But you had to learn to control the traffic. You had to keep it uncluttered, resist the temptation to cry wolf. Privacy in our family was a birthright, a union card granted with family membership. The card said you're one of us but also certified your separateness, your obligation to keep much of what defined your separateness to yourself.

An almost aesthetic consideration's involved. Okay, let's live together. Let's each build a hut and for security we'll arrange the individual dwellings in a circle and then build an outer ring to enclose the whole village. Now your hut is your own business, but let's in general agree on certain outward forms. Since we all benefit from the larger pattern, let's compromise, conform to some degree on the materials, the shape of each unit. Because symmetry and harmony please the eye. Let's adopt a style, one that won't crimp anybody's individuality, one that will buttress and enhance each member's image of what a living place should be.

So Robby and I faced each other in the prison visiting lounge as familiar strangers, linked by blood and time. But how do you begin talking about blood, about time? He's been inside his privacy and I've been inside mine, and neither of us in thirty-odd years had felt the need to exchange more than social calls. We shared the common history, values, and style developed within the tall stockade of family, and that was enough to make us care about each other, enough to insure a profound depth of mutual regard, but the feelings were undifferentiated. They'd seldom been tested specifically, concretely. His privacy and mine had been exclusive, sanctioned by family traditions. Don't get too close. Don't ask too many questions or give too many answers. Don't pry. Don't let what's inside slop out on the people around you.

The stories I'd sent to Robby were an attempt to reveal what I thought about certain matters crucial to us both. Our shared roots and destinies. I wanted him to know what I'd been thinking and how that thinking was drawing me closer to him. I was banging on the door of his privacy. I believed I'd shed some of my own.

We were ready to talk. It was easy to begin. Impossible. We were neophytes, rookies. I was a double rookie. A beginner at this kind of intimacy, a beginner at trying to record it. My double awkwardness kept getting in the way. I'd hidden the borrowed pen by dropping my hand below the level of the table where we sat. Now when in hell would be the right moment to raise it? To use it? I had to depend on my brother's instincts, his generosity. I had to listen, listen.

Luckily there was catching up to do. He asked me about my kids, about his son, Omar, about the new nieces and nephews he'd never seen. That helped. Reminded us we were brothers. We got on with it. Conditions in the prisons. Robby's state of mind. The atmosphere behind the prison walls had been particularly tense for over a year. A group of new, younger guards had instituted a get-tough policy. More strip searches, cell shakedowns, strict enforcement of penny-ante rules and regulations. Grown men treated like children by other grown men. Inmates yanked out of line and punished because a button is undone or hair uncombed. What politicians demanded in the free world was being acted out inside the prison. A crusade, a war on crime waged by a gang of gung-ho guards against men who were already certified casualties, prisoners of war. The walking wounded being beaten and shot up again because they're easy targets. Robby's closest friends, including Cecil and Mike, are in the hole. Others who were considered potential troublemakers had been transferred to harsher prisons. Robby was warned by a guard. We ain't caught you in the shit yet, but we will. We know what you're thinking and we'll catch you in it. Or put you in it. Got your buddies and we'll get you.

The previous summer, 1980, a prisoner, Leon Patterson, had been asphyxiated in his cell. He was an asthma sufferer, a convicted murderer who depended on medication to survive the most severe attacks of his illness. On a hot August afternoon when the pollution index had reached its highest count of the summer, Patterson was locked in his cell in a cellblock without windows and little air. At four o'clock, two hours after he'd been confined to the range, he began to call for help. Other prisoners raised the traditional distress signal, rattling tin cups against the bars of their cells. Patterson's cries for help became screams, and his fellow inmates beat on the bars and shouted with him. Over an hour passed before any guards arrived. They carted away Patterson's limp body. He never revived and was pronounced dead at 10:45 that evening. His death epitomized the polarization in the prison. Patterson was seen as one more victim of the guards' inhumanity. A series of incidents followed in the ensuing year, hunger strikes, melees between guards and prisoners, culminating in a near massacre when the dog days of August hung once more over the prison.

One of the favorite tactics of the militant guards was grabbing a man from the line as the prisoners moved single-file through an archway dividing the recreation yard from the main cell blocks. No reason was given or needed. It was a simple show of force, a reminder of the guards' absolute power, their right to treat the inmates any way they chose, and do it with impunity. A sit-down strike in the prison auditorium followed one of the more violent attacks on an inmate. The prisoner who had resisted an arbitrary seizure and strip search was smacked in the face. He punched back and the guards jumped him, knocked him to the ground with their fists and sticks. The incident took place in plain view of over a hundred prisoners and it was the last straw. The victim had been provoked, assaulted, and surely would be punished for attempting to protect himself, for doing what any man would and should do in similar circumstances. The prisoner would suffer again. In addition to the physical beating they'd administered, the guards would attack the man's record. He'd be written up. A kangaroo court would take away his *good time*, thereby lengthening the period he'd have to wait before becoming eligible for probation or parole. Finally, on the basis of the guards' testimony he'd probably get a sixty-day sojourn in the hole. The prisoners realized it was time to take a stand. What had happened to one could happen to any of them. They rushed into the auditorium and locked themselves in. The prisoners held out till armed state troopers and prison guards in riot gear surrounded the building. Given the mood of that past year and the unmistakable threat in the new warden's voice as he repeated through a loudspeaker his refusal to meet with the prisoners and discuss their grievances, everybody inside the building knew that the authorities meant business, that the forces of law and order would love nothing better than an excuse to turn the auditorium into a shooting gallery. The strike was broken. The men filed out. A point was driven home again. Prisoners have no rights the keepers are bound to respect.

That was how the summer had gone. Summer was bad enough in the penitentiary in the best of times. Warm weather stirred the prisoners' blood. The siren call of the streets intensified. Circus time. The street blooming again after the long, cold winter. People outdoors. On their stoops. On the corners. In bright summer clothes or hardly any clothes at all. The free-world sounds and sights more real as the weather heats up. Confinement a torture. Each cell a hotbox. The keepers take advantage of every excuse to keep you out of the yard, to deprive you of the simple pleasure of a breeze, the blue sky. Why? So that the pleasant weather can be used as a tool, a boon to be withheld. So punishment has a sharper edge. By a perverse turn of the screw something good becomes something bad. Summer a bitch at best, but this past summer as the young turks among the guards ran roughshod over the prisoners, the prison had come close to blowing, to exploding like a piece of rotten fruit in the sun. And if the lid blew, my brother knew he'd be one of the first to die. During any large-scale uprising, in the first violent, chaotic seconds no board of inquiry would ever be able to reconstruct, scores would be settled. A bullet in the back of the brain would get rid of troublemakers, remove potential leaders, uncontrollable prisoners the guards hated and feared. You were supremely eligible for a bullet if the guards couldn't press your button. If they hadn't learned how to manipulate you, if you couldn't be bought or sold, if you weren't into drug and sex games, if you weren't cowed or depraved, then you were a threat.

Robby understood that he was sentenced to die. That all sentences were death sentences. If he didn't buckle under, the guards would do everything in their power to kill him. If he succumbed to the pressure to surrender dignity, self-respect, control over his own mind and body, then he'd become a beast, and what was good in him would die. The death sentence was unambiguous. The question for him became: How long could he survive in spite of the death sentence? Nothing he did would guarantee his safety. A disturbance in a cell block halfway across the prison could provide an excuse for shooting him and dumping him with the other victims. Anytime he was ordered to go with guards out of sight of other prisoners, his escorts could claim he attacked them, or attempted to escape. Since the flimsiest pretext would make murdering him acceptable, he had no means of protecting himself. Yet to maintain sanity, to minimize their opportunities to destroy him, he had to be constantly vigilant. He had to discipline himself to avoid confrontations, he had to weigh in terms of life and death every decision he made; he had to listen and obey his keepers' orders, but he also had to determine in certain threatening situations whether it was better to say no and keep himself out of a trap or take his chances that this particular summons was not the one inviting him to his doom. Of course to say no perpetuated his reputation as one who couldn't be controlled, a bad guy, a guy you never turn your back on, one of the prisoners out to get the guards. That rap made you more dangerous in the keepers' eyes and therefore increased the likelihood they'd be frightened into striking first. Saying no put you in no less jeopardy than going along with the program. Because the program was contrived to kill you. Directly or indirectly, you knew where you were headed. What you didn't know was the schedule. Tomorrow. Next week. A month. A minute. When would one of them get itchy, get beyond waiting a second longer? Would there be a plan, a contrived incident, a conspiracy they'd talk about and set up as they drank coffee in the guards' room or would it be the hair-trigger impulse of one of them who held a grudge, harbored an antipathy so elemental, so irrational that it could express itself only in a burst of pure, unrestrained violence?

If you're Robby and have the will to survive, these are the possibilities you must constantly entertain. Vigilance is the price of survival. Beneath the vigilance, however, is a gnawing awareness boiling in the pit of your stomach. You can be as vigilant as you're able, you can keep fighting the good fight to survive, and still your fate is out of your hands. If they decide to come for you in the morning, that's it. Your ass is grass and those minutes, and hours, days and years you painfully stitched together to put off the final reckoning won't matter at all. So the choice, difficult beyond words, to say yes or say no is made in light of the knowledge that in the end neither your yes nor your no matters. Your life is not in your hands.

The events, the atmosphere of the summer had brought home to Robby the futility of resistance. Power was absurdly apportioned all on one side. To pretend you could control your own destiny was a joke. You learned to laugh at your puniness, as you laughed at the stink of your farts lighting up your cell. Like you laughed at the seriousness of the masturbation ritual that romanticized, cloaked in darkness and secrecy, the simple, hungry shaking of your penis in your fist. You had no choice, but you always had to decide to go on or stop. It had been a stuttering, stop, start, maybe, fuck it, bitch of a summer, and now, for better or worse, we were starting up something else. Robby backtracks his story from Garth to another beginning, the house on Copeland Street in Shadyside where we lived when he was born.

. . .

I know that had something to do with it. Living in Shadyside with only white people around. You remember how it was. Except for us and them couple other families it was a all-white neighborhood. I got a thing about black. See, black was like the forbidden fruit. Even when we went to Freed's in Homewood, Geraldine and them never let me go no farther than the end of the block. All them times I stayed over there I didn't go past Mr. Conrad's house by the vacant lot or the other corner where Billy Shields and them stayed. Started to wondering what was so different about a black neighborhood. I was just a little kid and I was curious. I really wanted to know why they didn't want me finding out what was over there. Be playing with the kids next door to Freed, you know, Sonny and Gumpy and them, but all the time I'm wondering what's round the corner, what's up the street. Didn't care if it was *bad* or good or dangerous or what, I had to find out. If it's something bad I figured they would have told me, tried to scare me off. But nobody said nothing except, No. Don't you go no farther than the corner. Then back home in Shadyside nothing but white people so I couldn't ask nobody what was special about black. Black was a mystery and in my mind I decided I'd find out what it was all about. Didn't care if it killed me, I was going to find out.

One time, it was later, I was close to starting high school, I overheard Mommy and Geraldine and Sissy talking in Freed's kitchen. They was talking about us moving from Shadyside back to Homewood. The biggest thing they was worried about was me. How would it be for me being in Homewood and going to Westinghouse? I could tell they was scared. Specially Mom. You know how she is. She didn't want to move. Homewood scared her. Not so much the place but how I'd act if I got out there in the middle of it. She already knew I was wild, hard to handle. There'd be too much mess for me to get into in Homewood. She could see trouble coming.

And she was right. Me and trouble hooked up. See, it was a question of being somebody. Being my own person. Like youns had sports and good grades sewed up. Wasn't nothing I could do in school or sports that youns hadn't done already. People said, Here comes another Wideman. He's gon be a good student like his brothers and sister. That's the way it was spozed to be. I was another Wideman, the last one, the baby, and everybody knew how I was spozed to act. But something inside me said no. Didn't want to be like the rest of youns. Me, I had to be a rebel. Had to get out from under youns' good grades and do. Way back then I decided I wanted to be a star. I wanted to make it big. My way. I wanted the glamour. I wanted to sit high up.

Figured out school and sports wasn't the way. I got to thinking my brothers and sister was squares. Loved youall but wasn't no room left for me. Had to figure out a new territory. I had to be a rebel.

Along about junior high I discovered Garfield. I started hanging out up on Garfield Hill. You know, partying and stuff in Garfield cause that's where the niggers was. Garfield was black, and I finally found what I'd been looking for. That place they was trying to hide from me. It was heaven. You know. Hanging out with the fellows. Drinking wine and trying anything else we could get our hands on. And the ladies. Always a party on the weekends. Had me plenty sweet little soft-leg Garfield ladies. Niggers run my butt off that hill more than a couple times behind messing with somebody's piece but I'd be back next weekend. Cause I'd found heaven. Looking back now, wasn't much to Garfield. Just a rinky-dink ghetto up on a hill, but it was the street. I'd found my place.

Having a little bit of a taste behind me I couldn't wait to get to Homewood. In a way I got mad with Mommy and the rest of them. Seemed to me like they was trying to hold me back from a good time. Seemed like they just didn't want me to have no fun. That's when I decided I'd go on about my own business. Do it my way. Cause I wasn't getting no slack at home. They still expected me to be like my sister and brothers. They didn't know I thought youns was squares. Yeah. I knew I was hipper and groovier than youns ever thought of being. Streetwise, into something. Had my own territory and I was bad. I was a rebel. Wasn't following in nobody's footsteps but my own. And I was a hip cookie, you better believe it. Wasn't a hipper thing out there than your brother, Rob. I couldn't wait for them to turn me loose in Homewood.

Me being the youngest and all, the baby in the family, people always said, ain't he cute. That Robby gon be a ladykiller. Been hearing that mess since day one so ain't no surprise I started to believing it. Youns had me pegged as a lady's man so that's what I was. The girls be talking the same trash everybody else did. Ain't he cute. Be petting me and spoiling me like I'm still the baby of the family and I sure ain't gon tell them stop. Thought I was cute as the girls be telling me. Thought sure enough, I'm gon be a star. I loved to get up and show my behind. Must have been good at it too cause the teacher used to call me up in front of the class to perform. The kids'd get real quiet. That's probably why the teacher got me up. Keep the class quiet while she nods off. Cause they'd listen to me. Sure nuff pay attention.

Performing always come natural to me. Wasn't nervous or nothing. Just get up and do my thing. They liked for me to do impressions. I could mimic anybody. You remember how I'd do that silly stuff around the house. Anybody I'd see on TV or hear on a record I could mimic to a T. Bob Hope, Nixon, Smokey Robinson, Ed Sullivan. White or black. I could talk just like them or sing a song just like they did. The class yell out a famous name and I'd do the one they wanted to hear. If things had gone another way I've always believed I could have made it big in show business. If you could keep them little frisky kids in Liberty School quiet you could handle any audience. Always could sing and do impressions. You remember Mom asking me to do them for you when you came home from college.

I still be performing. Read poetry in the hole. The other fellows get real quiet and listen. Sing down in there too. Nothing else to do, so we entertain each other. They always asking me to sing or read. "Hey, Wideman. C'mon man and do something." Then it gets quiet while they waiting for me to start. Quiet and it's already dark. You in your own cell and can't see nobody else. Barely enough light to read by. The other fellows can hear you but it's just you and them walls so it feels like being alone much as it feels like you're singing or reading to somebody else.

Yeah. I read my own poems sometimes. Other times I just start in on whatever book I happen to be reading. One the books you sent me, maybe. Fellows like my poems. They say I write about the things they be thinking. Say it's like listening to their own self thinking. That's cause we all down there together. What else you gonna do but think of the people on the outside. Your woman. Your kids or folks, if you got any. Just the same old sad shit we all be thinking all the time. That's what I write and the fellows like to hear it.

Funny how things go around like that. Go round and round and keep coming back to the same place. Teacher used to get me up to pacify the class and I'm doing the same thing in prison. You said your teachers called on you to tell stories, didn't they? Yeah. It's funny how much we're alike. In spite of everything I always believed that. Inside. The feeling side. I always believed we was the most alike out of all the kids. I see stuff in your books. The kinds of things I be thinking or feeling.

Your teachers got you up, too. To tell stories. That's funny, ain't it.

. . .

I listen to my brother Robby. He unravels my voice. I sit with him in the darkness of the Behavioral Adjustment Unit. My imagination creates something like a giant seashell, enfolding, enclosing us. Its inner surface is velvet-soft and black. A curving mirror doubling the darkness. Poems are Jean Toomer's petals of dusk, petals of dawn. I want to stop. Savor the sweet, solitary pleasure, the time stolen from time in the hole. But the image I'm creating is a trick of the glass. The mirror that would swallow Robby and then chime to me: You're the fairest of them all.

The voice I hear issues from a crack in the glass. I'm two or three steps ahead of my brother, making fiction out of his words. Somebody needs to snatch me by the neck and say, Stop. Stop and listen, listen to him.

The Behavioral Adjustment Unit is, as one guard put it, "a maximum-security prison within a maximum-security prison." The "Restricted Housing Unit" or "hole" or "Home Block" is a squat, two-story cement building containing thirty-five six-by-eight-foot cells. The governor of Pennsylvania closed the area in 1972 because of "inhumane conditions," but within a year the hole was reopened. For at least twenty-three hours a day the prisoners are confined to their cells. An hour of outdoor exercise is permitted only on days the guards choose to supervise it. Two meals are served three hours apart, then nothing except coffee and bread for the next twenty-one. The regulation that limits the time an inmate can serve in the BAU for a single offense is routinely sidestepped by the keepers. "Administrative custody" is a provision allowing officials to cage men in the BAU indefinitely. Hunger strikes are one means the prisoners have employed to protest the harsh conditions of the penal unit. Hearings prompted by the strikes have produced no major changes in the way the hole operates. Law, due process, the rights of the prisoners are irrelevant to the functioning of this prison within a prison. Robby was sentenced to six months in the BAU because a guard suspected he was involved in an attempted escape. The fact that a hearing, held six months later, established Robby's innocence, was small consolation since he'd already served his time in the hole.

Robby tells me about the other side of being the youngest: Okay, you're everybody's pet and that's boss, but on the other hand you sometimes feel you're the least important. Always last. Always bringing up the rear. You learn to do stuff on your own because the older kids are always busy, off doing their things, and you're too young, left behind because you don't fit, or just because they forget you're back here, at the end, bringing up the rear. But when orders are given out, you sure get your share. "John's coming home this weekend. Clean up your room." Robby remembers being forced to get a haircut on the occasion of one of my visits. Honor thy brother. Get your hair cut, your room rid up, and put on clean clothes. He'll be here with his family and I don't want the house looking like a pigpen.

The voice I hear issues from a crack in the glass. I'm two or three steps ahead of my brother, making fiction out of his words. Somebody needs to snatch me by the neck and say, Stop. Stop and listen, listen to him.

The Behavioral Adjustment Unit is, as one guard put it, "a maximum-security prison within a maximum-security prison." The "Restricted Housing Unit" or "hole" or "Home Block" is a squat, two-story cement building containing thirty-five six-by-eight-foot cells. The governor of Pennsylvania closed the area in 1972 because of "inhumane conditions," but within a year the hole was reopened. For at least twenty-three hours a day the prisoners are confined to their cells. An hour of outdoor exercise is permitted only on days the guards choose to supervise it. Two meals are served three hours apart, then nothing except coffee and bread for the next twenty-one. The regulation that limits the time an inmate can serve in the BAU for a single offense is routinely sidestepped by the keepers. "Administrative custody" is a provision allowing officials to cage men in the BAU indefinitely. Hunger strikes are one means the prisoners have employed to protest the harsh conditions of the penal unit. Hearings prompted by the strikes have produced no major changes in the way the hole operates. Law, due process, the rights of the prisoners are irrelevant to the functioning of his prison within a prison. Robby was sentenced to six months in the BAU because a guard suspected he was involved in an attempted escape. The fact that a hearing, held six months later, established Robby's innocence, was small consolation since he'd already served his time in the hole.

Robby tells me about the other side of being the youngest: Okay, you're everybody's pet and that's boss, but on the other hand you sometimes feel you're the least important. Always last. Always bringing up the rear. You learn to do stuff on your own because the older kids are always busy, off doing their things, and you're too young, left behind because you don't fit, or just because they forget you're back here, at the end, bringing up the rear. But when orders are given out, you sure get your share. "John's coming home this weekend. Clean up your room." Robby remembers being forced to get a haircut on the occasion of one of my visits. Honor thy brother. Get your hair cut, your room rid of, and put on clean clothes. He'll be here with his family and I don't want the house looking like a pigpen.

figured they would have told me, tried to scare me off. But nobody said nothing except, No. Don't you go no farther than the corner. Then back home in Shadyside nothing but white people so I couldn't ask nobody what was special about black. Black was a mystery and in my mind I decided I'd find out what it was all about. Didn't care if it killed me, I was going to find out.

One time, it was later, I was close to starting high school, I overheard Mommy and Geraldine and Sissy talking in Freed's kitchen. They was talking about us moving from Shadyside back to Homewood. The biggest thing they was worried about was me. How would it be for me being in Homewood and going to Westinghouse? I could tell they was scared. Specially Mom. You know how she is. She didn't want to move. Homewood scared her. Not so much the place but how I'd act if I got out there in the middle of it. She already knew I was wild, hard to handle. There'd be too much mess for me to get into in Homewood. She could see trouble coming.

And she was right. Me and trouble hooked up. See, it was a question of being somebody. Being my own person. Like youns had sports and good grades sewed up. Wasn't nothing I could do in school or sports that youns hadn't done already. People said, Here comes another Wideman. He's gon be a good student like his brothers and sister. That's the way it was spozed to be. I was another Wideman, the last one, the baby, and everybody knew how I was spozed to act. But something inside me said no. Didn't want to be like the rest of youns. Me, I had to be a rebel. Had to get out from under youns' good grades and do. Way back then I decided I wanted to be a star. I wanted to make it big. My way. I wanted the glamour. I wanted to sit high up.

Figured out school and sports wasn't the way. I got to thinking my brothers and sister was squares. Loved youall but wasn't no room left for me. Had to figure out a new territory. I had to be a rebel.

Along about junior high I discovered Garfield. I started hanging out up on Garfield Hill. You know, partying and stuff in Garfield cause that's where the niggers was. Garfield was black, and I finally found what I'd been looking for. That place they was trying to hide from me. It was heaven. You know. Hanging out with the fellows. Drinking wine and trying anything else we could get our hands on. And the ladies. Always a party on the weekends. Had me plenty sweet little soft-leg Garfield ladies. Niggers run my butt off that hill more than a couple times behind messing with somebody's piece but I'd be back next weekend. Cause I'd found heaven. Looking back now, wasn't much to Garfield. Just a rinky-dink ghetto up on a hill, but it was the street. I'd found my place.

Having a little bit of a taste behind me I couldn't wait to get to Homewood. In a way I got mad with Mommy and the rest of them. Seemed to me like they was trying to hold me back from a good time. Seemed like they just didn't want me to have no fun. That's when I decided I'd go on about my own business. Do it my way. Cause I wasn't getting no slack at home. They still expected me to be like my sister and brothers. They didn't know I thought youns was squares. Yeah. I knew I was hipper and groovier than youns ever thought of being. Streetwise, into something. Had my own territory and I was bad. I was a rebel. Wasn't following in nobody's footsteps but my own. And I was a hip cookie, you better believe it. Wasn't a hipper thing out there than your brother, Rob. I couldn't wait for them to turn me loose in Homewood.

Me being the youngest and all, the baby in the family, people always said, ain't he cute. That Robby gon be a ladykiller. Been hearing that mess since day one so ain't no surprise I started to believing it. Youns had me pegged as a lady's man so that's what I was. The girls be talking the same trash everybody else did. Ain't he cute. Be petting me and spoiling me like I'm still the baby of the family and I sure ain't gon tell them stop. Thought I was cute as the girls be telling me. Thought sure enough, I'm gon be a star. I loved to get up and show my behind. Must have been good at it too cause the teacher used to call me up in front of the class to perform. The kids'd get real quiet. That's probably why the teacher got me up. Keep the class quiet while she nods off. Cause they'd listen to me. Sure nuff pay attention.

Performing always come natural to me. Wasn't nervous or nothing. Just get up and do my thing. They liked for me to do impressions. I could mimic anybody. You remember how I'd do that silly stuff around the house. Anybody I'd see on TV or hear on a record I could mimic to a T. Bob Hope, Nixon, Smokey Robinson, Ed Sullivan. White or black. I could talk just like them or sing a song just like they did. The class yell out a famous name and I'd do the one they wanted to hear. If things had gone another way I've always believed I could have made it big in show business. If you could keep them little frisky kids in Liberty School quiet you could handle any audience. Always could sing and do impres-

sions. You remember Mom asking me to do them for you whe[n] came home from college.

I still be performing. Read poetry in the hole. The other fello[ws] real quiet and listen. Sing down in there too. Nothing else to do entertain each other. They always asking me to sing or read[.] Wideman. C'mon man and do something." Then it gets quie[t] they waiting for me to start. Quiet and it's already dark. You in y[our] cell and can't see nobody else. Barely enough light to read by. T[he] fellows can hear you but it's just you and them walls so it f[eels] being alone much as it feels like you're singing or reading to s[omeone] else.

Yeah. I read my own poems sometimes. Other times I jus[t] on whatever book I happen to be reading. One the books you[ ] maybe. Fellows like my poems. They say I write about the th[ings] be thinking. Say it's like listening to their own self thinki[ng] cause we all down there together. What else you gonna do b[ut] the people on the outside. Your woman. Your kids or folks, [if] any. Just the same old sad shit we all be thinking all the ti[me] what I write and the fellows like to hear it.

Funny how things go around like that. Go round and [ ] keep coming back to the same place. Teacher used to get m[e to] cify the class and I'm doing the same thing in prison. Yo[ur] teachers called on you to tell stories, didn't they? Yeah. It's [ ] much we're alike. In spite of everything I always believed [ ] The feeling side. I always believed we was the most alike [of the] kids. I see stuff in your books. The kinds of things I be thin[k]ing.

Your teachers got you up, too. To tell stories. That's f[unny]

• • •

I listen to my brother Robby. He unravels my voice. I sit w[ith] darkness of the Behavioral Adjustment Unit. My imagi[nation] something like a giant seashell, enfolding, enclosing us. [ ] face is velvet-soft and black. A curving mirror doubling [ ] Poems are Jean Toomer's petals of dusk, petals of dawn. [ ] Savor the sweet, solitary pleasure, the time stolen from ti[me] But the image I'm creating is a trick of the glass. The mi[rror] swallow Robby and then chime to me: You're the fair[est]

I have to laugh at the image of myself as somebody to get a haircut for. Robby must have been fit to be tied.

. . .

Yeah, I was hot. I mean, you was doing well and all that, but shit, you were my brother. And it was my head. What's my head got to do with you? But you know how Mommy is. Ain't no talking to her when her mind gets set. Anything I tried to say was "talking *back*," so I just went ahead to the man and got my ears lowered.

I was trying to be a rebel but back then the most important thing still was what the grown-ups thought about me. How they felt meant everything. Everything. Me and Tish and Dave were the ones at home then. You was gone and Gene was gone so it was the three of us fighting for attention. And we fought. Every crumb, everytime something got cut up or parceled out or it was Christmas or Easter, we so busy checking out what the other one got wasn't hardly no time to enjoy our own. Like a dogfight or cat fight all the time. And being the youngest I'm steady losing ground most the time. Seemed like to me, Tish and Dave the ones everybody talked about. Seemed like my time would never come. That ain't the way it really was, I know. I had my share cause I was the baby and ain't he cute and lots of times I know I got away with outrageous stuff or got my way cause I could play that baby mess to the hilt. Still it seemed like Dave and Tish was the ones really mattered. Mommy and Daddy and Sis and Geral and Big Otie and Ernie always slipping some change in their pockets or taking them to the store or letting them stay over all night in Homewood. I was a jealous little rascal. Sometimes I thought everybody thought I was just a spoiled brat. I'd say damn all youall. I'd think, Go on and love those square turkeys, but one day I'll be the one coming back with a suitcase full of money and a Cadillac. Go on and love them good grades. Robby gon do it his own way.

See, in my mind I was Superfly. I'd drive up slow to the curb. My hog be half a block long and these fine foxes in the back. Everybody looking when I ease out the door clean and mean. Got a check in my pocket to give to Mom. Buy her a new house with everything in it new. Pay her back for the hard times. I could see that happening as real as I can see your face right now. Wasn't no way it wasn't gon happen. Rob was gon make it big. I'd be at the door, smiling with the check in my hand and Mommy'd be so happy she'd be crying.

Well, it's a different story ain't it. Turned out different from how I used to think it would. The worst thing I did, the thing I feel most guilty behind is stealing Mom's life. It's like I stole her youth. Can't nothing change that. I can't give back what's gone. Robbing white people didn't cause me to lose no sleep back then. Couldn't feel but so bad about that. How you gon feel sorry when society's so corrupt, when everybody got their hand out or got their hand in somebody else's pocket and ain't no rules nobody listens to if they can get away with breaking them? How you gon apply the rules? It was dog eat dog out there, so how was I spozed to feel sorry if I was doing what everybody else doing. I just got caught is all. I'm sorry about that, and damned sorry that guy Stavros got killed, but as far as what I did, as far as robbing white people, ain't no way I was gon torture myself over that one.

I tried to write Mom a letter. Not too long ago. Should say I did write the letter and put it in a envelope and sent it cause that's what I did, but I be crying so much trying to write it I don't know what wound up in that letter. I wanted Mom to know I knew what I'd done. In a way I wanted to say I was sorry for spoiling her life. After all she did for me I turned around and made her life miserable. That's the wrongest thing I've done and I wanted to say I was sorry but I kept seeing her face while I was writing the letter. I'd see her face and it would get older while I was looking. She'd get this old woman's face all lined and wrinkled and tired about the eyes. Wasn't nothing I could do but watch. Cause I'd done it and knew I done it and all the letters in the world ain't gon change her face. I sit and think about stuff like that all the time. It's better now. I think about other things too. You know like trying to figure what's really right and wrong, but there be days the guilt don't never go away.

I'm the one made her tired, John. And that's my greatest sorrow. All the love that's in me she created. Then I went and let her down.

When you in prison you got plenty of time to think, that's for damned sure. Too much time. I've gone over and over my life. Every moment. Every little thing again and again. I lay down on my bed and watch it happening over and over. Like a movie. I get it all broke down in pieces then I break up the pieces then I take the pieces of the pieces and run them through my hands so I remember every word a person said to me or what I said to them and I weigh the words till I think I know what each and every one meant. Then I try to put it back together. Try to understand where I been. Why I did what I did. You got time for that in here. Time's all you got in here.

Going over and over things sometimes you can make sense. You know. Like the chinky-chinky Chinaman sittin' on the fence. You put it together and you think, yes. That's why I did thus and so. Yeah. That's why I lost that job or lost that woman or broke that one's heart. You stop thinking in terms of something being good or being evil, you just try to say this happened because that happened because something else came first. You can spend days trying to figure out just one little thing you did. People out there in the world walk around in a daze cause they ain't got time to think. When I was out there, I wasn't no different. Had this Superfly thing and that was the whole bit. Nobody could tell me nothing.

Seems like I should start the story back in Shadyside. In the house on Copeland Street. Nothing but white kids around. Them little white kids had everything, too. That's what I thought, anyway. Nice houses, nice clothes. They could buy pop and comic books and candy when they wanted to. We wasn't that bad off, but compared to what them little white kids had I always felt like I didn't have nothing. It made me kinda quiet and shy around them. Me knowing all the time I wanted what they had. Wanted it bad. There was them white kids with everything and there was the black world Mommy and them was holding back from me. No place to turn, in a way. I guess you could say I was stuck in the middle. Couldn't have what the white kids in Shadyside had, and I wasn't allowed to look around the corner for something else. So I'd start the story with Shadyside, the house on Copeland.

. . .

Another place to start could be December 29, 1950—the date of Robby's birth. For some reason—maybe my mother and father were feuding, maybe we just happened to be visiting my grandmother's house when my mother's time came—the trip to the hospital to have Robby began from Finance Street, from the house beside the railroad tracks in Homewood. What I remember is the bustle, people rushing around, yelling up and down the stairwell, doors slammed, drawers being opened and shut. A cold winter day so lots of coats and scarves and galoshes. My mother's face was very pale above the dark cloth coat that made her look even bigger than she was, carrying Robby the ninth month. On the way out the front door she stopped and stared back over her shoulder like she'd forgotten something. People just about shoving her out the house. Lots of bustle and noise getting her through the crowded hallway into the vestibule. Somebody opened the front door and December rattled the glass panes. Wind gusting and whistling, everybody calling out last-minute instructions, arrangements, good-byes, blessings, prayers. My mother's white face calm, hovering a moment above it all as she turned back toward the hall, the stairs where I was planted, halfway to the top. She didn't find me, wasn't looking for me. A thought had crossed her mind and carried her far away. She didn't know why so many hands were rushing her out the door. She didn't hear the swirl of words, the icy blast of wind. Wrapped in a navy-blue coat, either Aunt Aida's or an old one of my grandmother's, which didn't have all its black buttons but stretched double over her big belly, my mother was wondering whether or not she'd turned off the water in the bathroom sink and deciding whether or not she should return up the stairs to check. Something like that crossing her mind, freeing her an instant before she got down to the business of pushing my brother into the world.

Both my grandfathers died on December 28. My grandmother died just after dawn on December 29. My sister lost a baby early in January. The end of the year has become associated with mournings, funerals; New Year's Day arrives burdened by a sense of loss, bereavement. Robby's birthday became tainted. To be born close to Christmas is bad enough in and of itself. Your birthday celebration gets upstaged by the orgy of gift giving on Christmas Day. No matter how many presents you receive on December 29, they seem a trickle after the Christmas flood. Plus there's too much excitement in too brief a period. Parents and relatives are exhausted, broke, still hung over from the Christmas rush, so there just isn't very much left to work with if your birthday comes four short days after Jesus'. Almost like not having a birthday. Or even worse, like sharing it with your brothers and sister instead of having the private oasis of your very own special day. So Robby cried a lot on his birthdays. And it certainly wasn't a happy time for my mother. Her father, John French, died the year after Robby was born, one day before Robby's birthday. Fifteen years and a day later Mom would lose her mother. The death of the baby my sister was carrying was a final, cruel blow, scaring my mother, jinxing the end of the year eternally. She dreaded the holiday season, expected it to bring dire tidings. She had attempted at one point to consecrate the sad days, employ them as a period of reflection, quietly, privately memorialize the passing of the two people who'd loved her most in the world. But the death of my father's father, then the miscarriage within this jinxed span of days burst the fragile truce my mother had effected with the year's end. She withdraws into herself, anticipates the worst as soon as Christmas decorations begin appearing. In 1975, the year of the robbery and murder, Robby was on the run when his birthday fell. My mother was sure he wouldn't survive the deadly close of the year.

Robby's birthday is smack dab in the middle of the hard time. Planted like a flag to let you know the bad time's arrived. His adult life, the manhood of my mother's last child, begins as she is orphaned, as she starts to become nobody's child.

I named Robby. Before the women hustled my mother out the door into a taxi, I jumped down the stairs, tugged on her coattail and reminded her she'd promised it'd be Robby. No doubt in my mind she'd bring me home a baby brother. Don't ask me why I was certain. I just was. I hadn't even considered names for a girl. Robby it would be. Robert Douglas. Where the Douglas came from is another story, but the Robert came from me because I liked the sound. Robert was formal, dignified, important. Robert. And that was nearly as nice as the chance I'd have to call my little brother Rob and Robby.

He weighed seven pounds, fourteen ounces. He was born in Allegheny Hospital at 6:30 in the evening, December 29, 1950. His fingers and toes were intact and quite long. He was a plump baby. My grandfather, high on Dago Red, tramped into the maternity ward just minutes after Robby was delivered. John French was delighted with the new baby. Called him Red. A big fat little red nigger.

. . .

December always been a bad month for me. One the worst days of my life was in December. It's still one the worst days in my life even after all this other mess. Jail. Running. The whole bit. Been waiting to tell you this a long time. Ain't no reason to hold it back no longer. We into this telling-the-truth thing so mize well tell it all. I'm still shamed, but here it is. You know that TV of youall's got stolen from Mommy's. Well, I did it. Was me and Henry took youall's TV that time and set the house up to look like a robbery. We did it. Took my own brother's TV. Couldn't hardly look you in the face for a long time after we done it. Was pretty sure youall never knowed it was me, but I felt real bad round youns anyway. No way I was gon confess though. Too shamed. A junkie stealing from his own family. See. Used to bullshit myself. Say I ain't like them other guys. They stone junkies, they hooked. Do anything for a hit. But me, I'm Robby. I'm cool. I be believing that shit, too. Fooling myself. You got to bullshit yourself when you falling. Got to do it to live wit yourself. See but where it's at is you be doing any goddamn thing for dope. You hooked and that's all's to it. You a stone junkie just like the rest.

Always wondered if you knew I took it.

Mom was suspicious. She knew more than we did then. About the dope. The seriousness of it. Money disappearing from her purse when nobody in the house but the two of you. Finding a syringe on the third floor. Stuff like that she hadn't talked about to us yet. So your stealing the TV was a possibility that came up. But to me it was just one of many. One of the things that could have happened along with a whole lot of other possibilities we sat around talking about. An unlikely possibility as far as I was concerned. Nobody wanted to believe it was you. Mom tried to tell us how it *could* be but in my mind you weren't the one. Haven't thought about it much since then. Except as one of those things that make me worry about Mom living in the house alone. One of those things making Homewood dangerous, tearing it down.

I'm glad I'm finally getting to tell you. I never could get it out. Didn't want you to think I'd steal from my own brother. Specially since all youall done to help me out. You and Judy and the kids. Stealing youall's TV. Don't make no sense, does it? But if we gon get the story down mize well get it all down.

It was a while ago. Do you remember the year?

Nineteen seventy-one was Greens. When we robbed Greens and got in big trouble so it had to be the year before that, 1970. That's when it had to be. Youns was home for Christmas. Mommy and them was having a big party. A reunion kinda cause all the family was together. Everybody home for the first time in a long time. Tish in from Detroit. David back from Philly. Youns in town. My birthday, too. Party spozed to celebrate my birthday too, since it came right along in there after

Christmas. Maybe that's why I was feeling so bad. Knowing I had a birthday coming and knowing at the same time how fucked up I was.

Sat in a chair all day. I was hooked for the first time. Good and hooked. Didn't know how low you could feel till that day. Cold and snowing outside. And I got the stone miseries inside. Couldn't move. Weak and sick. Henry too. He was wit me in the house feeling bad as I was. We was two desperate dudes. Didn't have no money and that Jones down on us.

Mommy kept asking, What's wrong with you two? She was on my case all day. What ails you, Robby? Got to be about three o'clock. She come in the room again: You better get up and get some decent clothes on. We're leaving for Geral's soon. See cause it was the day of the big Christmas party. Geral had baked a cake for me. Everybody was together and they'd be singing Happy Birthday Robby and do. The whole bit and I'm spozed to be guest of honor and can't even move out the chair. Here I go again disappointing everybody. Everybody be at Geral's looking for me and Geral had a cake and everything. Where's Robby? He's home dying cause he can't get no dope.

Feeling real sorry for myself but I'm hating me too. Wrapped up in a blanket like some damned Indin. Shivering and wondering how the hell Ima go out in this cold and hustle up some money. Wind be howling. Snow pitching a bitch. There we is. Stuck in the house. Two pitiful junkies. Scheming how we gon get over. Some sorry-assed dudes. But it's comical in a way too, when you look back. To get well we need to get money. And no way we gon get money less we go outside and get sicker than we already is. Mom peeking in the room, getting on my case. Get up out that chair, boy. What are you waiting for? We're leaving in two minutes.

So I says, Go on. I ain't ready. Youns go on. I'll catch up with youns at Geral's.

Mommy standing in the doorway. She can't say too much, cause youns is home and you ain't hip to what's happening. C'mon now. We can't wait any longer for you. Please get up. Geral baked a cake for you. Everybody's looking forward to seeing you.

Seem like she stands there a hour begging me to come. She ain't mad no more. She's begging. Just about ready to cry. Youall in the other room. You can hear what she's saying but you can't see her eyes and they tearing me up. Her eyes begging me to get out the chair and it's tearing me up to see her hurting so bad, but ain't nothing I can do. Jones sitting on my chest and ain't no getup in me.

Youns go head, Mommy. I'll be over in a little while. Be there to blow them candles out and cut the cake.

She knew better. Knew if I didn't come right then, chances was I wasn't coming at all. She knew but wasn't nothing she could do. Guess I knew I was lying too. Nothing in my mind cept copping that dope. Yeah, Mom. Be there to light them candles. I'm grinning but she ain't smiling back. She knows I'm in trouble, deep trouble. I can see her today standing in the doorway begging me to come with youns.

But it ain't meant to be. Me and Henry thought we come up with a idea. Henry's old man had some pistols. We was gon steal em and hock em. Take the money and score. Then we be better. Wouldn't be no big thing to hustle some money, get the guns outa hock. Sneak the pistols back in Henry's house, everything be alright. Wouldn't even exactly be stealing from his old man. Like we just borrowing the pistols till we score and take care business. Henry's old man wouldn't even know his pistols missing. Slick. Sick as we was, thinking we slick.

A hundred times. Mom musta poked her head in the room a hundred times.

What's wrong with you?

Like a drum beating in my head. What's wrong with you? But the other thing is stronger. The dope talking to me louder. It says get you some. It says you ain't never gon get better less you cop.

We waited long as we could but it didn't turn no better outside. Still snowing. Wind shaking the whole house. How we gon walk to Henry's and steal them pistols? Henry live way up on the hill. All the way up Tokay then you still got a long way to go over into the projects. Can't make it. No way we gon climb Tokay. So then what? Everybody's left for Geral's. Then I remembers the TV youns brought. A little portable Sony black-and-white, right? You and Judy sleeping in Mom's room and she has her TV already in there, so the Sony ain't unpacked. Saw it sitting with youall's suitcases over by the dresser. On top the dresser in a box. Remembered it and soon's I did I knew we had to have it. Sick as I was that TV had to go. Wouldn't really be stealing. Borrow it instead of borrowing the pistols. Pawn it. Get straight. Steal some money and buy it back. Just borrowing youall's TV.

Won't take me and Henry no time to rob something and buy back the TV. We stone thieves. Just had to get well first so we could operate. So we took youns TV and set the house up to look like a robbery.

•   •   •

I'm remembering the day. Wondering why it had slipped completely from my mind. I feel like a stranger. Yet as Robby talks, my memory confirms details of his recollection. I admit, yes. I was there. That's the way it was. But *where* was I? Who was I? How did I miss so much?

His confessions make me uncomfortable. Instead of concentrating on what he's revealing, I'm pushed into considering all the things I could be confessing, should be confessing but haven't and probably won't ever. I feel hypocritical. Why should I allow my brother to repose a confidence in me when it's beyond my power to reciprocate? Shouldn't I confess that first? My embarrassment, my uneasiness, the clinical, analytic coldness settling over me when I catch on to what's about to happen.

I have a lot to hide. Places inside myself where truth hurts, where incriminating secrets are hidden, places I avoid, or deny most of the time. Pulling one piece of that debris to the surface, airing it in the light of day doesn't accomplish much, doesn't clarify the rest of what's buried down there. What I feel when I delve deeply into myself is chaos. Chaos and contradiction. So how up front can I get? I'm moved by Robby's secrets. The heart I have is breaking. But what that heart is and where it is I can't say. I can't depend on it, so he shouldn't. Part of me goes out to him. Heartbreak is the sound of ice cracking. Deep. Layers and layers muffling the sound.

I listen but I can't trust myself. I have no desire to tell everything about myself so I resist his attempt to be up front with me. The chaos at my core must be in his. His confession pushes me to think of all the stuff I should lay on him. And that scares the shit out of me. I don't like to feel dirty, but that's how I feel when people try to come clean with me.

Very complicated and very simple too. The fact is I don't believe in clean. What I know best is myself and, knowing what I know about myself, clean seems impossible. A dream. One of those better selves occasionally in the driver's seat but nothing more. Nothing to be depended upon. A self no more or less in control than the countless other selves who each, for a time, seem to be running things.

Chaos is what he's addressing. What his candor, his frankness, his confession echo against. Chaos and time and circumstance and the old news, the bad news that we still walk in circles, each of us trapped in his own little world. Behind bars. Locked in our cells.

But my heart can break, does break listening to my brother's pain. I just remember differently. Different parts of the incident he's describing come back. Strange thing is my recollections return through the door he opened. My memories needed his. Maybe the fact that we recall different things is crucial. Maybe they are foreground and background, propping each other up. He holds on to this or that scrap of the past and I listen to what he's saved and it's not mine, not what I saw or heard or felt. The pressure's on me then. If his version of the past is real, then what's mine? Where does it fit? As he stitches his memories together they bridge a vast emptiness. The time lost enveloping us all. Everything. And hearing him talk, listening to him try to make something of the nothing, challenges me. My sense of the emptiness playing around his words, any words, is intensified. Words are nothing and everything. If I don't speak I have no past. Except the nothing, the emptiness. My brother's memories are not mine, so I have to break into the silence with my own version of the past. My words. My whistling in the dark. His story freeing me, because it forces me to tell my own.

I'm sorry you took so long to forgive yourself. I forgave you a long time ago, in advance for a sin I didn't even know you'd committed. You lied to me. You stole from me. I'm in prison now listening because we committed those sins against each other countless times. I want your forgiveness. Talking about debts you owe me makes me awkward, uneasy. We remember different things. They set us apart. They bring us together searching for what is lost, for the meaning of difference, of distance.

For instance, the Sony TV. It was a present from Mort, Judy's dad. When we told him about the break-in and robbery at Mom's house, he bought us another Sony. Later we discovered the stolen TV was covered by our homeowner's policy even though we'd lost it in Pittsburgh. A claim was filed and eventually we collected around a hundred bucks. Not enough to buy a new Sony but a good portion of the purchase price. Seemed a lark when the check arrived. Pennies from heaven. One hundred dollars free and clear since we already had the new TV Mort had surprised us with. About a year later one of us, Judy or I, was telling the story of the robbery and how well we came out of it. Not until that very moment when I caught a glimpse of Mort's face out of the corner of my eye did I realize what we'd done. Judy remembers urging me to send Mort that insurance check and she probably did, but I have no recollection of an argument. In my mind there had never been an issue. Why shouldn't we keep the money? But when I saw the look of surprise and hurt flash across Mort's face, I knew the insurance check should have gone directly to him. He's a generous man and probably would have refused to accept it, but we'd taken advantage of his generosity by not offering the check as soon as we received it. Clearly the money belonged to him. Unasked, he'd replaced the lost TV. I had treated him like an institution, one of those faceless corporate entities like the gas company or IRS. By then, by the time I saw the surprise in Mort's face and understood how selfishly, thoughtlessly, even corruptly I'd behaved, it was too late. Offering Mort a hundred dollars at that point would have been insulting. Anything I could think of saying sounded hopelessly lame, inept. I'd fucked up. I'd injured someone who'd been nothing but kind and generous to me. Not intentionally, consciously, but that only made the whole business worse in a way because I'd failed him instinctively. The failure was a measure of who I was. What I'd unthinkingly done revealed something about my relationship to Mort I'm sure he'd rather not have discovered. No way I could take my action back, make it up. It reflected a truth about who I was.

That memory pops right up. Compromising, ugly. Ironically, it's also about stealing from a relative. Not to buy dope, but to feed a habit just as self-destructive. The habit of taking good fortune for granted, the habit of blind self-absorption that allows us to believe the world owes us everything and we are not responsible for giving anything in return. Spoiled children. The good coming our way taken as our due. No strings attached.

Lots of other recollections were triggered as Robby spoke of that winter and the lost TV. The shock of walking into a burgled house. How it makes you feel unclean. How quickly you lose the sense of privacy and security a house, any place you call home, is supposed to provide. It's a form of rape. Forced entry, violation, brutal hands defiling what's personal, and precious. The aftershock of seeing your possessions strewn about, broken. Fear gnawing at you because what you thought was safe isn't safe at all. The worst has happened and can happen again. Your sanctuary has been destroyed. Any time you walk in your door you may be greeted by the same scene. Or worse. You may stumble upon the thieves themselves. The symbolic rape of your dwelling place enacted on your actual body. Real screams. Real blood. A knife at your throat. A stranger's weight bearing down.

Mom put it in different words but she was as shaken as I was when we walked into her house after Geral's party. Given what I know now, she must have been even more profoundly disturbed than I imagined. A double bind. Bad enough to be ripped off by anonymous thieves. How much worse if the thief is your son? For Mom the robbery was proof Robby was gone. Somebody else walking round in his skin. Mom was wounded in ways I hadn't begun to guess at. At the root of her pain were your troubles, the troubles stealing you away from her, from all of us. The troubles thick in the air as that snow you are remembering, the troubles falling on your head and mine, troubles I refused to see . . .

● ● ●

Snowing and the hawk kicking my ass but I got to have it. TV's in a box under my arm and me and Henry walking down Bennett to Homewood Avenue. Need thirty dollars. Thirty dollars buy us two spoons. Looking for One-Arm Ralph, the fence. Looking for him or that big white Cadillac he drives.

Wind blowing snow all up in my face. Thought I's bout to die out there. Nobody on the avenue. Even the junkies and dealers inside today. Wouldn't put no dog out in weather like that. So cold my teeth is chattering, talking to me. No feeling in my hands but I got to hold on to that TV. Henry took it for a little while so's I could put both my hands in my pockets. Henry lookin bad as I'm feeling. Thought I was gon puke. But it's too goddamn cold to puke.

Nobody in sight. Shit and double shit's what I'm thinking. They got to be somewhere. Twenty-four hours a day, seven days a week somebody doing business. Finally we seen One-Arm Ralph come out the Hi Hat.

This TV, man. Lemme hold thirty dollars on it.

Ralph ain't goin for it. Twenty-five the best he say he can do. Twenty-five don't do us no good. It's fifteen each for a spoon. One spoon ain't enough. We begging the dude now. We got to have it, man. Got to get well. We good for the money. Need thirty dollars for two hits. You get your money back.

Too cold to be standing round arguing. The dude go in his pocket and give us the thirty. He been knowing us. He know we good for it. I'm telling him don't sell the TV right away. Hold it till tomorrow we have his money. He say, You don't come back tonight you blow it. Ralph a hard motherfucker and don't want him changing his mind again about the thirty so I say, We'll have the money tonight. Hold the TV till tonight, you get your money.

Now all we got to do is find Goose. Goose always be hanging on the set. Ain't nobody else dealing, Goose be out there for his people. Goose an alright dude, but even Goose ain't out in the street on no day like this. I know the cat stays over the barbershop on Homewood Avenue. Across from Murphy's five-and-ten. I goes round to the side entrance, the alleyway tween Homewood and Kelly. That's how you get to his place. Goose lets me in and I cop. For some reason I turn up the alley and go toward Kelly instead of back to Homewood the way I came in. Don't know why I did it. Being slick. Being scared. Henry's waiting on the avenue for me so I go round the long way just in case somebody pinned him. I can check out the scene before I come back up the avenue. That's probably what I'm thinking. But soon's I turn the corner of Kelly, Bam. Up pops the devil.

Up against the wall, Squirrel.

It's Simon and Garfunkel, two jive undercover cops. We call them that, you dig. Lemme tell you what kind of undercover cops these niggers was. Both of em wearing Big Apple hats and jackets like people be wearing then but they both got on police shoes. Police brogans you could spot a mile away. But they think they slick. They disguised, see. Apple hats and hippy-dip jackets. Everybody knew them chumps was cops. Ride around in a big Continental. Going for bad. Everybody hated them cause everybody knew they in the dope business. They bust a junkie, take his shit and sell it. One them had a cousin. Biggest dealer on the Hill. You know where he getting half his dope. Be selling again what Simon and Garfunkel stole from junkies. Some rotten dudes. Liked to beat on people too. Wasn't bad enough they robbing people. They whipped heads too.

Soon's I turn the corner they got me. Brams me up against the wall. They so lame they think they got Squirrel. Think I'm Squirrel and they gon make a big bust. We got you, Squirrel. They happy, see, cause Squirrel dealing heavy then. Thought they caught them a whole shopping bag of dope.

Wearing my double-breasted pea coat. Used to be sharp but it's raggedy now. Ain't worth shit in cold weather like that. Pockets got holes and the dope dropped down in the lining so they don't find nothing the first time they search me. Can tell they mad. Thought they into something big and don't find shit. Looking at each other like, What the fuck's going on here? We big-time undercover supercops. This ain't spozed to be happening to us. They roughing me up too. Pulling my clothes off and shit. Hands all down in my pockets again. It's freezing and I'm shivering but these fools don't give a fuck. Rip my goddamn pea coat off me. Shaking it. Tearing it up. Find the two packs of dope inside the lining this time. Ain't what they wanted but they pissed off now. Take what they can get now.

What's this, Squirrel? Got your ass now.

Slinging me down the alley. I'm stone sick now. Begging these cats for mercy. Youall got me. You got your bust. Lemme snort some the dope, man. Little bit out each bag. You still got your bust. I'm dying. Little taste fore you lock me up.

Rotten motherfuckers ain't going for it. They see I'm sick as a dog. They know what's happening. Cold as it is, the sweat pouring out me. It's sweat but it's like ice. Like knives cutting me. They ain't give back my coat. Snowing on me and I'm shaking and sweating and sick. They can see all this. They know what's happening but ain't no mercy in these dudes. Henry's cross the street watching them bust me. Tears in his eyes. Ain't nothing he can do. The street's empty. Henry's bout froze too. Watching them sling my ass in their Continental. Never forget how Henry looked that day. All alone on the avenue. Tears froze in his eyes. Seeing him like that was a sad thing. Last thing I saw was him standing there across Homewood Avenue before they slammed me up in the car. Like I was in two places. That's me standing there in the snow. That's me so sick and cold I'm crying in the empty street and ain't a damn thing I can do about it.

By the time they get me down to the Police Station, down to No. 5

in East Liberty, I ain't no more good, sure nuff. Puking. Begging them punks not to bust me. Just bout out my mind. Must have been a pitiful sight. Then's when Henry went to Geral's house and scratched on the window and called David out on the porch. That's when youall found out I was in trouble and had to come down and get me. Right in the middle of the party and everything. Henry's sick too and he been walking round Homewood in the cold didn't know what to do. But he's my man. He got to Geral's so youall could come down and help me. Shamed to go in so he scratched on the window to get Dave on the porch.

Party's over and youns go to Mommy's and on top everything else find the house broke in and the TV gone. All the stuff's going through my mind. I'm on the bottom now. Low as you can go. Had me in a cell and I was lying cross the cot staring at the ceiling. Bars all round. Up cross the ceiling too. Like in a cage in the zoo. Miserable as I could be. All the shit staring me in the face. You're a dope fiend. You stole your brother's TV. You're hurting Mommy again. Hurting everybody. You're sick. You're nothing. Looking up at the bars on the ceiling and wondering if I could tie my belt up there. Stick my neck in it. I wanted to be dead.

Tied my belt to the ceiling. Then this guard checking on me he starts to hollering.

What you doing? Hey, Joe. This guy's trying to commit suicide.

They take my clothes. Leave me nothing but my shorts. I'm lying there shivering in my underwear and that's the end. In a cage naked like some goddamn animal. Shaking like a leaf. Thinking maybe I can beat my head against the bars or maybe jump down off the bed head first on the concrete and bust my brains open. Dead already. Nothing already. Low as I can go.

Must have passed out or gone to sleep or something, cause it gets blurry round in here. Don't remember much but they gave back my clothes and took me Downtown and there was a arraignment next morning.

Mommy told me later, one the cops advised her not to pay my bond. Said the best thing for him be to stay in jail awhile. Let him see how it is inside. Scare im. But I be steady beggin. Please, please get me out here. Youns got soft-hearted. Got the money together and paid the bond.

What would have happened if you left me to rot in there till my hearing? Damned if I know. I probably woulda went crazy, for one thing. I do know that. Know I was sick and scared and cried like a baby for Mommy and them to get me out. Don't think it really do no good letting them keep me in there. I mean the jail's a terrible place. You can get everything in jail you get in the street. No different. Cept in jail it's more dangerous cause you got a whole bunch of crazies locked up in one little space. Worse than the street. Less you got buddies in there they tear you up. Got to learn to survive quick. Cause jail be the stone jungle. Call prison the House of Knowledge cause you learns how to be to be a sure nuff criminal. Come in lame you leave knowing all kinds of evil shit. You learn quick or they eats you up. That's where it's at. So you leave a person in there, chances are they gets worse. Or gets wasted.

But Mom has that soft heart anyway and she ain't leaving her baby boy in no miserable jail. Right or wrong, she ain't leaving me in no place like that. Daddy been talking to Simon and Garfunkel. Daddy's hip, see. He been out there in the street all his life and he knows what's to it. Knows those guys and knows how rotten they is. Ain't no big thing they catch one pitiful little junkie holding two spoons. They wants dealers. They wants to look good Downtown. They wants to bust dealers and cop beaucoup dope so's they can steal it and get rich. Daddy makes a deal with them rats. Says if they drop the charges he'll make me set up Goose. Finger Goose and then stay off Homewood Avenue. Daddy says I'll do that so they let me go.

No way Ima squeal on Goose but I said okay, it's a deal. Soon's I was loose I warned Goose. Pretend like I'm trying to set him up so the cops get off my ass but Goose see me coming know the cops is watching. Helped him, really. Like a lookout. Them dumb motherfuckers got tired playing me. Simon got greedy. Somebody set him up. He got busted for drugs. Still see Garfunkel riding round in his Continental but they took him off the avenue. Too dangerous. Everybody hated them guys.

My lowest day. Didn't know till then I was strung out. That's the first time I was hooked. Started shooting up with Squirrel and Bugs Johnson when Squirrel be coming over to Mom's sometimes. Get up in the morning, go up to the third floor, and shoot up. They was like my teachers. Bugs goes way back. He started with Uncle Carl. Been shooting ever since. Dude's old now. Call him King of the Junkies, he been round so long. Bugs seen it all. You know junkies don't hardly be getting old. Have their day then they gone. Don't see em no more. They in jail or dead. Junkie just don't have no long life. Fast life but your average dopehead ain't round long. Bugs different. He was a pal of Uncle Carl's back in the fifties. Shot up together way back then. Now here he is wit Squirrel and me, still doing his thing. Everybody knows Bugs. He the King.

Let me shoot up wit em but they wouldn't let me go out in the street and hustle wit em. Said I was too young. Too green.

Learning from the King, see. That's how I started the heavy stuff. Me and Squirrel and Bugs first thing in the morning when I got out of bed. Mom was gone to work. They getting theyselves ready to hit the street. Make that money. Just like a job. Wasn't no time before I was out there, too. On my own learning to get money for dope. Me and my little mob. We was ready. Didn't take us no time fore we was gangsters. Gon be the next Bugs Johnson. Gon make it to the top.

Don't take long. One day you the King. Next day dope got you and it's the King. You ain't nothing. You lying there naked bout to die and it don't take but a minute. You fall and you gone in a minute. That's the life. That's how it is. And I was out there. I know. Now they got me jammed up in the slammer. That's the way it is. But nobody could tell me nothing then. Hard head. You know. Got to find out for myself. Nobody could tell me nothing. Just out of high school and my life's over and I didn't even know it. Too dumb. Too hardheaded. I was gon do it my way. Youns was squares. Youns didn't know nothing. Me, I was gon make mine from the curb. Hammer that rock till I was a supergangster. Be the one dealing the shit. Be the one running the junkies. That's all I knew. Street smarts. Stop being a chump. Forget that nickel-dime hoodlum bag. Be a star. Rise to the top.

You know where that got me. You heard that story. Here I sit today behind that story. Nobody to blame but my ownself. I know that now. But things was fucked up in the streets. You could fall in them streets, Brother. Low. Them streets could snatch you bald-headed and turn you around and wring you inside out. Streets was a bitch. Wake up some mornings and you think you in hell. Think you died and went straight to hell. I know cause I been there. Be days I wished I was dead. Be days worser than that.

• • •

Robby was the rebel. He was always testing our parents, seeing how much he could get away with. Hanging on the coattails of his big brother Dave, he hit the streets earlier, harder than the rest of us, partied on weekends, stretched his curfew past midnight. He was grounded countless times, but he ignored the groundings just as he'd ignored the house rules that he'd broken to get himself in trouble in the first place. At thirteen he was a tallish, skinny kid. He began to let his hair grow out into an Afro. Facial hair began to sprout and he logged hours in front of the bathroom mirror, picking his bush, measuring, prodding the curly hairs on his chin, the shadow darkening his upper lip. My mother's warnings, threats, pleas, had no effect on him. He learned to ride out the storms of her anger, to be sullen and stubborn till his hardheaded persistence wore her down. Only so many privileges she could take away before she had no cards to play. Hitting him was a waste of energy. She'd hurt herself on his hard, bony body; neither her hands, nor her words, made dents in the wall he was fashioning around himself.

Daddy could still shake him up. Edgar Wideman was six foot tall and weighed around two hundred hard pounds. Robby knew Daddy could tear up his behind and knew that if he pushed the wrong way at the wrong time, Edgar would punch him out. My father's rage, his fists were the atom bomb, the nuclear deterrent. Robby feared him so he gauged his misconduct with a diplomat's finely honed sensitivity to consequence and repercussion. Yet Robby understood that he had launched himself on a collision course. His determination to become an independent power setting his own rules would bring on a confrontation with Daddy. The shit had to hit the fan sooner or later, so it became a question of biding his time, of marshaling his forces, and convincing himself that he'd survive the holocaust generally intact.

One of the worst parts of being grounded was losing phone privileges. With a stable of young girls to keep happy, a phone was an indispensable tool, especially since Robby's ladies were scattered all over the city and he had neither time nor money to make his rounds in person. When he was stuck in the house the phone was the only pipeline to his world, so when Mom said no calls in or out, Robby was in exile, a monarch languishing while enemies nibbled away at his undefended turf. Predictably, the last great battle between Robby and my father was fought about the phone.

In the house on Marchand Street the phone sat on a three-legged stand just inside the front door. The phone cord would stretch halfway up the front hall steps so you could climb them and stake out a sanctuary, lean your back against the wall or banister, and escape the confines of the house, talk yourself and the one listening into a dreamlike place where you could be whoever you wanted to be. Mom was exactly right when she said, That boy lives on the phone. Like his music, his dancing, the dark basements and street corners, the phone allowed Rob to practice the magic powers he knew he possessed, those powers the world outside his skin denied or threatened.

For a series of trespasses Robby had been absolutely, positively prohibited from using the phone. He observed the ban for most of one day, then the walls started closing in. A particularly sweet thing in Penn Hills had beaucoup hard legs hitting on her day and night. Robby'd laid a mean rap on her and was just starting to get over. But a day without a call might undo his work. He waited till Mom went grocery shopping, then dialed Penn Hills. Everything was beautiful. He was rapping hard and heavy; the lady was coming on strong. In just a few minutes she'd squeeze through the telephone wire. He'd have that fine thing curled lovey-dovey on his lap. The conversation got so good to him he missed the clatter of Mom returning through the front door.

What do you think you're doing? Hang up and get down off those steps. You know you're not supposed to touch the phone.

She stomped straight to the kitchen with her armload of Giant Eagle bags, but the fire in her voice, her eyes said she'd be right back.

Sure enough as soon as the grocery bags hit the kitchen table she was hotfooting it back into the hall. Robby scooted up two more stairs and blocked the stairwell with his leg.

Just a minute, Mom. I'm almost through now. She'd have to knock down the barrier of his outstretched leg and fight through his body before she got to the phone.

Come down off the stairs, boy. Hang up that phone and come down this instant.

He hunched over, cradling, protecting his love. It was difficult to keep his voice soft, insinuating, cool, and still drown out his mother's screeching. He cupped the receiver with his palm. Shielded his love in a corner of the steps, his chest, his heart almost touching the dial.

Mom was screaming and starting up the steps, and Robby stiffened his leg. She'd hit there first, knock his leg down and fight him for the phone. He needed just a little more time. He had this sweet thing's nose wide open. Just a minute now. If Mom could just be cool a minute, he'd finish his business and she could snatch the phone if she wanted it. Beat him over the head with it if she wanted. So he got his leg up and his arm too, a second line of defense to buy another few seconds—time for the three or four good-byes he needed to sew up the fine lady on the other end of the line.

Yeah, baby, I miss you, too. Yeah, it's just somebody, just my mama wants to use the phone, babe, but that's alright. I ain't gon give it up while I got something sweet as you on the wire.

No way he'd kick his mother, but he'd wave that leg and keep it in her path long's he could. He had five or six things going at once. Leg and arm stiffened for protection and heavy breathing and heavy rapping through his fingers so his hand could smother the racket coming up the steps after him. He's so busy he doesn't notice right away the front door swing open again.

He knows something's up when he hears the thump, thumple, thump of his ass hitting the steps one by one as he's dragged by the leg from his perch. Bram, bram, bram. Then the phone disappears, flies through the air and strikes the floor ringing once, louder than he's ever heard it. His father bends over to recover the phone, picks it up off the hall floor, sets it on the stand, slams the receiver back on the base. That big nigger had snatched the phone out his hand. That was my baby he flattened like a pancake when he bashed the two pieces of black phone together. Robby thinks this while he scrambles to his feet and leaps up the stairs. This is it, he thinks, and for a millisecond he considers jumping on his father's broad back, pummeling, kicking, settling once and for all the matter of who's boss. But that was a lot of hard nigger in the hall. And though his hands ached with fury, with sudden emptiness where a moment before he'd been holding his baby, he grabbed banister instead of his father's tough meat and scatted up the steps three at a time to the room he shared with brother David. He needed an equalizer. Something hard or heavy or sharp in his hand when that herd of elephants pursuing him got to the top of the steps.

Leave him alone. Don't go up there now. His mother's voice, then the steps bending, creaking, sighing, as slowly, in no hurry or rush or nothing, Edgar Wideman mounted them.

Robby slammed the door of his room. To buy time, to muffle the footsteps he hears anyway louder and louder pounding in his ears as he flings open a drawer and pulls out the scissors he knew were there. Long scissors. Black loops and thick, mismatched blades, the longer, wider one rounding to a point, the other tapering like a dagger. How should he hold them? Should he put his fingers through the holes or clutch both round eyes together like the handle of a knife? Cold steel in hand he faces the closed door waiting for it to burst open. How long had the scissors been lying in the drawer? Did he know he was after them when he bounced off his butt in the hall and catapulted up the stairs? Did he know then what he was after? Where he was headed? Had he been the one who had cached the weapon in the top bureau drawer? Did he know when he did it that he'd need them today? Did he know when he dialed Valery Jackson that he'd need the scissors to avenge her honor, his dignity? Was getting in her drawers tied to what he knew he could lay his hands on in the top drawer of the tall, slew-foot bureau?

Somebody was sobbing. The door flies open and it's not his Daddy in tears. It's not his mother either, because he can hear her running up the steps shouting for his father to stop, to let him alone, to come back downstairs. The sobbing has something to do with the rhythm of the scissors, the beat shaking his hand so the weapon is a blur of black and silver through his tears. The tears are messing up everything and they go with the sobs, like the trembling goes with somebody sobbing so it's him backed up against the wall, sobbing like a baby, facing the big man who looms in the space where the door used to be.

I'll kill you if you come in here. Swear to God I'll kill you.

And it's him talking, screaming at Edgar Wideman and talking to the scissors, calmly, coolly like he tried to get to Valery Jackson under his mother's shouts. Steady. Steady. Rise up like a weapon. Don't act like something pointed at me. Don't act like I'm the one should be scared of these blades.

I hate you. I hate your guts. You come over here and I'll kill you. Swear I'll kill you if you touch me. You ain't gon whip me no more. It's his voice shaky with sobs. He's spitting tears from his lips. His eyes are rolling down his cheeks. But he's got his hand up and it stabs the air with the points of the scissors.

You ain't gon touch me. You ain't never whipping me again.

Edgar doesn't. He never smacks his son in anger again. He stands in the doorway, a puzzled look on his face. It's like he keeps putting two and two together and it comes out four, but four's wrong so he adds two and two again and gets four but four's wrong again, so he patiently does the sum again, two plus two equals . . . He doesn't hurry, concentrates as hard as he can on getting the answer right even though he knows it's a simple problem, the easiest kind of problem, and he's produced the answer a million times before, everybody in their right mind, everybody with good sense or less knows the answer but he stands in the door staring at his son, staring at the scared kid with the load of scissors in his hand and the snot and tears and trembling lips and thinks, yes, I brought you into the world and, yes, I could take you out, thinks that thought facing his son, watches the pointy scissors bob and thinks, yes, I've faced cold steel before, killed before, and unclenches his fist and feels the air go out of his chest, the cold stinging air that had risen to block his nostrils so they flared for breath, and a sigh goes out of him and memories drain until he's back to the problem, back to the only solution he knows and knows it will be wrong again.

Why are you doing this? Why don't you listen to what anybody tells you? You're just a rebel. A damned rebel. You don't listen to anybody.

He can hear his mother saying his father's name. Softly, rising in the stairwell, filtering into the room, little soft bubbles of his father's name. Edgar, Edgar, then, *Oh, God. Please stop this*, bursting against his father's rage, his father's shouts as he hesitates at the threshold of his son's room. The puzzled, hurt look doesn't leave his father's eyes even though his mouth twists and his lips curl, and his words explode like shots in the little bedroom.

A rebel. A damned rebel.

Then the space is empty. The stairs bend under two people descending.

. . .

I was scared. Scared as I ever been in my life. He could have took those scissors and made me eat them. I didn't know what Ida done if he called my bluff. He must of taked pity on me. He seen I got myself in too far to back away. Had those scissors in my hand but I was wishing I didn't. Wished I'd never hid them in the drawer. Wished I never been born.

Edgar didn't do a thing. He was as mad as I ever seen him but he just stood there yelling at me and didn't take a step until he turned around and went back downstairs. Called me a rebel. Said I wouldn't listen. I guess he decided it wasn't worth it. I guess he told me what he thought of me and didn't have no more to say.

Anyway that's part of the beginning. I can look back now and see it must have been funny in a way. I can laugh at how I must have looked. My scrawny ass quivering and crying so much I must have looked like a drowned rat to Daddy. But he never hit me again. He told me what he thought and let me slide that day. Never mentioned the phone or the scissors or nothing about that day ever.

■ ■ ■

At about the time I was beginning to teach Afro-American literature at the University of Pennsylvania, back home on the streets of Pittsburgh Robby was living through the changes in black culture and consciousness I was reading about and discussing with my students in the quiet of the classroom. Not until we began talking together in prison did I learn about that side of his rebelliousness. *Black Fire* was a book I used in my course. It was full of black rage and black dreams and black love. In the sixties when the book was published, young black men were walking the streets with, as one of the *Black Fire* writers put it, dynamite growing out of their skulls. I'd never associated Robby with the fires in Homewood and in cities across the land, never envisioned him bobbing in and out of the flames, a constant danger to himself, to everyone around him because "dynamite was growing out of his skull." His plaited naps hadn't looked like fuses to me. I was teaching, I was trying to discover words to explain what was happening to black people. That my brother might have something to say about these matters never occurred to me. The sad joke was, I never even spoke to Robby. Never knew until years later that he was the one who could have told me much of what I needed to hear.

■ ■ ■

It was a crazy summer. The summer of '68. We fought the cops in the streets. I mean sure nuff punch-out fighting like in them Wild West movies and do. Shit. Everybody in Homewood up on Homewood Avenue duking with the cops. Even the little weeny kids was there, standing back throwing rocks. We fought that whole summer. Cop cars all over the place and they'd come jumping out with night sticks and fists balled up. They wore leather jackets and gloves and sometimes they be wearing them football helmets so you couldn't go upside they heads without hurting your hand. We was rolling. Steady fighting. All you need to be doing was walking down the avenue and here they come. Screeching the brakes. Pull up behind you and three or four cops come busting out the squad car ready to rumble. Me and some the fellas just minding our business walking down Homewood and this squad car pulls up. Hey, you. Hold it. Stop where you are, like he's talking to some silly kids or something. All up in my face. What you doing here, like I ain't got no right to be on Homewood Avenue, and I been walking on Homewood Avenue all my life an ain't no jive police gon get on my case just cause I'm walking down the avenue. Fuck you, pig. Ain't none your goddamn business, pig. Well, you know it's on then. Cop come running at Henry and Henry ducks down on one knee and jacks the motherfucker up. Throw him clean through that big window of Murphy's five-and-dime. You know where I mean. Where Murphy's used to be. Had that cop snatched up in the air and through that window before he knew what hit him. Then it's on for sure. We rolling right there in the middle of Homewood Avenue.

That's the way it was. Seem like we was fighting cops every day. Funny thing was, it was just fighting. Wasn't no shooting or nothing like that. Somebody musta put word out from Downtown. You can whip the niggers' heads but don't be shooting none of em. Yeah. Cause the cops would get out there and fight but they never used no guns. Might bust your skull with a nightstick but they wasn't gon shoot you. So the word must have been out. Cause you know if it was left to the cops they would have blowed us all away. Somebody said don't shoot and we figured that out so it was stone rock 'n' roll and punch-up time.

Sometimes I think the cops dug it too. You know like it was exercise or something. Two or three carloads roll up and it's time to get it on. They was looking for trouble. You could tell. You didn't have to yell pig or nothing. Just be minding your business and here they come piling out the car ready to go ten rounds. I got tired of fighting cops. And getting whipped on. We had some guys go up on the rooves. Brothers was gon waste the motherfuckers from up there when they go riding down the street but shit, wasn't no sense bringing guns into it long as they wasn't shooting at us. Brothers didn't play in those days. We was organized. Cops jump somebody and in two minutes half of Homewood out there on them cops' ass. We was organized and had our own weapons and shit. Rooftops and them old boarded-up houses was perfect for snipers. Dudes had pistols and rifles and shotguns. You name it. Wouldna believed what the brothers be firing if it come to that but it didn't come to that. Woulda been stone war in the streets. But the shit didn't come down that way. Maybe it woulda been better if it did. Get it all out in the open. Get the killing done wit. But the shit didn't hit the fan that summer. Least not that way.

Lemme see. I woulda been in eleventh grade. One more year of Westinghouse left after the summer of '68. We was the ones started the strike. Right in the halls of good old Westinghouse High School. Like I said, we had this organization. There was lots of organizations and clubs and stuff like that back then but we had us a mean group. Like, if you was serious business you was wit us. Them other people was into a little bit of this and that, but we was in it all the way. We was gon change things or die trying. We was known as bad. Serious business, you know. If something was coming down they always wanted us wit them. See, if we was in it, it was some mean shit. Had to be. Cause we didn't play. What it was called was Together. Our group. We was so bad we was having a meeting once and one the brothers bust in. Hey youall. Did youall hear on the radio Martin Luther King got killed? One the older guys running the meeting look up and say, We don't care nothing bout that ass-kissing nigger, we got important business to take care of. See, we just knew we was into something. Together was where it was at. Didn't nobody dig what King putting down. We wasn't about begging whitey for nothing and we sure wasn't taking no knots without giving a whole bunch back. After the dude come in hollering and breaking up the meeting we figured we better go on out in the street anyway cause we didn't want no bullshit. You know. Niggers running wild and tearing up behind Martin Luther King getting wasted. We was into planning. Into organization. When the shit went down we was gon be ready. No point in just flying around like chickens with they heads cut

off. I mean like it ain't news that whitey is offing niggers. So we go out
the meeting to cool things down. No sense nobody getting killed on no
humbug.

Soon as we got outside you could see the smoke rising off Homewood Avenue. Wasn't that many people out and Homewood burning already, so we didn't really know what to do. Walked down to Hamilton
and checked it out around in there and went up past the A & P. Say to
anybody we see, Cool it. Cool it, brother. Our time will come. It ain't today, brother. Cool it. But we ain't really got no plan. Didn't know what
to do, so me and Henry torched the Fruit Market and went on home.

Yeah. I was a stone mad militant. Didn't know what I was saying
half the time and wasn't sure what I wanted, but I was out there
screaming and hollering and waving my arms around and didn't take
no shit from nobody. Mommy and them got all upset cause I was in the
middle of the school strike. I remember sitting down and arguing with
them many a time. All they could talk about was me messing up in
school. You know. Get them good grades and keep your mouth shut and
mind your own business. Trying to tell me white folks ain't all bad. Asking me where would niggers be if it wasn't for good white folks. They
be arguing that mess at me and they wasn't about to hear nothing I had
to say. What it all come down to was be a good nigger and the white
folks take care of you. Now I really couldn't believe they was saying
that. Mommy and Geral got good sense. They ain't nobody's fools. How
they talking that mess? Wasn't no point in arguing really, cause I was
set in my ways and they sure was set in theirs. It was the white man's
world and wasn't no way round it or over it or under it. Got to get down
and dance to the tune the man be playing. You know I didn't want to
hear nothing like that, so I kept on cutting classes and fucking up and
doing my militant thing every chance I got.

I dug being a militant cause I was good. It was something I could
do. Rap to people. Whip a righteous message on em. People knew my
name. They'd listen. And I'd steady take care of business. This was
when Rap Brown and Stokely and Bobby Seale and them on TV. I identified with those cats. Malcolm and Eldridge and George Jackson. I read
their books. They was Gods. That's who I thought I was when I got up
on the stage and rapped at the people. It seemed like things was changing. Like no way they gon turn niggers round this time.

You could feel it everywhere. In the streets. On the corner. Even in jive Westinghouse High people wasn't going for all that old, tired bullshit they be laying on you all the time. We got together a list of demands. Stuff about the lunchroom and a black history course. Stuff like that and getting rid of the principal. We wasn't playing. I mean he was a mean nasty old dude. Hated niggers. No question about that. He wouldn't listen to nobody. Didn't care what was going on. Everybody hated him. We told them people from the school board his ass had to go first thing or we wasn't coming back to school. It was a strike, see. Started in Westinghouse, but by the end of the week it was all over the city. Langley and Perry and Fifth Avenue and Schenley. Sent messengers to all the schools, and by the end of the week all the brothers and sisters on strike. Shut the schools down all cross the city, so they knew we meant business. Knew they had to listen. The whole Board of Education came to Westinghouse and we told the principal to his face he had to go. The nasty old motherfucker was sitting right there and we told the board, He has to go. The man hates us and we hate him and his ass got to go. Said it right to his face and you ought to seen him turning purple and flopping round in his chair. Yeah. We got on his case. And the thing was they gave us everything we asked for. Yes . . . Yes . . . Yes. Everything we had on the list. Sat there just as nice and lied like dogs. Yes. We agree. Yes. You'll have a new principal. I couldn't believe it. Didn't even have to curse them out or nothing. Didn't even raise my voice cause it was yes to this and yes to that before the words out my mouth good.

We's so happy we left that room with the Board and ran over to the auditorium and in two minutes it was full and I'm up there screaming. We did it. We did it. People shouting back Right on and Work out and I gets that whole auditorium dancing in they seats. I could talk now. Yes, I could. And we all happy as could be, cause we thought we done something. We got the black history course and got us a new principal and, shit, wasn't nothing we couldn't do, wasn't nothing could stop us that day. Somebody yelled, Party, and I yelled back, Party, and then I told them, Everybody come on up to Westinghouse Park. We gon stone party. Wasn't no plan or nothing. It all just started in my head. Somebody shouted party and I yelled Party and the next thing I know we got this all-night jam going. We got bands and lights and we partied all night long. Ima tell you the truth now. Got more excited bout the party than anything else. Standing up there on the stage I could hear the music and see the niggers dancing and I'm thinking, Yeah. I'm thinking bout getting high and tipping round, checking out the babes and grooving on the sounds. Got me a little reefer and sipping out somebody's jug of sweet wine and the park's full of bloods and I'm in heaven. That's the way it was too. We partied all night long in Westinghouse Park. Cops like to shit, but wasn't nothing they could do. This was 1968. Wasn't nothing they could do but surround the park and sit out there in they cars while we partied. It was something else. Bands and bongos and niggers singing, *Oh bop she bop* everywhere in the park. Cops sat out in them squad cars and Black Marias, but wasn't nothing they could do. We was smoking and drinking and carrying on all night and they just watched us, just sat in the dark and didn't do a thing. We broke into the park building to get us some lectricity for the bands and shit. And get us some light. Broke in the door and took what we wanted, but them cops ain't moved an inch. It was our night and they knew it. Knew they better leave well enough alone. We owned Westinghouse Park that night. Thought we owned Homewood.

In a way the party was the end. School out pretty soon after that and nobody followed through. We come back to school in the fall and they got cops patrolling the halls and locks on every door. You couldn't go in or out the place without passing by a cop. They had our ass then. Turned the school into a prison. Wasn't no way to get in the auditorium. Wasn't no meetings or hanging out in the halls. They broke up all that shit. That's when having police in the schools really got started. When it got to be a regular everyday thing. They fixed us good. Yes, yes, yes, when we was sitting down with the Board, but when we come back to school in September everything got locks and chains on it.

We was just kids. Didn't really know what we wanted. Like I said. The party was the biggest thing to me. I liked to get up and rap. I was a little Stokely, a little Malcolm in my head but I didn't know shit. When I look back I got to admit it was mostly just fun and games. Looking for a way to get over. Nothing in my head. Nothing I could say I really wanted. Nothing I wanted to be. So they lied through their teeth. Gave us a party and we didn't know no better, didn't know we had to follow through, didn't know how to keep our foot in they ass.

Well, you know the rest. Nothing changed. Business as usual when we got back in the fall. Hey, hold on. What's this? Locks on the doors. Cops in the halls. Big cops with big guns. Hey, man, what's going down? But it was too late. The party was over and they wasn't about to give up nothing no more. We had a black history class, but wasn't nobody eligible to take it. Had a new principal, but nobody knew him. Nobody could get to him. And he didn't know us. Didn't know what we was about except we was trouble. Troublemakers; and he had something for that. Boot your ass out in a minute. Give your name to the cops and you couldn't get through the door cause everybody had to have an I.D. Yeah. That was a new one. Locks and I.D.'s and cops. Wasn't never our school. They made it worse instead of better. Had our chance, then they made sure we wouldn't have no more chances.

It was fun while it lasted. Some good times, but they was over in a minute and then things got worser and worser. Sixty-eight was when the dope came in real heavy too. I mean you could always get dope but in '68 seems like they flooded Homewood. Easy as buying a quart of milk. Could cop your works in a drugstore. Dope was everywhere that summer. Cats ain't never touched the stuff before got into dope and dope got into them. A bitch, man. It come in like a flood.

Me. I start to using heavy that summer. Just like everybody else I knew. The shit was out there and it was good and cheap, so why not? What else we supposed to be doing? It was part of the fun. The good times. The party.

We lost it over the summer, but I still believe we did something hip for a bunch of kids. The strike was citywide. We shut the schools down. All the black kids was with us. The smart ones. The dumb ones. It was hip to be on strike. To show our asses. We had them honkies scared. Got the whole Board of Education over to Westinghouse High. We lost it, but we had them going, Bruh. And I was in the middle of it. Mommy and them didn't understand. They thought I was just in trouble again. The way I always was. Daddy said one his friends works Downtown told him they had my name down there. Had my name and the rest of the ringleaders'. He said they were watching me. They had my name Downtown and I better be cool. But I wasn't scared. Always in trouble, always doing wrong. But the strike was different. I was proud of that. Proud of getting it started, proud of being one the ringleaders. The mad militant. Didn't know exactly what I was doing, but I was steady doing it.

The week the strike started, think it was Tuesday, could have been Monday but I think it was Tuesday, cause the week before was when some the students went to the principal's office and said the student council or some damn committee or something wanted to talk to him about the lunchroom and he said he'd listen but he was busy till next week, so it could have been Monday, but I think it was Tuesday cause knowing him he'd put it off long as he could. Anyway, Mr. Lindsay sitting in the auditorium. Him and vice-principal Meers and the counselor, Miss Kwalik. They in the second or third row sitting back and the speakers is up on stage behind the mike but they ain't using it. Just talking to the air really, cause I slipped in one the side doors and I'm peeping what's going on. And ain't nothing going on. Most the time the principal whispering to Miss Kwalik and Mr. Meers. Lindsay got a tablet propped up on his knee and writes something down every now and then but he ain't really listening to the kids on stage. Probably just taking names cause he don't know nobody's name. Taking names and figuring how he's gon fuck over the ones doing the talking. You. You in the blue shirt, Come over here. Don't none them know your name less you always down in the office cause you in trouble or you one the kiss-ass, nicey-nice niggers they keep for flunkies and spies. So he's taking names or whatever, and every once in a while he says something like, Yes. That's enough now. Who's next? Waving the speakers on and off and the committee, or whatever the fuck they calling theyselves, they ain't got no better sense than to jump when he say jump. Half of them so scared they stuttering and shit. I know they glad when he wave them off the stage cause they done probably forgot what they up there for.

Well, I get sick of this jive real quick. Before I know it I'm up on the stage and I'm tapping the mike and can't get it turned on so I goes to shouting. Talking trash loud as I can. Damn this and damn that and Black Power and I'm somebody. Tell em ain't no masters and slaves no more and we want freedom and we want it now. I'm stone preaching. I'm chirping. Get on the teachers, get on the principal and everybody else I can think of. Called em zookeepers. Said they ran a zoo and wagged my finger at the chief zookeeper and his buddies sitting down there in the auditorium. Told the kids on the stage to go and get the students. You go here. You go there. Like I been giving orders all my life. Cleared the stage in a minute. Them chairs scraped and kids run off and it's just me up there all by my ownself. I runs out of breath. I'm shaking, but I'm not scared. Then it gets real quiet. Mr. Lindsay stands up. He's purple and shaking worse than me. Got his finger stabbing at me now. Shoe's on the other foot now. Up there all by myself now and he's doing the talking.

Are you finished? I hope you're finished cause your ass is grass. Come down from there this instant. You've gone too far this time, Wideman. Get down from there. I want you in my office immediately.

They's all three up now, Mr. Lindsay and Miss Kwalik and Meers, up and staring up at me like I'm stone crazy. Like I just pulled out my dick and peed on the stage or something. Like they don't believe it. And to tell the truth I don't hardly believe it myself. One minute I'm watching them kids making fools of theyselves, next minute I'm bad-mouthing everything about the school and giving orders and telling Mr. Lindsay to his face he ain't worth shit. Now the whiteys is up and staring at me like I'm a disease, like I'm Bad Breath or Okey Doke the damn fool and I'm looking round and it's just me up there. Don't know if the other kids is gone for the students like I told them or just run away cause they scared.

Ain't many times in life I felt so lonely. I'm thinking bout home. What they gon say when Mr. Lindsay calls and tells them he kicked my ass out for good. Cause I had talked myself in a real deep hole. Like, Burn, baby burn. We was gon run the school our way or burn the motherfucker down. Be our school or wasn't gon be no school. Yeah, I was yelling stuff like that and I was remembering it all. Cause it was real quiet in there. Could of heard a pin drop in the balcony. Remembering everything I said and then starting to figure how I was gon talk myself out this one. Steady scheming and just about ready to cop a plea. I's sorry boss. Didn't mean it, Boss. I was just kidding. Making a joke. Ha. Ha. I loves this school and loves you Mr. Lindsay. My head's spinning and I'm moving away from the mike but just at that very minute I hears the kids busting into the balcony. It's my people. It's sure nuff them. They bust in the balcony and I ain't by myself no more. I'm hollering again and shaking a power fist and I tells Mr. Lindsay:

You get out. You leave.

I'm king again. He don't say a word. Just splits with his flunkies. The mike starts working and that's when the strike begins.

Your brother was out there in the middle of it. I was good, too. Lot of the time I be thinking bout the party afterward, my heart skipping forward to the party, but I was willing to work. Be out front. Take the weight. Had the whole city watching us, Bruh.

II

*D*ark when we got to Detroit. Sammy is Marcus's nephew and he sorta knowed the way. He's giving directions till we get to this phone booth across from the projects where we supposed to call Marcus. Marcus is the Twinkies' brother. A half brother or something, cause he don't look nothing like the Twinkies. That's what everybody call William and his brother Charles. The Twinkies. They bring in most the dope in Homewood. Stone Little Caesar gangsters with cigars. Call them Twinkies. You know. Cause they black and look alike. That's their street name. Marcus is the Twinkies' brother in Detroit and we supposed to call him to get the dope.

It's me, Cecil, Michael, Sowell, and Sammy in Mike's deuce and a quarter. This is our big chance. Making our play for the big time like Garth said we should. Everything seems right. Back in Pittsburgh ain't nobody on top. No big-time dealers on the scene. I got me a good rep. Everybody knows me. I been selling for the few main cats that's out there. But ain't none of them worth shit when you got down to it. This one guy, Billy Sims. He used to be bad but all his brothers got killed so he ain't got no backup, and people taking off his dealers. Sims ain't respected no more. He gorillas people. You know. Coming down hard on dudes and shooting people and that's bad business. Everybody knows it's just a matter of time cause you got to have that respect. So I'm out there on the set, you dig. I'm a young guy coming up and the Twinkies like me. I'm almost family cause I'm going out with Tanya and she's the Twinkies' niece. They know me as a together dude. They know I can take care of business and stay cool, so one day I hit on William Twinky, "Hey, man, can you hook me up?"

Like I say, he's digging me. He been watching me more than I know. I guess he talked to Tanya about me. Whatever he been hearing or seeing he likes it cause he says yeah. Says his nephews been begging him to hook them up but them niggers ain't worth nothing. Dopeheads, he calls them. Says he could have made them rich but they too foolish. He tells me he likes my style. Right away he calls up Marcus in Detroit and Marcus says yeah. Come on up and get it tomorrow. That quick. Tomorrow.

I talk to Mike and Cecil. That's our little crew. Them two and Sowell and Chunky who's gon deal for us when we get the dope. We all been working and saving up our cash. We put our money together and it's enough to make the buy. Talk about some happy dudes. We know our time is come. We just know we gon get our foot in the door and won't be no stopping us. We're on our way to the top just like Garth said.

Couldn't help but think of Gar while we riding up to Detroit. Wishing he was with us. Wishing he could make the trip. We had to bring Sammy cause he knew the way. Sammy's a funny cat. I mean like comical funny. Fun to be with cause he keeps you laughing but nobody really liked the dude cause he's a stone junkie. Sammy had one them dope-fiend faces. All sunken in and bleary-eyed. The cat was way out. You be on the corner you hear somebody say, "Sammy, get the fuck out the middle of the street, man." Sammy be on another planet. Nodding off in the middle of Homewood Avenue like it's his living room. He was what you call a classic dope fiend. Skinny. Running around frantic and jittery, always looking for a fix. Hey, man . . . Hey, man . . . Where's it at, man? But he knew what he was and played the part. That's what make him so funny. Nobody else really dug him but he was my man. Yeah. He was cool by me. He was Sammy the dope fiend and he could crack me up acting the part. Anyway, he was the one knew how to get to the restaurant in Detroit where we supposed to call Marcus. We got there and Marcus said go down the street and turn here and turn there and go two blocks and turn right you see a phone booth. A bunch of foreign-intrigue mysterious shit like that so we did and come to this phone booth across from the projects.

I'm trying to remember, but nothing special about the projects. It was dark. They looked like projects look anywhere. They was high rises. Nighttime so the lights was on. Must have been late October. Trees beside the highway was bare. Wasn't no trees around the project.

Just this phone booth in the middle of nowhere and these tall black buildings across the street.

Yeah, it was cold. Not wintertime cold but the wind was whipping. I had on a jacket. My tan leather jacket but I could feel the wind. Hear it beating on the phone booth when I was inside. This guy on the line tells me get rid of my crew. They should go back to the restaurant and wait. He wants me to stay by myself in the booth. Now shit. I ain't crazy. Here I am in the middle of nowhere, in a strange city and it's dark and I got two thousand dollars in my pocket and he's telling me to send my people away. He says it's cool. He says we got to trust each other to do business. Well, I come back and say Sammy wants to come. He wants to see his uncle. Sammy ain't no whole lotta help but I figure two is better than me standing out there alone, but the cat says, No good. You got to come by yourself. And no guns.

We come this far, I'm thinking. We come this far and we ain't going no further less we willing to take some chances. That's where it's at. Don't get something for nothing, so I goes back to the car and tell the fellows what's going down. They don't like it neither, but they put it on me. Mike says, It's your ass out here. You do what you think is cool. I look at them and look at my gun on the backseat. I want that sucker but the cat said no. We too close to getting over to turn back now, so I say, Shit. Youall drive on back to the restaurant. Ima take care of business. I say it like I mean it and I did but I ain't gon try and bullshit you, Bruh, I was scared. When the car lights get halfway down the block, I wants to run after it. I wants to get in with the fellows and call the whole thing off. But they rolling away and I goes back inside the booth and wait.

Didn't have to wait too long. They must of been watching from one the windows in the project cause soon as Michael and them gone a few minutes I see this shadow come out from around the side of a building. Then this shadow whistles and waves for me to come over. Hey, Bruh, I got as much heart as the next dude but I'm not liking nothing that's going down. My boys is gone, my piece gone, and I got this fat wad of dough in my back pocket. Now, somebody I ain't never seen in my life is whistling and waving me over to a place I ain't never been and it's black as Sambo's ass over there by them buildings. I looks around and don't see nothing. I'm having second and third and fourth thoughts about the whole mess. These niggers might be setting me up. Take my money and what I'm gon do about it? The whole trip's feeling real shaky right then. Pittsburgh's a long way off and I'm wishing I was back in the Burgh digging TV with my lady, but this cat's waving me cross the street and I come this far and Garth is depending on me. The crew's depending on me. I got to take the chance. I follow the dude. He don't say a word. Just walks real slow, checking every now and then to see if I'm behind him. It's around one building and through another, then back where there's garbage cans and around to another building with steps up the side. Tried to keep track of where he was taking me but the point of going round and round like that was to make sure I'd never find my way back again. Had to keep following the dude cause after a while I didn't know where the fuck I was.

We went up some steps and knocked on the first door. Standing there in the dark, a funny thing happened. I started thinking about my clothes. For some fool reason that's what I was thinking of then and now I can see my leather jacket and blue jeans and red boots. I can see the zippers up the side of the boots, the fancy stitching on the jeans. Wondering if I'd look good dead in that shit, probably.

The dude still ain't said word the first. I'm up beside him and he knocks. I hear Marcus's voice and that helps a little bit. Chains start sliding loose on the other side of the door. Then I see Marcus's face and I feel a whole lot better. Seen Marcus before in Pittsburgh when he blew in to see the Twinkies, so I knew who he was and I felt better cause if they was gon take me off it wouldn't be Marcus doing it. He get some his thugs for the heavy work. I ain't over yet but I start relaxing some, checking out where I'm at.

It's a little project house. Marcus shuts the door and I think we alone till a woman's voice come from one the inside rooms. They go back and forth about something. I figure it's probably the woman's pad and Marcus use it for business. No way Marcus be as big as he is in dope and living in no stomp-down project apartment.

We in this tiny little kitchen. Marcus don't waste no time. He gets out the dope. Says it's good stuff. Says it take a five cut.

The "P" is in pill bottles. It's "P" cause it's pure heroin. Marcus had all his shit in a case, like a tape case. You know. Just a brown case with snaps. The cuts in plastic bags. A mix of quinine and milk sugar. A ring of measuring spoons in the case with the P and the cut. A scale too. Nothing fancy. The kind of stuff you get in a dime store or a supermarket. Ring of metal spoons. Dime-store scale. Marcus had the shit hooked up in five minutes. Mixed me a light street bag. A eighth spoon P and cut.

I shot it. It checked out good. Prime shit. Real nice.

Marcus threw in a ounce of cut for free. The dude was being fair. Better than fair. Good price on the dope, and he just gimme the other stuff for nothing. I'm digging Marcus more and more all the time. He's good with his hands. While he was hooking me up he talked real friendly.

Have you seen so and so in Pittsburgh. How's William and Charles. How's my sweet niece, Tanya. What's happening on the set. Stuff like that. Like he's an old friend been knowing me all my life. Like family. I'm thinking, Yeah. Yeah, the cat's digging me and I'm really into something. I'm in the family business. Marcus talking, being sociable, but he let some things drop. Marcus play a real deep third base. Never gon let on too much. But he let me know they been keeping track of me. Watching how I handle myself. Marcus talk like my uncle or something. Don't get hooked, Rob. If you want to be the man you got to stay cool. You could be the one take Billy Sims's spot. I'm listening to every word. And it's sweet. My dream's coming true. Ain't nothing in the way. I can see myself rising straight to the top.

Marcus says, I'll front you. You do right and you're on your way. The big time. I want to jump up and holler. Marcus saying the very same thing I'm thinking so it got to be true. He tells me to sell the shit and bring him back the money right away. Flip it. Turn it back to dope. You know. Flip money. Bring it back to him for more dope and flip it again and flip it again and I'm standing there in somebody's jive little kitchen a rich man counting all the money I'm gon make.

We got two thousand and that will turn seven thousand on the street. Chunky can get us seven thousand dealing the shit and then we come back to big D and buy more dope and it's the big time. Fat city. I'm tripping on the good times we gon have.

There's this table where Marcus was working and a sink full of dirty dishes. Two chairs. Them bargain-basement kind with plastic seats that pop open and got dirty cotton inside. One them undersize project stoves and a project refridge. The woman's calling Marcus again. I'm feeling good but this apartment is hurting. It's greasy-looking and the lights too bright. I goes in my back pocket and pull out the stake. Old money. Lots of tens and fives and twenties in a rubber band. A fistful of wrinkled-up money we been saving off our jobs and shit. I slip it on the table for Marcus. He smile and don't even count it. He smiles a little Uncle Ben smile and I know I'm grinning back. I can see the sun. I can see me rising straight to the top.

I call Michael and them. Tell them meet me back at the booth where they dropped me. See, that tripping round the project wasn't nothing but a trick to get me lost. The phone booth right outside Marcus's place. Walked out the front door of the apartment and there it was.

Did I say Mike's car? Wasn't Mike's car that time. Got that wrong. Was Sowell's car. Triple blue Chevy Impala. Dark blue vinyl top, baby blue outside, blue interior. Tape deck, wire wheels, and all that kinda stuff. Sowell liked to go first class. He knew how to spend money. So the fellows come back and I gets in and we're on our way. Isley Brothers on the stereo. The album with lots of slow songs. What's it called. I can't remember. I can hear the songs though. Sweet, slow stuff and everybody's happy. Everybody's feeling good. Talking up dreams. What we gon spend our riches on. Passing round a jug of Thunderbird. Getting real happy. Hey. What's the word. Hey, what's the price. You know, being silly and dreaming up on new cars and new pads and how we gon keep our number-one ladies in fine apartments. How they gon lay up in there all perfumed and nice waiting for us and we the only one got the key. Goodtiming and laughing and mellow all the way back to Pittsburgh.

Sammy the only one who's a pain in the ass. He's bugging everybody to let him shoot some the dope. C'mon, man. Gimme some, man. That's all he wants. Couldn't care less about no women and apartments. Sammy wants him a fix. Wants to get high. His uncle was right on. You couldn't trust that fool with nothing. He was my man but he couldn't carry no dope around the corner without getting into it. You hook him up in Detroit you never see Sammy again. Be done O.D.'d. Be looking for a fix in junkie heaven or junkie hell or wherever a junkie go he leaves here.

When I look back it seems like that ride was the best time. We was happy. We had our dreams. Everything went downhill after that. The roof falls in when we get back to Pittsburgh.

Sunday morning when we finally drive in. Early. Early morning. Sun just breaking through. No traffic. We got off the Turnpike at Monroeville and came in on 22. Rode up the back way to East Hills. Nobody out in the street. Everything quiet and still. We's all still up. Been on the road a day and a half but nobody ready to go to bed yet. We still too high. We still tripping on that Superfly fantasy. I mean we on our way, ain't we? We got the dope. Marcus in our corner. The Twinkies in our corner. No hitches. Our shit be on the street next morning gobbling up money. So we still high. We all ready to test the dope now.

Except Sowell. Sowell don't never shoot up. Says he's tired from driving and drops us at my pad. We make him take Sammy home. Sammy's mad but Mike and Cecil don't want to be bothered with Sammy. Sowell splits and we lay at my house. Mike had left his car parked outside so there's a way home when people ready. We sat around and got high. Divided the dope into street bags. Mixed in the cut. Finished fixing about half of it. Then we had to figure where to stash it. Took it over to Sowell's cause he never been in no trouble. His place be the safest. Like I said before, Sowell was in it for the money. He didn't hang out like the rest of us. You'd see his car up on the set but he just be dropping by. Like a businessman checking his store. Cause that's all he wanted to do. Make that quick money. Sowell wasn't in the life. He worked every day. Dope money was something extra. So we took it over to his place, then Michael dropped me back home and I slept like a baby till evening.

Had nine half-spoons of dope at my place already. Stuff I was selling for Sims. Could of gone out and sold them Sunday night but Tanya come over. We trying to get it back together. Had a light falling out early in the week. Needed a little time together get things mellow again. So Tanya slept over my place and I didn't do no Sunday work. Not on the corner, anyway. We be making mellow love and I wasn't thinking about selling them nine half-spoons. Monday morning soon enough. I'm king that night. Got a fine lady beside me all brown and warm and being special nice cause she knows she was wrong, knows the little falling out was her fault and she's trying to make it up. Got Tanya beside me and the dope ready to go. Monday ain't kicked my ass yet. The roof ain't caved in yet so I'm King Rat. I'm thinking in just a few hours the world's gon open her big legs and say, Come on. Come get you some. Come on and take it all if you want it.

Monday morning I hear this knocking. Tanya's sleep and I'm still half drugged. Think I hear something, then again I'm not sure. I rolls over and say fuck it to whatever it was. Then I hear them pounding again. Somebody at my front door. .

What you want? Ain't got no clothes on. Talking through the door.

You got a yellow Cadillac out here. It's blocking the driveway.

No. Shit no. I'm pissed off cause somebody bugging me over nothing. Waking me up when sleep was feeling so good. But once I'm up, I'm up. Hear Tanya in the bathroom. Figured I mize well get rid of Sims's shit early. Then I'd help cover Chunky's back while he dealed our stuff. Washed up. Got my clothes on. Called me a jitney. Done forgot all about that yellow Cadillac.

When the jitney blows I step outside into the hall. My building was on the corner, 3332 East Hills Drive. I had the first apartment on the ground floor just inside the front door. Soon as I step in the hall I hear shotguns pumping. Once you heard that sound you never forget it. I'm in the hall and I hear them. Half a dozen shotguns pumped. All of them pumping and aiming at my chest.

Halt.

Nine packs of dope in my pocket so I never stop. Can't let them find that shit on me. All I can think is I gotta get rid of this dope and from my door I jumps straight out the door of the building. Zoom. I takes off. Flies through the air till I hit the front door. Then I leap down the steps. Flying again when these cops catch me. Grab me right out the midair.

Hustled my ass back into the apartment. Then they tear the place up looking for dope. They find some reefer in Tanya's purse. Funny thing is, they ain't searched me yet. Them nine packs make a fat package and I'm wearing tight jeans. Kind with straight pockets in the front, more like slits than pockets. For decoration cause you can't get nothing down in them. You know, like two watch pockets in front with stitching to match the stitching down the legs and on the back pockets. The kind of jeans they was wearing then. Tight-assed and tight-legged, so the dope's bulging in my back pocket. They searching and I'm standing in the middle of the room with my hand over my ass trying to hide the shit. Seemed like anybody could see it poking out back there. But they didn't search me for the longest time. Tore up the place looking for dope and I'm standing there with nine bags stashed in my pocket plain as day. I was looking for a chance to break away and flush the shit down the toilet or throw it out a window. But the cops was too close on me. A million of them. They had the place surrounded. Pump guns in the hallway and patrol cars all up and down the drive. Then I remembered the voice waking me up. Must of been them trying to trick me out the house. Cops ain't shit. Playing Dick Tracy games. Can't find dope when it's staring them in the face. Finally, one searched me. I was tired of patting my ass anyway. Arrested me and Tanya. Took us down to No. 5. Jammed me up over the nine bags. Tanya ain't had nothing but a joint in her purse so they let her go. Wasn't ten o'clock in the morning of the first day of the big time, and I'm jammed up in the slammer.

Now this is weird. Real weird. Mike finally came down and got me out of jail that day and later on while we in the bar talking we can't figure out why the cops busted me. And add to that the cops was talking about Detroit. One kept asking me, Where's the shit you picked up in Detroit? We know you copped in Detroit. Now how in hell the cops know about Detroit? We ain't hardly back yet and they talking about the run to Detroit. Don't make no sense at all unless somebody who made the run snitching to the cops. Didn't nobody else know about it.

Cecil and Mike figure it had to be Sammy. They want to go and off the nigger right away. They was mad and they thinking Sammy ain't shit anyway. Nobody but me liked him. Lots of people just looking for an excuse to waste the dude. Cecil and Mike was mad as I ever seen em. They was probably right, too. Who else it be but Sammy.

Me, I'm mad too, but I'm shook up. I been in jail all day and worrying. We so close and now it starts to raining shit on our big play. I tell them guys cool it. Wasting Sammy ain't what it's about. All our money tied up in this dope and we got to take care of business. The cops is probably watching me. They know something's up. It's a bad scene all round. Election time and the set's tight. They busting people to look good for the voters. Be's like that every election so it's risky to do business. Ain't no sense going down on Sammy. Just make things tighter. I say cool it. I say keep the shit stashed at Sowell's a week or so till I ain't hot. Till election's over. We can wait. A week or two won't change nothing. We waited this long so let's take our time and do it right. That's what I'm trying to get across and the fellows see my point but they's still pissed at Sammy. Leave Sammy be. He ain't nothing. Anyway we ain't even sure it was him.

Who else it gon be? Wring that punk's neck.

Yeah. Simple-assed Sammy lucky he didn't walk in the bar that night. Funny thing is, Sammy ain't opened his mouth. Cops busted me that morning cause the roommate of one my old girl friends dropped a dime on me. Never knew till much later. Till I was in the joint. That's when I found out what really happened. See this girl I used to hang with. She was a trifling bitch. Had to put her down and after that she's always bad-mouthing me. Putting my name in shit every chance she gets. According to her, I'm the worst cat in the world. Number one on the Ugly list. Well, she talks that kinda trash all the time. Robby this and Robby that and Robby ain't no good. Her roommate listening to that mess all the time and one day in the grocery store she sees Tony and Tony knows all us and knows we was going to Detroit and the chick asks him, Where's Robby? She ain't seen Robby in a while. Like she's my friend and shit and maybe want to give me some pussy. Tony don't make nothing of it one way or another. He says Robby's in Detroit this weekend. Just a casual conversation in the A & P, you know. But the bitch she knows she got something good. She's scheming. She been out on the set and figures we ain't driving to Detroit for no picnic. Bitch calls the cops and sets me up.

That's why the cops knew about Detroit. That's why they staked me out. Figured they was on to a super bust. Well, them nine half-spoons they found wasn't what they was hoping for but it was enough to get me jammed up and we had to keep our shit off the street two weeks. And them two weeks blew the whole scheme. But I ain't to the weird part yet. See this girl. What's she trying to do? She don't even know me except what she's heard from her roomie. She's just taking it on herself to do her friend a favor. Then look what happens. I'm here in this motherfucking slammer today cause that bitch dropped a dime. Don't know what would have happened if she'd of minded her own business. Maybe we would have sold our dope and flipped the money and sold some more. Maybe we'd have made it big. Got to the top. Niggers see us and say, "Those dudes made theirs from the curb." Maybe I woulda been Superfly for a day. Who knows? What did happen was the bitch blew our tip before it even got started good. By holding back that dope it spoiled, and then we didn't have nothing. No money, no dope, no jobs. Nothing. We was stone broke and didn't have no choice but to rob us some money. So we did. And Stavros got killed, and here I am. All on account that bitch dropped a dime.

Now I don't know what all that means. And I can't sit here and say what might have been if she had minded her own business. What I do know is, the broad is sitting in a wheelchair today, paralyzed from the neck down. A car accident. Ain't that something? So in a way she's worser off than me. She may have put me in a world of trouble but trouble got a way of turning around, of coming back at you when you puts it on somebody else. I ain't saying it was punishment. And I sure ain't saying she deserves to be a cripple cause she did dirt to me. But the fact is she dropped that dime and I'm where I am today and she's where she is.

Could be she did me a favor. At least I'm alive. If we had made the big time it just be a matter of time before somebody off us. Wheel's always turning. You can *get* to the top but ain't no way you gon *stay* at the top. Too much bullshit. Too many cats want what you got. Everybody shooting at you. The life is hard. It's hard and fast. That's why everybody trying to get over in a hurry. Here today and gone tomorrow. Ain't nothing to it, really. It ain't the money or the cars or the women. It's about all that but that ain't what it's deep down about. Cats blow a thousand a night when they on top. The money ain't nothing. You just use the money to make your play. To show people you the best. Yeah. Look at me. I got mine. I melted the rock to get mine. You got money and money ain't nothing. You throw it away cause it's here today and gone tomorrow. You out there to show your ass. To let people know you're somebody. Yeah. You out there to shine. To be a star.

Straight people don't understand. I mean, they think dudes is after the things straight people got. It ain't that at all. People in the life ain't looking for no home and grass in the yard and shit like that. We the show people. The glamour people. Come on the set with the finest car, the finest woman, the finest vines. Hear people talking about you. Hear the bar get quiet when you walk in the door. Throw down a yard and tell everybody drink up. See. It's rep. It's glamour. That's what it's about. What else a dude gon do in this fucked-up world. You make something out of nothing.

So maybe the bitch did me a favor. Wasn't going nowhere in that gangster bag. Be just a matter of time before somebody wasted me. All the big-time niggers get wasted. My life ain't shit now but at least I got a life. Maybe I ought to thank the bitch.

The world's a weird place. Got plenty of time on my hands to think about how weird it is. We was sitting blaming Sammy. Sammy close to getting his head blowed off over nothing. That's the way things happen.

Somebody I don't even know hurts me worse than I ever been hurt. And maybe doing me a favor at the same time. And she winds up a cripple in a wheelchair.

See. Ain't all of us out there in the street crazy. We know what's going down. We look round and what do we see? Homewood look like five miles of bad road. Ain't nothing happening. We see that. We know it. So what we supposed to do? Go to church like the old folks? Be O.J. or Dr. J? Shit. Ain't everybody in the street crazy. We see what's going down. We supposed to die. Take our little welfare checks and be quiet and die. That ain't news to nobody. It's what's happening every day in Homewood. Them little checks and drugs. What else is out there? The streets out there. The hard-ass curb. That's why the highest thing you can say about a cat is he made his from the curb. That's a bad cat. That's a cat took nothing and made something. When a dude drive up in a big hog and goes in the bar with a fox on his arm and drops a yard on the counter, he's bad. Got to be bad. What else he be but bad if he made all his shit from that hard rock?

Don't matter if it's gone tomorrow. If he's dead tomorrow. The cat was bad. He made it the only way he could.

The glamour. The rep. That's what I wanted. Coming home one day with my pockets full of hundred-dollar bills and buying Mommy a house and anything else she wants. I knew I was doing wrong. Knew I was hurting people. But then I'd look around and see Homewood and see what was going down. Shit. I ain't gon lay down and die. Shit. Ima punch that rock with my bare hand till it bleeds money.

See. There we was. No dope, no jobs, no money. I take it back to that bitch dropped the dime on me. Cause that Monday when the cops raided my place, we had it all together. I mean, wasn't no stopping us. Then I got busted. Tried to fly out of there but them cops caught me in midair. You should of seen it. I was flying. Hit my door and heard them guns pump and I ain't never stopped. I leaps the little railing so I can get away but they're down there too. Two of em alongside the building. I swear they grabbed me right out the air cause I was flying. Trying to make it to the grass, to the open place beside the building, but must of been a million cops out there. I'll never forget how them guns sounded in the hall. Pump em just like you seen in cop shows on TV. Shlkdump. Shlkdump. Them pumpguns all aiming at my heart and it skipped a beat but I ain't never stopped. I'm gone till they tackled me out the air.

Yeah. It's kinda funny to think back on it. A lot of stuff we did was funny. We was crazy. Had to be. Doing stuff all the time that didn't make no sense. Lemme tell you, though. I wasn't laughing when they carried me back up in the house. Had all that dope on me. Never gave me a chance to ditch it. I'm thinking bout the shit in my pocket but what I'm really worrying about is our plans. We was uptight. Everything was alright. We had it together and this spozed to be the day we put our shit on the street and start to making big money. But I'm jammed up. Got me in the police station and I'm thinking, What the fuck is happening? This ain't spozed to be happening. Shooting for the big time and they got me for them nine half-spoons in my back pocket. Ain't no way, I'm thinking. This ain't where it's at. Like, my feelings was hurt. Like, shit. Ima big-time gangster and they jamming me over this little jive-time shit of Billy Sims's.

Then, like I said, Mike came down to No. 5 and got me out. We all met in the bar that night. Me and Cecil and Mike and Sowell. We decided to cool it till the heat was off. Bunch of busts coming down cause it's election time and I'm hot as a pistol so it ain't hardly time to move no dope. We decide to put the shit away. Sowell says he'll drop it at his sister's. She got a basement and ain't never been in no trouble. I mean, ain't no choice really. Ain't safe to move it on the set. Two weeks and things be cool again, so that's how it goes down.

There's two kinds of dope. One's the natural kind. You know. Make it from berries, them little poppy-flower berries. That's the natural shit. And there's the other kind. Synthetic. Chemicals and do. Whatever it is, it's different than the natural kind. One kind won't keep, is the biggest difference. Well, whatever it is, we had the wrong kind. Cause when them two weeks up I get a jitney over to Sowell's and he takes me to his sister's. Nice house. Real straight, you know. She ain't had no idea what's in that paper bag in her basement. A real clean, nice house. The shit's in a brown paper bag and we go downstairs to cop and it's even clean down there. She hand it to us just as nice. Like it's a sandwich or something.

Sowell drops me back to my pad. I finish cutting the stuff up cause we only did half of it before. Get it all ready in street bags. It's ready but I ain't hardly gon let it out the door without trying a little taste. Mize well do it up right. You know. Greedy. Put a three cut on some. Bam.

But wait a minute. Ain't nothing happening. Do a two cut and try again. A two now and it's spozed to take a five. Bam. Do the two and I know something's wrong. Two cut should take me out but nothing again. Cept I start to shaking. Shakes get worse and worse. Can't stop shaking. My whole body shaking so bad I can't even stand up. I'm lying on the floor out of control. Nothing I can do. My mind's racing. I'm flashing on all kinds of shit. Mostly just scared. Panicky. Don't know what the fuck's happening. Think I'm dying. See, it's like you get if you shoot water. You start shaking and can't stop. Like the chills. Chills just tearing your body up till your heart can't take it no more. On my back bouncing on the floor and I can't do shit. I figure that's it. Figure I bought the big one. But then it don't get no worser. Get a little better. I crawl over to the phone and call my girl. Still trembling so bad I can't even talk. Get the phone dialed and get her on the line but I can't say shit. My body still out of control all I can do is holler help. Holler it two or three times into the phone. She's screaming on the other end. Robby . . . Robby . . . what's wrong, what's the matter, where are you, and I'm choking and sputtering and can't say shit but help . . . help. You ever had one of them nightmares so bad you all tangled up in it you can't get loose? It's some damn thing or another chasing your ass and it just about got you so you scream but nothing comes out. Just this little squeaky nothing like you can't get your throat open. Trying hard as you can but you can't scream and the bogeyman dead on your ass. That's what it was like. Musta scared the daylight out of Wanda. She told me later it did. Said I sounded like I was gargling or something. Like I was drowning.

Anyway, I didn't die. Mike and Cecil come by. By that time Wanda had me wrapped in blankets and I could sit up. Just about alright again when they come in with Chunky. I could talk then and the shakes almost gone but I didn't want to say what I had to say. Had to tell them the dope was bad.

Wanda don't know what's happening. She don't know about the dope or the plan or nothing. She know something real bad had hold to me and she was upset and cried a little bit, but Wanda's cool. She ain't asking no questions after she sees I'm gon be alright. Tell her to go out in the kitchen and make some coffee. Then I got to say what have to be said to my crew.

But damn, man. I can't even say it to myself, let alone tell Cecil and Mike. They know something's up. They know it's bad business. They my partners. We been through all kinds of stuff together. They my main men. Still are. Ain't no bullshit between us, so I got to lay it on em.

The shit's bad, man. I shot it and it ain't no good. Like to killed me, man.

That's it. That's the end of the dream right there. But Mike don't want to hear it. Mike got to find out for hisself. Maybe it just ain't strong. Maybe we can put a one cut on it. He don't listen to nothing. Got to do it hisself. Mike's gon put the shit in the street no matter what.

Hey, man. I did a two cut and it nearly killed me.

Mike ain't listening. He's gon do it his way. Shoots the shit and I'm waiting for his eyeballs start dancing but don't nothing happen. Nothing.

We gon sell this shit, anyway. It's dope, ain't it. We bought it and we gon sell it. It's dope. Niggers will buy it and shoot it. I don't care if they get high or die or turn to purple-ass baboons. That's my money in those bags. That's all the money I got in the world.

Mike is wrong. Stone wrong. The shit is bad and you can't be selling people no bad shit. You got to get a reputation. Be reliable. You got to be there and stand behind your shit. We can't be jiving. We want to go all the way to the top. I say to Mike, Look, man. We can't blow, man. Too much at stake, I'm trying to tell him, but he can't see past the money we got tied up in that bad shit.

It's out there. It's out there on the street today, so mize well stop talking about it. It's gon out there today. Just cause this bag's bad don't mean it's all bad.

You can't talk to the cat. He's in his hardhead bag. It's in his eyes. His eyes doing the talking and his eyes ain't got no ears, so no sense in saying nothing. He's wrong, but he's right too. Cause every penny in the world we got is tied up in dope. Good or bad, that's where our money is. Took us all summer to get it together. Working jobs and hustling any way we could. Took us three months to get a stake together and ain't no way we gon just give it away. So Mike's wrong but he's right, too. We got to get back as much as we can from our money.

Three dudes cop right away. Things been tight on the set so niggers happy to see some new shit. Half an hour they're back on the corner looking for Chunky, wanting their money back. This shit ain't shit. Cats is mad. Gon put the word out. Want my money, man. Ain't nothing to this shit, man. Don't take a half hour and we know it's over. It's bad shit. No way to move it. Them two weeks waiting did it to us. Two weeks killed the dope and killed the dream. Talk about sorry asses. Talk about some wasted, pitiful, sorry-assed cats. Threw the shit in a garbage can. Took two thousand dollars and lifted the lid and dropped it in and said good-bye.

Now what we gon do? No jobs, no money, no dope. Winter's coming. Hard times on the way. I'm low as I can go. I'm desperate. It's worse cause we built up the dream. Seemed like things was going our way. You know. We got so close. I could taste it, brother John. Like, it so close I had my hands all down in the drawers. It was that close. Then nothing. Just all blowed away. Wasn't even no dream no more. Shit. And to make it worse, me and Mike both lost our jobs.

Ima tell you another one of those weird things. One them things don't make no sense but they just happen anyway. It was the day after I got busted. They been on my butt at my job. I was working at the center with retarded kids. Best job I ever had. Shoulda stayed with that job but my head was off into the gangster thing. No small-time shit would do. So I be messing over my job. Being late and missing a day here and there. Supervisor called me in. Said she give me one more chance. Only reason she's giving me another chance is them kids. Them kids loved me. I could get them to do things nobody else could. This one named Timmy. Ain't nobody ever heard him say a word. He just sit like a bump on a log. Autistic, you know. That's what they called him. Him and some the other ones that was always spaced out. Yeah. It's some sad shit. Little wee kids and they gone already. Just sit all day staring off in space. Don't even move to go to the bathroom. Pee and shit all over theyself. You could stick a pin in them they wouldn't cry. I seen staff people do that too. You wouldn't believe how they treat those kids. Some the stuff goes on make you sick at the stomach. You work with a kid all day and get him halfway settled down and acting like a human being, and next morning he get off the bus crazier than he was the day before. It's pitiful. Just kids but they treat em like animals. You wouldn't believe the shit I've seen. They stay at night at the home and bring em to the center in the morning. Belt marks and burns and bruises all over their bodies. I know. I seen it. You work all day to get one quiet and feeling good and next morning his lip busted and he's wild again.

I loved them kids, liked to work with em, but it was hard to see em come piling off that bus drugged up and beat down every morning. Wasn't nothing really wrong with most those kids. You just treat em nice and they act nice. They was crazy cause they got treated like dogs. Little Timmy used to make a sound for me. Think he called hisself saying my name. Little squeaky sound when he wanted me or when I do something for him he like. They said he was autistic. Said he'd never be nothing but a vegetable all his life. But if I could get him to make a sound then Timmy was in there somewhere. Supervisor didn't believe me till she heard him herself.

Now see, if my head had been together I would have stayed with that job. I liked the kids and they liked me. Felt like I owed them something. Always a little something I could do for them. It was hard. Ain't gon tell you no lie. You know I never liked to smoke but I went round with a cigarette in my mouth all the time. Had to. No way to get close to some of them less you got that smoke to breathe. They be messing they pants. Big ones and little ones. I'm talking bout ten-, eleven-, twelve-year-old kids and they stink just like you or me going to the bathroom. One everybody call Icky Ricky. A happy little dude but he smell like a skunk. Eat his own dookey, you didn't keep an eye on him. C'mon over here, Ricky. Let me change them nasty things. I'd get me a cigarette lit up and take care of business. That's the only way you could get close to ole Ricky. Blow a cloud of smoke.

Center was a hard place to work. They didn't pay no money. Most the staff ain't shit. Some worse than that. Some sicker in the head than any them kids. Don't know nothing but how to hurt. Punch kids or kick em. Scream at em or push em when they want them to move. I had to tell em, you know. Don't do that shit in front of me. You do it in front of me and Ima knock you out. And the so-called professionals ain't much better. Got their little certificates and titles. Walking round high and mighty like they God in them white coats. They just as ignorant as the hard legs. It's all just bullshit. Them professionals know what I know. They see them knots and bruises all over the kids. Long as they keep sending them back to the home at night it don't matter what they do at the center. It's two steps up and three back. They know but they don't care. They got their little jobs and their little titles. They living off those kids, so they ain't about to mess up a good thing.

Worked out there at the center a year and a half. Had to be that long cause it wasn't till the second year Timmy started squeaking at me. Just about jumped out my shoes the first time I seen his eyeballs rolling at me. You could wave your hand in his face and he wouldn't blink. Like he had this glass wall all round him. You could go up to it and peek in but Timmy in outer space somewhere minding his own business. Then one day he followed me with his eyes. A whole year after I started messing with him. Kind of a game, you know. Messing with him. Couldn't hurt nothing. Didn't take no time. Just something to do so I kept at it. Played with him a little bit every day. That was my thing. I'd be sick of changing dirty drawers, sick of the stink, sick of the evil, ugly-acting people in there. Sometimes I'd go off by myself and hide for a while but most the time I'd mess with Timmy. Like me and him had this thing. Really my thing, cause Timmy ain't never looked up. He don't care what I be doing. Then, like I say, one day them little green marbles followed me. Didn't believe it at first. Thought I was getting loony like the rest of them. But it happened again. Got to be a everyday thing. Then one day he squeaked. Wasn't as big a shock as his eyes following me that first time. You'd think him making a sound would have shocked me more but by that time I knew me and Timmy was friends. Knew he was hiding behind that wall and he could come out if he wanted to, so when he made that little squeaky sound I just laughed and answered back cause me and Timmy was buddies by then.

I let them kids down. Many a time I've wondered how they are. If things is better for them. They sure do need somebody but I let them down. Like I let everybody else down. No room for no kids. Room for nobody or nothing cause my head was full of the big time. Steady messing up but the lady said she'd give me one more chance on account of the kids liking me and do.

Got one more chance and blew it. I'm talking with the lady Friday. Monday I don't come in. It ain't even my fault. It's the Monday they jam me up and the cops hold me all day so how I'm spozed to be at work. I call over to the center Tuesday but she don't want to hear nothing. I'm fired. Got some money coming to me so I go downtown that day to get it. Ain't much but, you know, all my money tied up in the dope so that little change get me through till we can deal our shit.

I'm on my way home now. They told me to sign this and that and they'd put what they owe me in the mail. Have it in a week or so they said, and I'm hot. Shit. I done pulled the time. The money's mine but I got to wait. So my lip's poked out. I'm mad anyway behind being busted and worried about waiting two weeks to put our dope in the street. You know. One evil nigger waiting to get the bus back to Homewood. I was crossing the street. Lemme see. It must of been Forbes. Yeah, crossing Forbes Street over to the bus stop and who do I see but Michael. What's Mike doing down here? Mike spozed to be working. I get over to where he's at and, Hey man, ain't you working today?

Funny thing is, Mike's jaw's just as tight as mine. I can see he's hot about something but then he sees me, and I tell him I lost my job and he starts to laughing. Laughing his ass off. Now I don't see nothing particularly funny. Then he tells me he was driving the truck and his boss was in there with him and his boss said some off-the-wall shit and Mike told him to fuck hisself and quit right there. Turned off the motor and left truck, sausages, and boss sitting there in the middle of traffic. Mike don't play. He said fuck it and that was it. So it's Tuesday and we both wind up losing our jobs and waiting at the same stop for the same damned bus back to Homewood. That's some weird shit, ain't it?

Next thing happens is, we find out the dope's rotten and we need to get us some money. Now we can't bop down to no bank and get no loan to buy dope. So where's it at? You know where it's at. Got to steal us some dough.

There was this dude named Smokey. He used to hang out on the set. Smokey was a older dude. Been around, you know. He done a bit at Western. Kinda cat mind his own business and stay cool. He was like a teacher. Take a young guy under his wing and show him the ropes. Smokey like you, he could turn you on to some heavy shit. He the one taught me the TV hustle. Did it with Smokey a couple times, then me and Mike and Cecil tried it that summer. Got good at it. Mike's just like me. He con you out the shirt on your back. Loved to act. Stone Hollywood just like me.

The con goes like this: Drive up in Mike's deuce and a quarter. Me and Mike fall out clean as beans. Big-time hustlers. Like we got money to burn. When we talk to a dude we flash our watches. Let him see our gold chains and shit. Mike he checking his watch. See we're busy. We got appointments. Just jiving up a storm. Got real good at the bullshit. Sometimes I believed it myself. Yeah. We was sure nuff actors and con artists. Laid down that big-time impression and them suckers ate it up.

Cause they was crooks theyselves. Natural-born crooks. That's what made it so funny. You could see it in them greedy eyes. They been cheating people and lying and bullshitting so long they think they the king. They think they the only one out there conning people. That's why we worked the scam on used-car dealers. Them little shabby lots with raggedy-ass cars. They ain't nothing but crooks theyselves. Always looking to get away with something or beat somebody out of something. So that's where we'd go. To them greedy motherfuckers don't care how they make money. Once in a while we'd try one them big gas stations on a busy corner. They be steady ripping off people so they got that greedy thing going too. We'd try them if we couldn't find no used-car lot.

First couple times when I went with Smokey he'd do most the work, most the talking, and I'd just watch and listen and learn the ropes. See, what you'd do was tell the dude you had some hot TVs and ask the cat do he want to buy the motherfuckers. It's like the Godfather, you know. Offer the dude a deal he can't refuse. Get that greed going. You can see it in their eyes. You say I got these TVs still in the box and Ima let you have them for next to nothing cause TVs ain't my thing, I deals in other business and these TVs just happen to come my way and I don't want to mess with em. Don't want to be bothered, you dig, cause I ain't into that, dig. I'm dealing in other business, so you got a bargain you take these TVs off my hands. In the crate. Untouched. Brand new.

Well the dude goes for it but he's a crook hisself so he's halfway slick and wants to see the TVs before he gives up his money; so you say, sure. Yeah, that's square business. You say my people got the TVs and tell the dude bring the money and you take him to the people so he can see the stuff before he buys. Carry the dude to the stone ghetto. He be nervous now. Nothing but niggers in sight so he's getting squirmy but you be bullshitting him the whole time. Take his mind off his worries. Everything gon be all right.

You be in a truck or a van. Something that will hold all them TVs.

You get to a house and go up the steps. Got to be a house with a back door and a front door. You be outside with the dude and knock on the door and somebody say, real nasty like, Who is it? Smokey say, It's me, Smokey, and the person inside say, What you want, and Smokey say I got a man here for them TVs. See, they be doing all this talking and the door ain't open yet. The cat inside is a surly-talking motherfucker like he don't appreciate what's going down. He gets on Smokey's case. Man, I told you not to bring no strangers here. And Smokey say, He's cool, man. This dude's all right.

Don't give a fuck who he is. I told you I ain't dealing with nobody but you.

My man's all right.

He a brother?

No, man, but he's cool.

Ain't no honkies coming in here.

Hey, soul, be cool now. The man's square business. He got the money and he's ready to deal. Man just wants to see the TVs first.

Shit. I want to see the money. I ain't opening this goddamn door to no stranger till I see green.

They shouting now. Loud talking back and forth through the door and the dude ain't so sure now he wants no TVs. He's in the middle of the ghetto and these niggers arguing and they liable to start cutting one another or shooting through the door and his honky ass smack dab in the middle. So he's fidgeting and starting to sweat. He's trying to get Smokey's attention and tell him forget it. Wants to get the hell out of there before the cops come or somebody busts out the door and slits his throat.

It's like you weakening the cat. Softening him up. So he's grateful when Smokey gets the dude on the other side of the door cooled down. Then Smokey says, Look here. He'll open up and let me in but he says you have to wait outside. He says he'll let you in after he sees the money.

Now the dude ain't liking this. He's thinking real hard. Maybe he ought to tip back down the steps and forget it. But Smokey's a stone con. He's doing the man a favor. He gon deal with the gorilla on the other side the door. The dude's thinking real hard but he's scared too. Seems like at least one these crazy niggers is on his side so he best better go along with the deal.

My man here will wait with you whiles I check it out.

Smokey's smiling at the dude then he looks at me real hard and I'm Fido the watchdog. I gets real serious too and look down the steps and stares all around and shake my head. Yeah, Smoke. Ima keep my eye out. Ima take care your main man here.

We stone acting and the dude taking everything in. He don't like it but he goes in his pocket and pulls out the money and hands it to Smokey and Smokey knocks and the door opens half a inch and Smokey says, Okay, Ima show you the green, and the door slides wide enough so Smokey brushes in and it slams behind him.

You hear them talking inside again then it gets real quiet. The white dude be smoking but he gets tired of that and throws down the weed and tramps it with his heel. We two stories above the street. On a wooden porch. It's the back of the building with wood steps up to each floor. The stone ghetto. Garbage and wrecked-up cars and all kinds of mess back there. That's all you see when you look down. That kinda shit and the backs of other apartment buildings raggedy as the one you're standing on. The dude's blue van's parked in the alley. He's keeping his eye on it. You think it'll hold ten TVs? Yeah, man. They in the boxes. Easy to load, man. Smokey had all the answers. Smokey a stone con.

The dude squashes his cigarette and in a few minutes starts to light another. But his hand's too shaky.

I'm cool. Like ain't nothing unusual even though Smokey been gone ten minutes and it must seem like ten hours to the dude cause his money been gone that long too.

What do you think's happening?

Don't know.

Well, why's it taking so long?

Don't know.

Do you know these people? Have you ever dealt with them before?

They just people. Nothing special.

You know. Acting like I'm in no hurry. Like it ain't no big thing Smokey's been gone fifteen minutes. I'm taking in the scenery. Lady in a brassiere moving round in one them windows cross the way. Cool, you know.

I think something's wrong.

Smokey's cool, man.

It's taking too long.

I'm checking out the window cross the way. The dude steps up closer to the door. He leans his ear to the door. It's funny cause he's scared. He's remembering that surly motherfucker who did all the bad-mouthing. Honky this and honky that. Don't allow no honky mother-fuckers in here.

Go ahead and check it out if you in a hurry.

He's like a traffic light. Go from red to white to red again. Like he stepped on a hot wire cause he jumps back from the door when I say "Go ahead" and look at me like I put his mama in the dozens.

Well . . . well . . . maybe *you* better check.

That's what I want to hear but act like I ain't in no hurry. I saunters over and knocks. Nothing. No answer. No sound. I look back at the dude. He's whiter than he was before but he's mad now too. His jaw's tight. He'd be cussing me if he wasn't so scared.

I knocks again. Harder, with my fist. Then I turn the knob and call Smokey.

Smokey. Hey, man, what's happening?

I'm in then and slam the door behind me. I'm calling Smokey again but I know he ain't there. Smokey's long gone. My feet tipping out the front door and I eases it shut and I'm gone too.

That's one way. The old-time Murphy way. Old-time Murphy pimp con. You know. Gimme some money, you can fuck the fine lady I keeps upstairs. Nothing upstairs but a knob and a door. Dude out to pull some leg and gets his leg pulled. Nothing but a TV Murphy con but Smokey had it down. Taught it to me and we used it that summer. Did it that way and another way. Same con only you bring the TVs to the dude in-stead of taking him to the TVs. Word gets round. Not everybody fool enough to jump in a car with a pocketful of money and two strange splibs. Got this other way of doing business. For the slick ones. Ones don't trust nobody.

Like I said, word gets around. Only so many places you can deal. Like the best kind of place is along a highway, or big road where they got a bunch of car lots and gas stations. A strip. Like out to Monroeville and Ardmore. We worked all them around here and in the tristate area and was running out of territory. Word gets around, so you got to keep moving. Sucker one dude and it ain't cool to go back to the same area. People suspicious. You got to find new places.

Some them dudes ain't dumb as they look. They just greedy. Get so greedy they get careless. One time we drive up in a empty rental truck spozed to be full of TVs. Nothing in it but Cecil with a shotgun waiting for the dude to check out the TVs. We drives up and this bald-head dude say, Come on in the office. He don't even ask to see what we got so I'm wondering what's up. You know. Specially since he was one suspicious dude. Never take his eye off you. And talking trash, too. Street talk. Like some them young white guys. But this dude a bald-head, potbelly chump. Talking that lame, Hey, man this and Hey, man that shit. Laying down his feeble rap like he goes for bad and do. I'm figuring he think he sure gon ask to check out the merchandise before he show us a dime. It's dark. He the only one around and there's two of us. Figure I got his number but the dude don't check out the van. He say, Come on in the office, fellows.

Then he mess up. See, he's gon get the money out his desk drawer. I'm watching him like a hawk all the time, you dig. He pulls out the top drawer. He thinks he's cool but he messes up. Opens the top drawer and all I see is silver. Something silver filling the whole damn drawer. He slams it shut real quick but I see something shiny in there and I'm on his ass. I'm holding in the top drawer before he gets the money drawer open.

What you got in there, my man?

Nothing's in there. Just opened the wrong drawer. See, here's the money. It's right here.

Yeah, but what's in there?

Got my piece in my hand and Michael backing me with that cowboy gun of his. Magnum look like the Liberty tubes when it's pointing at you.

You sure did open the wrong drawer.

I slides it open and there's the biggest, shiniest gun I ever seen. Bigger than Mike's magnum. I'm talking about a wide desk drawer and that piece filled it. I picks it out the drawer. It was a heavy Johnson with a silver barrel and fancy silver hand grip.

Look here.

Damn. My man got him a silver cannon. What was you gon do with that cannon, my friend, if we turned our backs on you? Mike's aiming at the dude's head.

The dude about to shit a brick. Starts stuttering about the wrong drawer . . . the wrong drawer.

Yes, you did open the wrong drawer. You sure did.

We left that fool up behind Greentree somewhere. Locked his ass in the truck and told him he better not open his mouth cause we was gon be right outside listening. Mike wanted to keep that pretty pistol but we sold it. We cracked up over that wrong-drawer shit.

Stuff like that happened all the time. You be in the middle of some dangerous shit but you got to laugh. You see a dude's face when he messes up. He knows he done messed up real bad. His ass in a sling and he's trying to cop a plea and his eyes is big and some old funny shit comes out. The wrong drawer. You got to laugh cause it's funny. He mighta blowed you away with that cannon but you don't think about nothing like that. Ain't nobody gon get killed. You just into cowboy and Indin shit like in the movies. You the gangsters but you the good guys too. No problem.

I'm telling you the whole bit now. Ain't holding nothing back. That's the way we was. Stone gangsters. Robbing people. Waving guns in people's face. Serious shit. But it was like playing too. A game. A big game and we was just big kids having fun. Guns wasn't real. Bullets wasn't real. Wasn't planning on hurting nobody. Pow. Pow. You know. Fall over. I got you. No, you didn't. You missed. Pow. Pow. I got you. You lying. I got you first. Cowboy and Indin shit like the old days on Finance with Gumpy and Sonny and them.

I ain't never told nobody all of it cause I didn't think I could. Fraid it would make you or Mommy or anybody think I was really bad, that I belonged in here with the criminals. Cause I did it all. Your brother was a stone gangster and that's what he wanted to be. I had things figured out. Needed a stake to start me on the way to the top. Robbing people was the only way, so that's what we did. Made up my mind to do whatever it took. Never thought I'd really have to hurt nobody. Never thought I'd get hurt. We was cool. We could bullshit our way out anything.

Well, that's who I was. I needed to tell you that. I come this far I don't want to hold nothing back.

We was desperate after the dope went bad. Everything gone, nothing coming in. I had a little bit of income-tax money due me and them nickels from my job but that wasn't nothing. See we'd got too close. We was close enough to taste it and we waited once and the dope turned rotten and no way we gon be patient and wait again.

See, we had to have some money. We was hooked up with Marcus. Had it all together but nothing happening till we got some dough. See, cause it's about money. Money talks. Marcus in my corner but Marcus ain't waiting forever. And Marcus ain't giving out no dope on credit. It's on us. We got to put up or shut up.

Took us ten days but we finally found this place over on the West Side after you come out the tunnel on Greys Pond Road. Stavros was the dude's name owned it. I can't remember what he looked like. When I think about it it's like I can remember what he said and what he had on but it's blank where his face supposed to be. He was about my height. Nothing really special about him. Nothing that would stick in your mind you pass him on the street. Kind of a hippy-looking guy. You know. Long scraggly hair. Had on jeans and one them scrufty blue work shirts. Thin guy. Spoke real soft. He wasn't suspicious or nothing. Just wanted to get it on. Yeah, he figured he had him a good thing. Stepped in shit, you know. Fast, easy money and he liked that, he liked the idea of getting over cause he was a known fence and dealing a little drugs on the side. He wasn't nobody's angel. Just an out-there dude trying to make it. Run a little dope, buy stuff off junkies, sell people them jive cars he had backed up on that lot. I can see the jeans and the blue work shirt and I can see lots of other things. Like this other guy. A mechanic. Clean-cut, nice-looking dude. Creases in his blue jeans and his hair cut shorter than Stavros's. Neat-looking cat sitting off to the side while we's negotiating. He's the one we talked to first. Kept acting like he didn't want nothing to do with two fly niggers. Like nigger might rub off on him or something if he got too close, but he called Stavros and we got it on. Yeah. I can see the other guy's face. I seen him then and seen him at the trial and if I close my eyes I could see him now but Stavros's face is empty. I remember the scraggly hair and them hippie-type clothes but ain't nothing where his face supposed to be. I can hear that soft voice but I can't see no mouth, no face.

Been that way since I heard he was dead. Didn't even know he was dead till Sunday morning. That's right. No way he could be dead cause the cat jumped up from the ground and ran. Watched him run all the way out to Greys Pond Road myself, so when Mike called me the morning after the job I didn't know what he was talking about. See, it was Sunday, the morning after we pulled the job, and my head was real bad. We'd been out celebrating, partying, you know, and I'm still groggy when the phone rings. I'm laying at my girl's house with a bad head but when the phone rings I grab it. Something tells me to grab it quick and it's Mike on the other end.

We bought one, man.

What you talking bout we bought one?

Did you see the paper? It's all in the paper.

Now the fog starts to clear. It's only one thing Mike can be talking bout. Then I'm stone wake. My heart's thumping so loud it's like it's inside the telephone and I'm listening through the receiver. Last time I saw the dude he was holding his shoulder and hauling ass. Could have blowed him away easy. A real easy shot cause I had run up to the front of the truck to catch him before he got away, but shit I wasn't about to shoot nobody unless they shooting at me so I just thought about how easy it would be to bring him down. Couldn't help thinking that standing there with my piece in my hand. Aimed at the cat but no way I'm gon shoot him down in cold blood. Just sighted over my pistol at him. I'm remembering how he looked and figuring couldn't be nothing wrong with a cat running hard as he was. He was grabbing at his shoulder but he was steady truckin.

How's he dead, man? The cat was running, man.

Stravros was close to me. But he was far away too. You sight down the barrel of a gun, a dude look real small. Like he's miles away but you know you can pull the trigger and boom. He's down. So he's close, but he's far away too. He's hauling ass but you know you could bring him down easy by pulling the trigger. He's running but he ain't going nowhere. He was just a few yards away cause I run up to the front of the truck to see what's happening after I hear the shots and Cecil yelling, *Stop, stop.* Dude never seen me. His head was facing toward the street so he didn't know I was close as I was. He woulda shit if he did, but his head turned to the street so he didn't see me and I couldn't see his face. And I still can't. It's still a blank.

Anyway, what I was starting to tell you was about the stickup. Thursday. That's the day we found Stavros's place and went over there and made arrangements. Set up the deal for Friday. Everything's cool. The dude's anxious to make a buy. He's ready that first day but it's too

quick. We say Friday cause it take us that long to get our shit together.
We got to cop a license so we can rent a truck. The license we got is hot
so we got to cop another one and Friday's soon enough. We been waiting all our lives and two days ain't gon change nothing, so me and Mike
run down some bullshit or another to Stavros. You know. Stone con.
Flashing our gold watches and jiving about all the heavy business we
got to take care of. We been desperate looking for a place to hit and
soon's I see all them shabby cars crowded up in that lot and this druggy-
type dude want to get rich quick, I know we got a good thing. So it's
Friday. Yeah, man, we be calling you Friday and biff bop bam it's a soul
shake, knuckles and thumbs hooked and squeezing meat, all that
bullshit to seal the deal.

• • •

My brother slows down. As slow as he talked the first few minutes the
first time he began to tell me his story. He's the one telling but he's looking too. I think of somebody fumbling through a drawer, trying to find
something important he knows is not in the drawer because he's
searched it before but he's also searched everyplace else where the
missing item could be, so he's started over again, looking where he's
looked before. Not paying strict attention now to the contents of the
drawer he's rifling because he knows deep down that what he wants is
not there. But it's not anyplace else he can think of, so it's almost mechanical, this searching again in a familiar place; he sifts distractedly,
slowly through what's there, his mind somewhere else, trying to imagine the one obvious place he's overlooked. He talks to me like that.
Slowly, long spaces between words and phrases while he searches for
what's missing.

I'm filling a sheet of yellow, lined paper with notes. The writing is
automatic. It will be difficult to read because I don't look down at what
I'm scribbling. I'm too busy watching my brother remember. Too busy
listening to what is unsaid, watching his shoulders and hands, the angle of his head tilting toward me, away, moving side to side absorbed by
its own drifting in time that has nothing to do with anyone, with being
anywhere. Not at a table in the visiting lounge, not in Western Penitentiary, not in the words spoken slowly, haltingly that I hear and try to
transcribe. My brother is searching in a place no one else will ever see,
for an answer no one else would ever understand. His head nods, his

hands pinch and pull atop the table, then they disappear under its pitted surface. His shoulders lean toward me, hunch, retreat. The rhythm has little to do with what he's saying but it's the key to what's really happening, to the real search words can only bump against and echo.

A day passes and Friday comes and is just about gone before a phone call is made. They've come up empty. No license, no rental truck so they have to call and make excuses. Saturday for sure. Just a little something that's come up and we have to handle it today. No sweat. No problem. The TVs packed in a truck already. Brand new Sonys still in the boxes. Untouched. Yeah. Course they's colored. Yeah. Colored as me, man. Copped them this morning like I said I would but something came up. You dig. Nothing to do with the TVs. All that's cool. Other business. You dig. Heavy, heavy business so we got to put off to tomorrow what we can't do today. Dig. I'll buzz you round noon tomorrow. Yeah. Square business.

    But Saturday's no better. Still no license. Michael's is suspended. Rob never owned one. And nobody to take Cecil's place if they use Cecil's license to rent a truck. Cecil will have to report his license stolen and hang out Saturday when they're pulling the job so he'd have an alibi. But nobody to take Cecil's place. Chunky in Canton, Ohio, at his grandmother's for the weekend. Robby calling all over Pittsburgh but can't find brother Dave. Dave would go if they could reach him but nobody knows where he is.

■ ■ ■

See, everybody's jaws getting tighter and tighter. Start to remembering the dope bit. How we waited too long and blew that and now we blowed Friday and time running out again Saturday and if the white boy don't hear from us today he gon back out, don't care how greedy he is you give a dude too long to think and he starts thinking something's shaky. You give him too much time he gon get scared. So bad shit's in the air. Is we gon fuck up again? Is that the story of our lives? Is we just spozed to fuck up and keep on fucking up and that's why we in the mess we in in the first place?

    But ain't really nothing to do, so we just sitting around my place getting uptight, getting ugly. I'm calling everywhere I can think of for Dave but no luck. No, I ain't seen Dave or no answer at all. Just ring,

ring, ring and I slams down the phone hard as I can like everything fucking with me is under there and I squash it like a bug. Goddamn. Goddamn. Got no money in the bank. Look around and Mike and Cecil just as hot as me. They both staring at Sowell cause he's in his usual punkass bag. He's coming up short and they blaming him. I'm ready to go upside his head my ownself cause he's trying to say ain't no reason for him to rob nobody. He can come up with his end of the dope money so why he need to be robbing people. Well, that's one way to look at it. Sowell got the dough for his share of the buy but shit, if there ain't no stickup, ain't no action for nobody. We all got to get our shares together and if we don't move on the car lot what Sowell's holding don't mean nothing. Naturally, Sowell don't want to hear it. His lip poked out a mile. Mike signifying and Cecil egging him on and Sowell knows they talking bout him like a dog but he ain't budging out his corner. I got my end, man. Youall the John Dillingers and shit. Youall get yours and we can do business. That's what he keep on saying but he ain't saying shit now cause he see Mike and Cecil ain't playing. They stone down on his case and taking it to court so Sowell's trying to look casual in his double knits, laid back in my easy chair but he ain't moving a feather and he sure ain't opening his mouth now. He just waiting a chance to get up and get the fuck gone. I know that. He knows it.

When Sowell halfway out the door Cecil says loud and nasty what we all thinking:

Who the hell is he? Nigger wants to get rich quick but ain't willing to take no risks. Who the fuck he think he is?

After the door slams I'm almost smiling cause I'm thinking of Garth. I say to him, You my main man, Gar. You a righteous dude but you sure do keep some jive company. I'm teasing Garth behind his no-heart nigger Sowell, and Garth can't do nothing but grin back. Cause Sowell ain't worth doo doo.

Everything be alright if I could bring Garth down off that cloud, but ain't no way. Ain't nobody can do that. When you're gone, you're gone; so it ain't gon be Garth but who the fuck it gon be? Can't mess up again. Can't let the dream slip away again.

Then I know. Ain't no question about it. It be's the way it always be. The three musketeers. Me and Cecil and Mike. We gon have to do it our ownselves. Can't find Dave. Chunky in goddamn Canton, Ohio. Sammy's too silly. Mike and Cecil still mad, anyway. They subject to break Sammy's neck he look at them cross-eyed. That leaves three. The three musketeers. So that's that.

Cecil calls the police station and tells them his license stolen. They tell him he got to come down in person to report it stolen.

Let's go, Cecil says. Me I say, Huh-uh. No-o-o . . . Hell no . . . I ain't gon down to no police station. Not today, man. No way they gon get this nigger's ass down to no No. 5.

What you worried about, man? Cecil the one should be worried. It's his license they be having for the truck.

Hey, Cecil says. Don't make me no difference. I ain't worried. What they gon do? They got my license. So what? What's that prove? Just told them it was stolen.

Mike come in: There ain't gon be no robbery reported. Just be a truck somebody finds out on the highway. Who's gon report a robbery? That white boy's a thief just like us. The dude's a fence. He ain't hardly calling no cops on us. He don't want no cops looking round there. That's bad for business.

Yeah, man. You right. But I ain't worried no way. What I got to be worried about? Things can't get no worser. Nowhere to go but up. Or out. Don't make me no nevermind.

Cecil, you crazy.

Cecil's cool, man, Cecil knows where it's at.

I still don't want to go to no police station. Something about it. On that day specially. A day we planning to do wrong. Heavy wrong. Holding people up and do. Just don't seem right to take your ownself down to no goddamn police station. All them cops running round inside. And the street full of cop cars. It's like jinxing yourself. Or being too goddamn bold for your own good. So I'm nervous. I don't like what's happening. We a man short and a day late and I can't figure all what else is wrong but I got a feeling and that feeling's telling me something I don't want to hear. I knew something bad was gonna happen. The license bit. Cecil coming along. Stopping at the police station on our way to pull a job. None of that was sitting right with me. I knew we was taking big chances, dumb chances, but like Cecil say, Damned if you do and damned if you don't. Thinking round in circles like that and knowing all the time I'm gon do what I have to do but I swear, Brother, it wasn't sitting right in my mind. Something trying to pull my coat, something trying to whisper in my ear, *No*, saying *no, no, no.* . . .

But we come too far to turn back now. Too far, too long, too much at stake. We got a sniff of the big time and if we didn't take our shot wouldn't be nobody to blame but ourselves. And that's heavy. You might live another day, you might live another hundred years but long as you live you have to carry that idea round in your head. You had your shot but you didn't take it. You punked out. Now how a person spozed to live with something like that grinning in his face every day? You hear old people crying the blues about they could have been this or done that if they only had the chance. Well, here was our chance. Our shot at the big time. How you gon pass that by? Better to die than have to look at yourself every day and say, Yeah. I blew. Yeah, I let it get away.

That's what I was thinking then. How else I'm spozed to think? Couldn't see myself on no porch in no rocking chair crying the blues. Like, what else I'm spozed to do? No way Ima be like the rest of them niggers scuffling and kissing ass to get by. Scuffling and licking ass till the day they die and the shame is they ain't even getting by. They crawling. They stepped on. Mize well be roaches or some goddamn waterbugs. White man got em backed up in Homewood and he's sprinkling roach powder on em. He's steady shaking and they steady dying. You know I ain't making nothing up. You know I ain't trying to be funny. Cause you seen it. You run from it just like I did. You know the shit's still coming down and it's falling on everybody in Homewood. You know what I'm talking about. Don't tell me you don't, cause we both running. I'm in here but it's still falling on me. It's falling on Daddy and Mommy and Dave and Gene and Tish and all the kids. Falls till it knocks you down.

So you better believe Ima go for it. I'm scared and I know something ain't right, something deep down and serious ain't right, but I got to go.

Across from the Channel Four Building, over the hill from Wilkinsburg, out Ardmore way where there's dividers in the road is a gas station rents U-Haul trucks. You know where I mean. Used Cecil's license to rent us a truck. Drove it back to my place and I got on the phone again. Tried Dave one more time but he still ain't nowhere to be found. It's nearly five by now. We been stalling and putting it off long as we could. It's down-and-dirty time now. When I talked to Stavros at twelve I told him it be early evening before we could come by with the

TVs. Told him I'd call again, 5:30 at the latest, to tell him exactly when we'd be there with the goods. It's after five so I got to call.

We be there by seven. Right around seven but no later. The cat sounds spacy. Like I woke him out a deep sleep or something. But everything cool. He's tired of hanging round but if we get there by seven he'll wait. Seven. Yeah. That's cool. Seven.

It's settled. Ain't nobody else available so it got to be Cecil. Funny thing is Cecil don't care. I'm worrying my ass off but Cecil he cool, calm, and collected. Cause that's Cecil. Nothing don't bother Cecil. He's ready to go. He jumps up in the truck and me and Mike follow him in Mike's car down to No. 5 police station in East Liberty.

Cecil parks the truck round the block and gets in wit us and then him and Mike go in the station. That's when it hits me. Chills. Chills all over my body so's I'm shaking like a leaf. I can't explain it. They just come down on me. Not no little nervous twitches or nothing like that. Not no rookie fever or nothing. Hard rocking chills, Brother. So bad I can barely open the door and crawl in the back. Cause that's what I had to do. I needed to hide. Crawled in the back of Mike's car and hid down in the seat. On my knees on the floor so wasn't nothing of me showing out the window. It's starting to get dark now. It's dusk and couldn't nobody see me from the police station but I'm scrunched down in the back in the shadows and them chills tearing me up so bad I'm thinking the whole car must be shaking. To this day I don't know what hit me. Wasn't all that cold. The windows up anyway. Maybe it was just being around so many damned cops. Cops everywhere around there and the last thing in the world I need to see is a cop. Maybe that's all it was or maybe it was . . . you know . . . a premonition. Maybe something inside me could see everything that was gonna come down. Maybe I knew somebody gon die.

It's good and dark by the time we get through the tunnel to the West Side. Left Mike's car in the Hill. The three musketeers all in the rental truck. Me and Mike in the cab. Cecil in back. Turning chilly but it ain't really that cold. Anyway I ain't shaking no more. Whatever it was hit me is gone bout its business and I'm trying to forget it happened. Halfway embarrassed. Wondering if Mike or Cecil saw me sneaking in the backseat. I got to tell you one more thing, though, about the time outside the police station. At the trial the desk sergeant swore I was one the men walked in to report the license. I wasn't in there. No way nobody get me inside. Almost died sitting outside so ain't no way in hell Ima strut up inside no police station. The cop lying through his teeth. But on the stand he swore on Jesus, Mary, and Joseph, and his mama, I was the one. That's how they do. They all get their shit together and tell the same lie and the jury wind up believing them cause they all got the same lie down pat. Said he remembered me cause I had one them African hairdos. Plaits sticking out my head. Same thing one the Kramer brothers said to the jury. Yes. That one. He's the one. Hair sticking out all over his head. Rattails or pigtails. He called my do something like that. But truth is, I was wearing a hat that night. My Big Apple hat and kept my hair pushed up under it. So how they remembering plaits? How they remember hair sticking out? I'll tell you how. They remember cause they was lying. They all looking at the lineup pictures. I'm the only one there with cornrows and plaits. In the mug shots, that is. They must have sat down in some little room and got their lie together looking at the picture. Dummies never thought of no hat. But I sure nuff be wearing my Apple hat all night. Never left my head. They was gon get them a nigger and didn't care if it was the right one or wrong one just so they got one they could hang.

III

---

*T*hey are riding in the dark going over their plans. It's fall. Days are shorter, nights longer and colder. The rental truck chugs and rattles over bad streets, roars so loud in the Liberty tunnels they give up trying to talk. When they arrive and drive past once, all the lights in the used-car lot are out. No lights in the office either. Just one hooded bulb burning in front of the garage.

Robby's thinking something's funny. Thinking, This don't make no sense. Why this cat sitting round in the dark? See, the wind's bucking up, too. Mike parked the truck up the street at a restaurant so it's just me and I'm walking cross the lot and the wind making them little flags pop and shaking the strings of lights and little pointy flags they got hanging out front where you come in off the street. Like it's sure nuff night now. Good and dark now and the wind blowing got everything moving. Little noises you can't see and things moving behind your back and them flags popping. Kind of spooky. Maybe the dude got tired of waiting. Maybe he's gone home to bed.

. . .

Yeah. I remember what I was wearing. Lemme see now. Yeah. I remember exactly. Like I said, my Apple hat. And my new leather jacket. One with a fur collar and a zipper up the front. Sharp. Fitted me real nice. Come down about ass length. And jeans, quilted jeans like they be wearing then with sailor pockets. Black-and-green shoes. High heels. Patchwork too, like a quilt, you know, fancy toes with black and green patches. Sharp. Stone sharp. That was your brother. Gon stick somebody up but I was clean. Stayed sharp. Had my do tucked up under my cap. And my eyes wide open cause I didn't like walking cross no dark lot. Couldn't see nobody till I got to the office. There's three of them inside. Two brothers, the Kramers, and Stavros sitting around in there with no lights on. Stavros was more like stretched out. Had a couch in the office and he's like napping and the other two looking puffy-eyed like they been sleep too.

Things ain't getting no better fast. Like I said, I ain't been feeling right since the get-go and now there's three dudes stead of one to deal with and that sure ain't gon make things no easier. I gets Stavros to come outside by his self. He ain't too happy about it but I let him know I ain't digging the fact that he got his boys hanging round neither.

Who are those guys?

Hey, man. It's okay. They're my partners. The Kramer brothers. They're in on it. Help me out around here sometimes. They'll gimme a hand loading the TVs.

Yeah, but that ain't part the deal. You didn't say nothing about no two guys hanging round while we dealing.

Keeps on his case, you dig, and whiles I'm talking I'm looking round real careful. Don't want no more surprises. Far as he knows I'm checking out the place for cops. For a setup. I mean them guys in the office might be cops for all I know. I say this and Stavros kinda laughs. He laughs and says, Cops. They ain't hardly cops. They'll get a kick out of that. I'm gon tell them guys you thought they was cops. Yeah. He's grinning and I grin back and kinda relaxes but I'm still scoping the layout. Getting it in my mind again. It been three days since I been there and I'm making sure it's like I remembered. The office. The garage. Cars parked out front on Greys Pond and some more junky-looking ones back beside the garage. A open place where we could pull in the truck and back it up to the garage. I'm checking all this out but the same time running con on Stavros. Like we're buddies now and I'm jiving the cat. You know. Where'd you go to high school and shit. And is the Steelers gon go all the way? Then we talk money. Get the deal straight again. He coming up short and poor-mouthing but it don't matter. I don't need to hear that shit. Say we better go back and call my buddy.

We's back inside a couple minutes. I go out again by myself to check the lot next door. There's a light next door and I check it out. Then I go back in the office. Call Mike.

Everything's cool, man. Yeah, solid. My man here's alright. Got two his boys to help with the loading. We's ready, man.

Them cats ain't turned on no lights yet. They still looking drugged. Like they all been sleep. Then I figure maybe they been sitting waiting all day just like we been. They tired and probably had a hit of something or other.

One them turns on a little desk lamp so Mike can see where we at. Nobody got nothing to say. Nothing to do but wait now till Mike gets here with the truck. Seems like hours but it don't really take no time at all and Mike's pulled up at the entrance. The brothers go out and get him backed up to the garage. Me and Stavros wait till the truck stops then we leave the office and walk over to the driver's side. Mike ain't hardly climbed down out the truck good before he's in Stavros's face. Mike don't play. Got that hard look in his eyes. He's all business. Ain't going for no bullshit.

Do you have the money?

Yeah.

Lemme see it.

Lemme see the TVs.

Lemme see the money.

They go back and forth like that a couple rounds but Mike ain't budgin. Mike's tall, you know. A basketball player. Woulda been the next Doctor J and shit if things had worked out different. To hear Mike tell it he was badder than the Doc. You done heard all that mess before. You know how it goes. Anyway Mike got this way of staring down at people. Intimidation is what it's about. Don't matter how tall a dude be, Mike can stare down at him. Get that hard look in his eyes and stand still as a statue. Nothing moving like he's froze or something. Just staring down at you and letting you know he owns you. Letting you know he could step on you and squash you like a bug and ain't nothing you could do about it. So they hit it back and forth a couple times like it's Ping-Pong. Money—TVs—Money—TVs. Then Stavros sees Mike ain't up for no game. He's dealing with one them hardhead, hard-leg niggers and ain't no win.

Money's in the office. I'll go get it.

Something tells me watch this dude. Watch him real close, Robby. Why he need to go *back* to the office by his ownself? Why ain't he brought the money with him to the truck where we dealing? Why it got to be dark in the office? I'm thinking a mile a minute. I'm watching him close as I can but I got to keep my eye on them other dudes too. Them brothers who ain't spozed to be here in the first place. When we was all in the office I'm remembering Stavros got up once and went to fumbling in his desk drawer. Had his back to me so I couldn't see what he was doing but I do know he ain't no child. A soft-talking dude, but he's halfway slick too. He got a piece somewhere. And it ain't gon be too far out of reach. Kinda jacket he's wearing you couldn't tell what he might have stuck down the front his pants. I'm hawking the dude but I ain't got a real clear view. One little light on in the office. All's I know is he's back at that desk drawer again. Like I can see his silhouette through the office window but I can't tell what he's doing down there in that drawer.

Mike got a better view. He's off to one side so he can watch everything. Like a statue standing back there in the shadows. He's taller than everybody. The way he was standing still in the dark not moving, not saying a word made you think he was ten feet tall. A big black statue is what I thought. And I know Mike wasn't missing a thing. Like he was all tense and coiled up. Ready to leap. Like he told me later. Rob, I was sure the dude had a gun. Just the way he come walking back from that office. If he ain't had one before, he got one now. Just knew it.

Which means Mike was thinking what I was thinking at the time. I ain't seen nothing but the dude's silhouette in the window before I went over to the other side of the truck where the Kramer brothers was standing, but Mike said he seen Stavros pull something out that desk and wasn't about to wait till he woke up in heaven or hell to find out what it was.

First thing I notice is Stavros got his jacket closed when he come back. I'm worried worse now. But in a funny way I ain't worried at all. See, it's happening now and I'm scared and nervous but it's happening now. The deal's going down. It's coming down hard and you got to go wit it. You got your mind on a million things at once and you can't let nothing bother you. You got to be ready. Ain't no time to be hemming and hawing. You out there and you got to go.

I done thought about the stickup so many times. Everything that happened that night. I been over it and over it in my mind and talked to Mike and Cecil so I know exactly what happened. The facts. What we said and what we did. And what them white boys did too. I got it all in my head but it ain't easy to say to you. It's hard like it's the first time every time I try to tell it.

Stavros's jacket's closed. We's all behind the truck now, under the garage light. Except Mike. Mike still ain't moved. He's off to one side in the shadows. So I ask the dude.

You got the money?

Don't know what I woulda done if he reached inside his jacket but that ain't what happened. He pulled the money out his back pocket. It's kinda wadded up in a ball.

Okay. Here's the money. Where's the TVs?

Cecil been inside the truck taking everything in. He got a sawed-off shotgun in there with him and when I open the gate the gun's the first thing you see. Sawed-off shotgun's a nasty, dangerous-looking piece. You better believe it. Make you pee just looking at it.

Everybody freeze.

Them white boys froze, and me and Mike drew our pieces.

Throw down your money on the ground.

Stavros says, Aw, fuck . . . shit, and drops the money. I bend down to pick it up. Wind's blowing and ain't no time to do nothing but chase the money. It's scooting and I'm down trying to scoop it up and I hear Mike yell, Robby, he's running. The money's blowing and I'm crawling after it and I don't know what the fuck is going on behind my back. Just hear Mike call my name and say, *He's running.*

Get em. That's what I yell cause my mind's on them bills and all the trouble it's taken and they about to fly away across the lot.

Then the shot. Boom. Like a cannon. Got to be Mike's .44 magnum. A warning shot in the air but I don't know that yet. I yell *Get em* and then the shot and I run up alongside the truck to cut off anybody trying to get away. Sounds like somebody's down. A loud, stumbling noise on the other side of the truck so I peel back to see what's happening. If anybody's shot or what. But I ain't made it to the back end of the truck before there's another shot. *Boom*. It's all happening fast. Three, four seconds all it took. Happening faster than I can tell it. I yell, then a shot. Start for the front of the truck, hear a noise and turn around. Then *boom* again and I go running to the front again.

What happened is Stavros fell down when Mike shot the first time. He stumbled or just plain scared shitless and his feet gave out under him. That's what I heard on the other side of the truck. Bram. Him hitting the pavement and scuffling to get up again. Funny thing is I can see him. How hard he hit. How he crumpled down the first time and looked like he was digging in his clothes for something. Didn't see none of this but it's strong in my imagination just as if I did see it. That's when Mike shot again. He was sure Stavros was going for a gun. Sure enough to pull the trigger. I'm not gonna wait till I wake up in heaven or hell to find out for sure if he had a gun. That's what Mike said. Stavros slipped down and he was reaching inside his clothes. I can see him down just like I was there. It's that clear in my mind.

When I hear the second shot I run all the way to the front of the truck. The dude's bounced up off the ground and steady hauling ass out toward Greys Pond Road. He's kind of running low to the ground, bent over like and holding his shoulder. I didn't even realize he was hit or nothing like that. Didn't think nothing really except he was running and things was fucked up. Had a clear shot but didn't take it. By then Mike is round the front of the truck too and he's got his pistol pointing at the dude's back and coulda blowed him away easy just like me but we let him go.

One thing certain. The shit had hit the fan. Wasn't nothing going down like it spozed to. Shooting. A dude running. We was in a mess and Cecil still holding them Kramer brothers lined up behind the truck. After we got the money the plan was to put Stavros in back the truck and drive it somewhere in Schenley Park and just leave him back there till somebody found him in the morning. That's the way we done it before. Give us time to get away. Give the cat time to cool his heels and think a little while fore he called the cops or did something else foolish. Well, them brothers still standing there staring down the barrels of the sawed-off shotgun. I'm scared but they scareder than me. And mad. Don't say shit but they mad. Put the shotgun in they hands it be three dead niggers sprayed all over the car lot. You could see it in their eyes. They don't know if Stavros is wasted or what. They don't know what we gon do with them. They mad and scared but that shotgun is keeping them in line.

We got to get out of here, man. What we gon do with these dudes? They be running just like the other one we turn them loose.

Put the motherfuckers in the back.

Up they go. I'm shoving and pushing and the tailgate bonks one the dudes in the head. Got them in the back where Stavros spozed to be if everything wasn't fucked up. But it's fucked up good now. One dude shot and running for the cops. Two stashed in the back of the truck. And the money ain't half what it ought to be. Ain't had time to count but when I was picking it up I could tell it wasn't what it supposed to be. Not half. Not even half of half, it turned out.

Wasn't worried about money, though. Was getting our asses away from there we was worried about.

All three us up in the cab now. Me and Cec and Mike. The Kramers in the back of the U-Haul truck. Mike slams that raggedy sucker in gear and we's rolling. Turned on Greys Pond and then turned again up a long windy street. One that goes all the way up the hill into Brownsville Road. Mike driving like a crazy man. Truth is we all's shook. We in a panic. Looking for cops. Listening for sirens. See it's lily white over in there. All white so we ain't gon be real hard to find. And Mike revving the truck like it's a bucking bronco. But nobody thinking straight. Just want to get away fast as we can.

When we first come out the lot had to stop at the light on Greys Pond. Heard this loud bang and it's them fools in the back. We ain't locked the door good and they's out and running down the middle of the street. Pushed the truck doors open when we stopped at the light and I can see them in the mirror running back the way we came. Now we really fucked up. Three white boys running loose. They gon have all West Side on our ass. Why the fuck didn't we lock those doors? Ain't nothing going the way it spozed to be. Wasn't spozed to be no shooting. All them big guns was to scare people. Scare the shit out them so we could take the money and run. But ain't nothing working right. Stavros gone. The brothers gone. White people everywhere. Feels like the goddamn street's trying to tear up the truck. I'm looking for a tire to blow or the damn truck to run outa gas. Sure now our ass is grass.

We gotta get out here, man. They be looking for a truck, man. That's the first thing they be looking for.

Fuck this goddamn truck, man. Pull the motherfucker over and let's get outa here.

We at the top of the hill now. Maybe four, five minutes since I seen them brothers running away in the mirror. Couldna been no longer than that. On the main drag now. Stores and restaurants and do. Drive down a block or so and park the truck on a side street. Getting our shit together best we can now. Leave it on a side street so the cops have to look to find it. So they don't trip over the big, burly motherfucker. Cause we need time. Don't know what's happening down the hill. Heard sirens but Cecil said them's fire engines. Nothing but fire engines.

Walk down the main drag a block or so and then duck in this store got kids standing around in front. A hangout joint, you know. Little soda fountain and some chairs and booths inside. Everybody look at us kinda funny. Don't say shit but they stone looking. Ain't no signs up or nothing saying, No Niggers Allowed. But we steady getting them You in the wrong place, ain't you? looks. See, but we clean and we cool. Walk through them kids and through the door like we been coming to this store every day for years. Old lady at the cash register staring too. Ask her just as nice if she got a pay phone we could use to call a cab. You know. Smiling and good manners and shit. She see we ain't no hoodlums. Ain't come to rob her or rape her or nothing like that. We some them nice nigger boys. All we need is a cab and we be gone.

I can call youns one but they take forever. Didn't used to be that way around here but now they make you wait. Your best bet's standing outside till one comes along.

Yeah, well, maybe she's right. I mean about cabs and do but here we is deep in white folks' territory and we ain't hardly gon stand in the middle of no main street flagging down no taxis. But I smiles and nods anyway. What she's saying is she prefers our black asses out her store.

Thank you, ma'am. Maybe we'll try hailing one outside. She smiles now. She's happy now. We on our way and she ain't had no trouble.

Kids still hanging out outside. Teenagers. We need a ride, I tells em. Any youns got a car? From out of town and don't know our way around the city. Need a ride back to where our car's parked. Pay somebody they give us a lift. They all giving me them dumb looks. Way kids do when they ain't paying no mind to what you saying. Like you speaking Watusi or some damned jibber-jabber talk they don't speak. Looking dumb and moving back out the way so we can get through. What these niggers doing here anyway? Why don't they go on and leave us alone? Dumb looks or I-don't-give-a-fuck looks or just, Go on, Sambo, go on back to the jungle where you belong.

But one. A young, skinny kid with a beard. Guess he was listening cause he says I know what it's like to be a stranger in town. I'll give you guys a ride. My car's just down the street.

Coulda kissed the little honky. He wouldn't even take no money. Said he knew what it was like being a stranger in a strange town. Said he wasn't doing nothing. Didn't have no place to go, he'd take us anywhere we wanted. He was one nice cat, really. But back then gas wasn't but fifty-some cents a gallon.

He takes us all the way over to the Hill to Mike's car. Kinda kid likes to talk so I run a conversation on him. We was best friends by the time he dropped us off. You know me. Kid asked a whole lot of questions so I'm steady making up lies. Feeding him buckets full of shit. Some fantastic story about being from out of town and the business we was in and how much we stay on the road and what it's like in places I ain't never seen the inside of. Making shit up as I go along. It got good to me. Like I'm half believing it, it sounds so good. Anyway we best buddies by the end of the trip. The kid taking it all in. Gee whiz, and Wow and Groovy and Far Out. That kind of kid. A good-hearted little white dude cause it's night and he got three niggers in his car he don't know from Adam. Took us to the Hill, too. Blackest part of town. Woulda took us to West Hell, I believe, long as I kept feeding him lies. You run into people like that every now and again. Like they in their own world and shit. They ain't got all the hang-ups most people got. See, to him it was just an adventure. Captain America rescuing three spooks and shit. A good deed and shit and he ain't thought nothing about being mugged or robbed or having his throat slit. Innocent. You know what I mean. Ain't gon tell you no lie now. We was scared. Me and Cec and Mike probably all thinking the same thing. Maybe we ought to knock this dude out and take his car. And he's a witness, right? He be taking us from the scene of a crime to Mike's car, right? Maybe he reads the papers tomorrow and shit. He figures out we the bad guys and he was driving the getaway car. We scared and we all thinking the same thing. Saving our asses. Getting the fuck off the West Side as clean and fast as we can.

We scared and the man after us, so we subject to do most anything but we ain't into hurting people and the little dude didn't seem like the kind be running to no cops. Just a nice hippie-type kinda kid. Ain't never seen him again. Never showed up at the trial or nothing, so I guess we guessed right. It was funny, really. We come rolling back down the hill. All hell was breaking loose. I mean cop cars and flashing lights and people crowding around. Seen Mike and Cec hunching down in the backseat. Here we is, riding past the scene of the crime, and they got every cop in West Side out there, and this kid goes:

Wow. Something must have happened here.

We riding past and Mike and Cecil trying to crawl under the floor-boards and he's saying, Wow. Something must have happened. Yeah, something happened alright and you about to have three niggers with heart attacks in your car you don't get the fuck away from here.

But we rolled on past the commotion and he let us off in the Hill. Wanted to take us farther but we said no. We can find the car from here. He couldn't figure that one out but I said, Thanks, man. You a real friend, man. If you ever in Cleveland you give me a buzz.

Lemme tell you. It felt good to get back to my girl's that night. Back to where there was niggers. Still shaking, but it seemed like we got away clean. Things ain't worked out exactly like we planned but we got some dough and we got away. Seemed like luck was finally wit us. Mike said he just winged the dude. Shot him in the shoulder, so ain't nothing to worry bout on that count. And the money ain't what we expected but it's something. We got something.

I seen the dude running my own self. Somebody hurt bad wouldn't be running like he was so I'm starting to feel better. Whole thing was a fuckup from the git but we coming out the other end now. Need to take my mind off it. Like when I was jiving that kid. Make-believe and shit. Get into lying so deep it's almost like real. Yeah, you call me when you in St. Louis or L.A. or wherever the fuck I said we from.

Got away. Back in the streets. Started to cool out. C'mon, man. Mize well go out and celebrate.

Cecil split for the North Side over to his girl's house. Mike dropped me at Wanda's, my girl's, and went home to change. Said he was gon throw away the clothes he had on. Wasn't nothing wrong with em but he was gon throw them away. A jinx or something like that. Pulled a job in them clothes, so out they go. Just didn't want them no more.

By the time Mike gets back to pick me up must been around 9:00, 9:30. We head out to the Fantastic Plastic but it's too early. Ain't nobody in the joint yet, so we drive downtown to Market Square. At the time the Plastic was the newest disco in Pittsburgh. Everybody be hanging out in there cause it was new, you know. They had it laid out real fancy. A nice place, always full of ladies. If you couldn't get over in the Plastic, you mize well give it up. But we's too early and them joints downtown usually be happening anytime on weekends, so we cruise down to Market Square but ain't no parking places. Have to go all the way back up to Forbes, round Forbes and Stanwix before we can find a place to park. Way back at the edge of town we don't feel like walking. We just sitting there a minute getting our shit together. Thinking, you know. Should we lay in town or ride back to Oakland and check out Fantastic Plastic again? Sitting there, you know, cooling out. What you want to do, Robby man? I don't know, Mike. Just sitting there by the corner of Forbes and Stanwix when chills come down on me again. Right around 9:30, 10:00. I remember the time cause later I found out Stavros died just about then. Terrible chills again, and that panicky feeling. Like I'm coming apart. Breaking up in little pieces. I can't stop shaking. My teeth chattering, I'm shaking so bad. But the worst thing is the feeling something awful's happening. Something so bad I can't even think of nothing to call it, can't give it no name, but I'm sure it's happening and ain't nothing I can do about it. Chills come down on me just like outside the police station when I was waiting for Mike and Cecil.

Chills didn't last but a minute or so but I was shook. Said to Mike, Turn around. Let's get away from here. Let's get out from Downtown. Like I was having a nightmare. Like I knew something was wrong and had to get away from there.

I thought at the time maybe it was just being close to Downtown set me off. You know. Like Downtown belonged to white folks and cops or something like that and it was West Side all over again and I didn't want no part of nothing like that. Still ain't sure what it was come down on me but I found out later I got the chills just about exactly the time they say Stavros died. A little bit before ten on Saturday. I'm slouching down in the car again and Mike says what's wrong, man? You sick or something? Wasn't nothing I could say. Just knew something terrible was wrong. I was worse than sick but I said, Naw, man. Let's just get the fuck away from here.

We riding again and I talked to myself. Calmed myself down. Told Mike my nerves bad and shit. Told him stop in the Hill and let's get a drink at the Hurricane. I'm steady telling myself ain't no reason to be uptight. We got away. Them white boys ain't talking to no cops. They gon tell the cops they trying to buy some hot TVs and got stuck up? Hell, no. They in the shit deep as we is. Crooks ain't telling on crooks. And we got some dough again. We got a handle on the dream again. So why I'm feeling so bad? So scared?

Two double hits of gin at the Hurricane and I'm cool. I'm over the shakes and got my head together. I'm ready for the Plastic.

Run into Chunky soon's we get in the door. Plastic's sure nuff crowded now. Wall-to-wall people and lights spinning and whole lotta boogying on the dance floor. Yeah. The joint's jumping now and I'm ready to celebrate.

Thought you was in Ohio.

I was, man. See my grandma. Been there and back today.

Well, we in business again. Everything gon be alright. Got some dough.

Hey, that's cool. That's righteous, brother. You the man.

He's laying skin on me and I'm doing it to him and then Mike's right there with his big ham hands and slapping and soul shaking in the middle of the Plastic. We got our shit together and we know people is watching us. We clean. We cool. They gon hear more about us. We headed for the big time. Number one. People's eyes on us and we ready to party party. Party hearty.

DOING TIME

I've decided to write notes to you; thoughts as well as stories. It's easier for me to write to you as I would talk, so please don't be a professor on my grammar. . . . That out of the way, my thoughts are real scattered about our visit today but one thing I remembered you asked me, did I ever worry that Mommy wouldn't accept the presents I would buy her in my gangster fantasies and I said no. To explain further, I didn't worry that she wouldn't want them, my worry was that she would be upset knowing where the money came from. Yet I believe she knew how bad I wanted things and that most avenues of success had been blocked or blown. Blown out of anger and frustration that was misdirected at the ones who did the blocking—and so to see me at least find success in the games that were left for me—despite the worry and anguish I knew she'd be feeling, I hoped her seeing that I was finally doing well would somehow bring ease.

Next Visit: Today we talked some about how I have done a lot of things in as far as the street thing is concerned—it was as if I slipped off and on different skins playing different roles as an actor does, always trying to shine and glitter as a star in my world, the world of the street, the world left for me. . . .

It's ten days or so since I wrote last yet my whole life has changed and again my whole outlook has been altered. Changed again by forces that are far removed and completely unaffected by me or my wants, wishes, *dreams, aspirations, feelings, or thoughts. Once again the man, that ever existing man, has reached out and smacked hope, joy, love, and the ability to have an effect on my life's destiny out of my ever grasping hands. I heard from the courts they denied my appeal, they denied my existence as being in any way meaningful or of having any worth at all. I received this devastating news last Friday the day after I saw you and have been in a state of depression ever since. I'm trying hard to keep it all together but right now it's really hard to find a reason to keep it together, for they seem to have taken away all reasons worth trying.*

Two weeks later: I haven't written or done anything in two weeks, sorry, but I'm just more or less recovering from my latest setback. You should hear from me by phone before receiving this. I think I'll be able to write more now; I really do have a lot to say and tell you. I'll write again soon in the same manner—until, give everyone there my

Love,
Rob

I. *November 16, 1975*

We bought one, man. We bought the whole farm. That's what Mike said, those were the words but it didn't sound like Mike. Wasn't his way of talking. Never heard him say nothing like that before. Sounded like somebody else talking. Funny thing, though, was I knew exactly what he meant. Asked him: What you talking about, man? But I knew all along, soon as I heard his voice over the phone. Stavros was dead. Seen the cat up and running so he should be alright, but I knew. Didn't need Mike telling me, really, cause it hit me the night before. Knew when I was sitting in Mike's car downtown. I knew Stavros was dead.

Mike called round nine. Then he went looking for Cecil over Cecil's girl's house on the North Side. They come back to Wanda's and we's all just sitting around. In shock, you know. The Steelers is on TV. Don't remember who they was playing. Didn't make no difference anyway. Just halfway paying attention cause everybody is shook up. What we gon do?

Cecil leaves. We tell him don't talk to nobody. Lay low. Nothing's in the newspaper except it says they're looking for Cecil behind his license being hooked up with the truck. No more information in the newspaper story. No name but Cecil's, so we don't know what they know.

In a hour or so Cecil comes back with his sister. Couldn't go home cause his sister said the cops was watching his mama's house. He's packed up a bag with some his things he keeps over at his sister's. I'm glad. I been saying all along we better get out of town. Fast as we can git. Let's get out of town. That's what I keep saying but somebody else

171

got the idea Cecil should go to the police. Tell em he seen the story in the newspaper and came down to the station cause his license been stolen. Bold face. You know. Like he ain't got nothing to hide. Like if he shaved off his beard and picked out his hair he'd be hard for anybody to identify. They ain't seen that much of Cecil anyway. He just popped out the back of the truck. They ain't had time to see that much of him. And it was dark. Any anybody got a shotgun poked up in they face gon see more of that gun than the man behind it. But I said don't do it. Said we got to leave town. And Cecil's sister says don't. Her boyfriend's in jail. If the cops just a little suspicious they throw your ass in jail. She knows. Her old man's still in jail. He thought he could just go down and talk to the cops. Cecil, don't you go nowhere near them dogs. Stay as far away as you can.

I know what I want to do but we sit around talking and arguing a long time, getting a plan together. Finally the women go and get our clothes. Except we figure the cops probably still watching Cecil's house so nobody goes over there. By eight that night we hit the road.

Next thing I know I'm waking up somewhere in the middle of goddamn Indiana. It's dark outside. The car's pulled off the road in one those rest areas and everybody else is sleep. At the time I didn't know where the fuck we was at. I could see the highway and a few trucks riding along but that's about it. No lights and I can't hear nothing but crickets so we's in the country. The stone boonies but I don't know where till I wake those other dudes up and we get rolling again and I see signs, Indiana road signs and a sign for Gary, which is where we're headed cause a friend of Cecil's sister lives in Gary and he can get us I.D.'s.

Gary turns out to be a bummer cause this guy who knows Cecil's sister ain't acting right. Yeah, he can get us I.D.'s. That's what he says, anyway. But there's something about the dude makes Mike and Cecil suspicious. We meet him at a McDonald's and he's supposed to be gone taking care of business but when we leave Mickey D's Mike says the dude's following us. We checked in a hotel anyway to wait. Cecil and Mike went out to get some wine. I'm kinda sick. On methadone, you know. And it's wearing off so I'm starting to feel miserable. Lay down on the bed waiting for the fellows to get back. They come in a nervous wreck.

Something's wrong, Rob.

Did you see how close that dude was watching us? Kept his eyes on us all the time.

I swear I seen him following us. Probably followed us here. Now why the cat got to do that? This whole bit ain't sitting right with me. Something's funny.

Well, I think they exaggerating. We scared and tired and in a strange city. But I'm getting sick as a dog so I ain't in no shape to figure out whether they just letting imagination run away with them or if the dude mean us some harm. Point is, Gary don't work. We on our way again early next morning.

You ever seen two grown men in a telephone booth fighting over a telephone? They waited till I was sleep then sneaked and found a telephone. We's in a parking lot outside Chicago and there they are like a couple of kids fighting over who's gon use the phone. They wake me up with that foolishness. All I can think is, Oh, my God. What they doing in a phone booth? Cause I made them promise not to call Pittsburgh. We running and don't want nobody knowing where we are. Cops be watching Cecil's. They probably be watching Mike's place and my apartment by now. And got the phones tapped listening in. What's the sense of running if you gon tell people where you running? I'm thinking, Shit. These fools done messed up for sure.

Get off the phone, man. Gimme the goddamn phone. You know better.

I can't believe it. Mike been on with his father. Then Cecil called his Mom. Trying their women next. Fighting over who's gon go first.

We heading back home. My Mom said it will be alright. We'll get off light. It's the first time.

Are you crazy, man? First time, shit. Ain't no going back. They catch us they'll put us under the jail and throw away the key.

No. She said come back. Come back and turn myself in. She said they'll give me a break cause I never been in trouble before.

Ain't no going back. Cops been lying to your mama. She's scared and wants you home cause the cops telling her you get killed if you don't turn yourself in.

I'm going back and take my chances.

I ain't arguing wit you. You do what you need to do. But lemme tell you. Ain't but one chance and that's getting somewhere and starting up a new life. You go back to Pittsburgh and that's it. Murder One is life. Ain't no breaks. Break your ass is what they'll do.

I'm gon too, Rob.

You guys is crazy. Don't you know what's waiting for you back there? Don't care what lies they be telling Cecil's mom.

Ima take my chances.

Well, leave me out of it. And stay off the goddamn phone. Youall don't need to advertise to the world where we at. You knew you was doing wrong. Waited till I was sleep before you got on the phone. Here. Youns want money for the bus?

We got to take the car.

The car . . . Fuck, man. We supposed to be getting away in the car. . . . Shit. Take the motherfucker. It's your goddamn car. . . . Damn, you got me hollering now. Lucky ain't nobody out here to see us acting like fools. Go on. Take the car. But you gon be sorry. You want the money too?

Just enough to get back. You keep the rest. You gon need it out here.

Think hard, man. Think what youns is doing. They might catch my ass tomorrow. Might be dead tomorrow. Then again, maybe not. If I get to L.A. and settle in, it's a new life. Poochie's out there. He can get us I.D.'s and whatnot. We all sat down and figured this thing out once before. We agreed on what we had to do and now all the sudden youns is changing your minds. L.A.'s bigger than Gary. A whole lot bigger. Fuck that simple cat back there. We can disappear in L.A. easy. That's what it's all about. A new life. We ain't got the money we thought we'd have, but it's enough to get started. Think about it, man. Ain't nothing back in the Burg.

Pleaded with the cats but they had their minds made up. Wasn't no moving em so I told em, If I don't see you no more in this world, see you in the next. And don't be late. That's Jimi Hendrix. My favorite line from one his songs. That's what I told them and I was sorry to see them go but no way I was going back. We come too far. Wasn't no back.

They leave me off at the bus station. I gets on the bus to L.A. Sit there with my eyes closed, crunched down in the seat. Getting sicker and sicker now. Don't want to see nothing or hear nothing. It's just me by myself and I'm trying to curl up so I'm halfway comfortable in the goddamn seat cause it's still a long way to L.A. I got a day, maybe two or three to ride. All's I know is I feel like shit and there's like this heavy, heavy cloud and my head's in the middle and it's stinking and hard to breathe but I just want to sink down in it deeper and forget everything. So many thoughts running through my brain afterwhile it's like everything gets all jammed together. I ain't really thinking about nothing then. Just sinking deeper and getting sicker. The motor starts up. The bus be shaking like it does when the engine's revving up. Then I hear the doors squeeze open and all this noise. Them fools changed their minds again. Here come Mike and Cecil flying on the bus. Ain't had time to pack the suitcases. Clothes hanging out, falling all over the place. They throwing suitcases up on the rack and picking up clothes and stuffing clothes back in the bags. Sick as I was, I had to laugh. Cause the driver ain't paying them fools no mind. They ain't on the bus good yet and their stuff is still flying around everywhere but the driver got his bus pulling out the station and Mike and Cecil trying to hold on and hold still and bouncing round like pool balls in the aisle. Everybody on the bus looking. Wondering what is this? What these simple niggers up to? Must be running from something. Acted like I didn't know them two. Stared at em scrambling around just like everybody else.

No sooner than we got to the outskirts of Chicago Mike gets off again. His seat ain't warm yet but he figures he better go back to the bus station and pick up his car and find someplace to park it. Left it at a meter. Talk about some lame shit. But he's right about going back. If they tow it, they'll check the license and registration. Might be hot by now. Don't know what they know back in Pittsburgh, so Mike gets off to take care of his car. He says he'll catch the next bus, meet us in L.A. Didn't know it then, but I won't see Mike again till after Christmas. Day after my birthday when he showed up in Johnny-Boy's room in Ogden. Hotel clerk told Mike, your friends not here, but Johnny-Boy might know where he's at. I screamed when I saw Mike. Like seeing a ghost. Like something magic bringing us together again. I'm thinking, where'd this nigger come from? Been six weeks since I seen him, then there he is sitting on Johnny-Boy's bed. Like I sure didn't know when he left he'd be gone that long. Didn't know he'd be in jail and outa jail and cops hot on his ass and he'd be smoking back and forth cross the whole damn country two or three times before we hooked up again.

Didn't know I wouldn't never get to L.A. Whole lot of things I didn't know when Mike split to get his car. Just said, Take care man. Later, man. Catch you in L.A. So it's just me and Cec. I'm glad for the company but it don't make me feel no better. Righteous sick now. Takes a hit of wine Cecil brought on board and that just makes me sicker for a while but then it puts me to sleep.

I lose track of time long about now. Sick as a dog. Nodding on and off. Don't know how long I was sitting in the bus. Night when I woke up. Or kinda woke up. Days and nights start running together about then. Didn't really get myself straight till I got to Ogden and copped. But first there's still me and Cecil on the bus. It's night and we're in Iowa or some damn place. Cecil tells me he thinks it's Iowa cause I don't be knowing from nothing. Could of been West Hell or New Mexico or the Promised Land. It was by me, that's for sure, cause my eyes wasn't focusing and my head was bad. What it comes down to is, I didn't give a fuck where I was. Cause I was nowhere. Nodding and drifting and sick. You know how hard it is to sleep on a bus anyway. The road keeps coming up through the wheels and jerking you awake. Well, when you sick it's that much worse. Thought I was gon puke a couple times. What saved me was having nothing in my stomach to bring up. Cept a hit of wine and it knew better. So I wasn't sleeping. Just kinda drifting. Rolling around and spinning and every now and then I'd snap wide awake. Like a flashbulb shot off in my brain and I could see something bright as day right in front my eyes. But it'd be gone in a second. Flashing just long enough to get me good and wake. Just enough to bust my sleep wide open. Then I'd try to nod off again. Feel the bus taking every bump on the road. Boom-boom-boom, like beating on a drum. So I wasn't wake but couldn't sleep neither. Kept having nasty little split-second dreams. Pictures of bad things, ugly things snatching at me, keeping me from really sleeping.

Think it was the fact we was standing still finally woke me out my daze. Bus was empty. Cecil's not in the seat cross the aisle where he been stretched out. I musta been talking to myself cause I heard voices and seemed like I was waiting for somebody to answer me. Dumb shit. Half wake and half sleep and having a conversation with myself. Where is we, man? But ain't a soul on the bus to answer.

Trying to get myself together. Sweating terrible inside my clothes but I'm cold, too. Flashed on one the dreams I been having. A nightmare really, cause everything in it turned around. Tanya was in it but she wasn't Tanya. She was a goat. All kinds of nasty goings-on but all I can remember now is Tanya was a goat.

Wherever we was, it was cold. Just a couple steps from the bus to the station but it was a different world outside. That cold air stone woke me up. Cleared my head right quick. Shivering by the time I got to the snack bar.

I remember trying to drink a cup of coffee to warm up. Sitting shivering at the counter. Shaking so much I spilled most the coffee in the saucer. Then what make it so bad I dumped the saucer. Thought to myself what the fuck am I doing here a thousand miles from nowhere spilling coffee all over this man's clean counter?

Then I spots Cecil. On the phone again. Thought he was in the bathroom or something, but there he is on the goddamn phone again.

I'm too miserable to say a word. Just stand there and stare at him.

It's gon be alright. My mom said they'll go easy if I turn myself in.

By now I'm disgusted. Just plain tired of this yo-yo back-and-forth shit. Tell him: If you got to go, you got to go. Cecil's my man so I had to say one more time what I said in the first place about going back. Then I just shook my head and let it be. He's a grown man. He got to make his own choice.

Turned out we's at a rest stop. Bus going in the opposite direction, headed for Pittsburgh, stopped there too. Cecil said one be through in the next couple hours and he was heading for home. My bus was ready to leave. Gave Cecil money to buy a ticket. It had started snowing. I got on my bus. Looked out the window and there was Cecil outside the station standing in the snow.

Somewhere in all that riding I remember a sign saying Lincoln, Nebraska. Funny how some things strike home. Stay with you. Like Cecil standing in the snow. Like this lesson in fourth grade on states and capitals. For some damned reason states and capitals was something I dug. Couldn't wait to get home so I could memorize them. Lincoln, Nebraska was special. Stuck in my mind. When I saw the sign saying Lincoln I remembered school and the lesson on states and capitals. Maybe it was something about Lincoln freeing the slaves. Maybe it was the funny way Nebraska sounded, Indian or something. Alls I know I got off on Lincoln. I was happy I seen that Lincoln sign. Seemed like my luck might turn.

One place we stopped had a liquor store cross the street. Copped two half-pints of gin and a quart of wine.

The bus pretty empty when I got on with my taste. Cecil was gone. Only one other black guy, an old dude sitting in the back. Loneliness starts to set in. My crew done split. I'm sick. In the worst trouble of my life. Thinking about the guy got killed. Just a young dude. Not much older than me. I don't know nobody and nobody don't know me. Out the window ain't nothing but miles and miles of nowhere. Maybe I can find Poochie in L.A. Maybe not. Everything's coming down on me. Thinking about home. Thinking about never seeing my people and my friends again. Feeling guilty. Feeling real sorry for myself. Know Ima get sicker before I get better. Just me and my gin. You know what I mean. The stone blues. Looking at myself and seeing how bad I done fucked up and how pitiful I was sitting on that damned bus going nowhere. About ready to cry, I was so sorry for myself.

Needed some company. Wasn't doing myself no good sitting there with all that heavy shit on my mind. The old dude looked like the type of guy be happy to crack a quart of wine with me. I goes back to where he's at and we get it on. Pretty soon we kills the wine and passing the gin back and forth. The old dude been everywhere. He's a storyteller. Every town we pass he knows somebody lives there or used to live there or heard about something crazy going on. He's hip. Got a bunch of hustles keep him in dough. Welfare checks coming in six or seven places. Little shady jobs he does for people. A real together old dude. All I got to do is ask a question and he's off on another story. Seems like he been traveling all his life. On the road. Half the time he just be bullshitting, making up lies. But he knows a lot. Don't matter to me whether he's lying or not cause the miles is going faster.

Asks me tell him a little bout myself. He's hip. He knows a guy like me, nice clothes, money in my pocket, a down rap, he knows I got to be running from something. So I tells him I'm Robin White. Big time pimp from New York. Had to leave the Apple fast. Stepped on some people's toes. Big, bad people. Had to split. Leave most my shit behind. On my way to the Coast. Got connections out there. Start my business up again in L.A. My lady's gon meet me. Yeah. Life's a bitch, ain't it? On top one day. Running the next. Had to leave all my pretty cars and pretty women behind. Yeah, I miss the good life but it's just a matter of time. Be back on top again.

We's laughing and joking and having a good old lying time. Best of buddies by the time the bus stops in Ogden, Utah. What I see out the window reminds me of home. For the first time in I don't know how long, it's the stone ghetto. I ask the old guy about Ogden. Tell him I got that old-home sensation when I looked out the window and seen the ghetto.

Oh, yeah. You got that right. It's the stone ghetto. And sure. He knows lots of people in Ogden. Ogden ain't a bad town. Yeah. Plenty black folk in Ogden. Been here for years. You find anything you want in Ogden. Niggers living everywhere out West. You just got to know where to find em. No trouble finding them in Ogden.

He's like a history book. Don't know why I can't remember his name. Maybe he never told me. Think he did but it won't come to me now. Don't matter. He's Tom or Sam. Something like that. I'll call him Pops. Old Pops. Well, Pops is steady rapping about Ogden. Seems like he lived there a long time. He's going on and on about how nice a place it is till we get to Salt Lake City. Talks me into paying a visit to Ogden. Talks hisself into going back. We get off the bus in Salt Lake. Catch another bus back to Ogden.

This Chinese lady in Ogden. She runs it, man. She owns a hotel and a restaurant, a store. She got the whole joint tied down. Collecting all the winos' welfare checks. See, they be eating in her restaurant and staying in her hotel. Pops, he's hipping me to what's going down. Used to work for the old Chinese bitch sometimes. We in her little restaurant drinking coffee and Pops telling me all kinda stuff about Ogden. I ain't never heard of Ogden before but the way he's talking it sounds just like home. Like the set at home.

Sitting drinking coffee. My jones down on me but it feels good being off that goddamn bus. Fulla gin and wine, I'm hurting but I'm feeling better cause Ogden be sounding like a place I can handle. You know. Get myself together. Looking round me and it's sure nuff the ghetto. What's different is it ain't full of niggers. Chinese people and cowboy-looking dudes and bums, but ain't no jitterbugs. Hey, Pops, man. Where's the young bloods? Gotta be some young guys hanging round somewhere.

Right when I'm asking Pops the question, Johnny-Boy bops by the window. Hip walk, process, Do Rag round his head. Trifling-looking dude in this trench coat trying to be with it but it's so dirty you know the cat ain't been nowhere and ain't going nowhere but the street. I'm thinking, Where's the niggers, and here come this trifling dude and Pops knocks on the window. Johnny-Boy strolls inside, sits down.

Johnny-Boy. How you doing, fella? This my man, Robin. He's new in town.

Pleased to meet you, man. You know where I can cop some reefer, man?

Sure, blood. I can get anything in this town. Reefer, boogie. Johnny-Boy get anything in this town.

The way he said "boogie," I knew just what he meant. Johnny-Boy ain't nothing but a street punk. I'm digging that from the front. Trifling little dude. But he would know where the boogie was. Got his slick head and high-water bell bottoms, he know he cool. Like something out the fifties. Like something the cat drug in. Typical hippy-dip ghetto brother. That was Johnny. Nothing to him. Strong wind get up under that raggedy trench coat and blow him away. But he's cool. He's hip. Yeah. Trying to get over. He knows where it's at. But you got to be careful with a brother like that. Turn on you in a minute. A snake. A street rat. He be round the action but he's trifling. Don't want to have no more to do with a dude like that than you got to.

Boogie. Reefer. Anything.

Me and Pops at the table in this Chinese lady's restaurant. It's getting late in the afternoon and the stone ghetto walks in and sits down wit us. A thousand miles from home and I'm thinking, I ain't been in town ten minutes and already I done found the action. Things is ready to start up again. Funny part about it is, we's drinking our coffee in the Lincoln Hotel. That's the name the place—Lincoln Hotel. Ain't that a bitch? I'm thinking maybe my luck is changing. Maybe things gon get better. . . .

II. Summer 1982

*O*ne more time. Summer 1982. The weather in Pittsburgh is unbearably hot. Two weeks of high temperatures and high humidity. Nights not much better than the days. Nights too hot for sleeping, days sapping what's left of the strength the sleepless nights don't replenish. You get sopping wet climbing in or out of a car. Especially if your car's little and not air-conditioned, like my mother's Chevette. Nobody remembers the last time they felt a cool breeze, nobody remembers pulling on clothes and not sweating through them in five minutes. "Unbearable" is my mother's word. She uses it often but never lightly. In her language it means the heat is something you can't escape. The sticky heat's a burden you wake up to every morning and carry till you're too exhausted to toss and turn anymore in your wet sheets. Unbearable doesn't mean a weight that gets things over with, that crushes you once and for all, but a burden that exerts relentless pressure. Whether you're lifting a bag of groceries from a shopping cart into the furnace your car becomes after sitting closed for twenty minutes in the Giant Eagle parking lot, or celebrating the birth of a new baby in the family, the heat is there. A burden touching, flawing everything. Unbearable is not that which can't be borne, but what must be endured forever.

Of course the July dog days can't last forever. Sooner or later they'll end. Abruptly. Swept away by one of those violent lightning-and-thunder storms peculiar to Pittsburgh summers. The kind signaled by a sudden disappearance of air, air sucked away so quickly you feel you're falling. Then nothing. A vast emptiness rubbing your skin. The air's gone. You're in a vacuum, a calm, still, vacated space waiting for the storm to rush in. You know the weather must turn, but part of the discomfort of being in the grip of a heat wave or any grave trouble is the fear that maybe it won't end. Maybe things will stay as miserable as they are.

Nothing changes. Nothing remains the same. One more visit to the prison, only this time, after I dropped my mother off at work, I tried a new route. The parkway had been undergoing repairs for two years. I'd used it anyway, in spite of detours and traffic jams. But this time I tried a shortcut my buddy Scott Payne had suggested. Scott was right; his way was quicker and freer of hassles. I'd arrived at Western Penitentiary in record time. Yet something was wrong. The new route transported me to the gates but I wasn't ready to pass through. Different streets, different buildings along the way hadn't done the trick, didn't have the power to take me where I needed to go because the journey to visit my brother in prison was not simply a matter of miles and minutes. Between Homewood and Woods Run, the flat, industrialized wasteland beside the river where the prison's hidden, there is a vast, uncharted space, a no-man's land where the traveler must begin to forget home and begin to remember the alien world inside "The Walls." At some point an invisible line is crossed, the rules change. Visitors must take leave of the certainties underpinning their everyday lives.

Using the parkway to reach Woods Run had become part of the ritual I depended upon to get me ready to see my brother. Huge green exit signs suspended over the highway, tires screaming on gouged patches of road surface, the darkness and claustrophobia of Squirrel Hill Tunnel, miles of abandoned steel-mill sheds, a mosque's golden cupola, paddle-wheeled pleasure boats moored at the riverbank, the scenes and sensations I catalogue now as I write were stepping stones. They broke the journey into stages, into moments I could anticipate. Paying attention to the steps allowed me to push into the back of my mind their inevitable destination, the place where the slide show of images was leading me.

I'd missed all that; so when I reached the last few miles of Ohio River Boulevard Scott's shortcut shared with my usual route, the shock of knowing the prison was just minutes away hit me harder than usual. I wasn't prepared to step through the looking glass.

Giving up one version of reality for another. That's what entering the prison was about. Not a dramatic flip-flop of values. That would be too easy. If black became white and good became bad and fast became slow, the players could learn the trick of reversing labels, and soon the upside-down world would seem natural. Prison is more perverse. Inside the walls nothing is certain, nothing can be taken for granted except the arbitrary exercise of absolute power. Rules engraved in stone one day will be superseded the next. What you don't know can always hurt you. And the prison rules are designed to keep you ignorant, keep you guessing, insure your vulnerability. Think of a fun-house mirror, a floor-to-ceiling sheet of undulating glass. Images ripple across its curved surface constantly changing. Anything caught in the mirror is bloated, distorted. Prison's like that mirror. Prison rules and regulations, the day-to-day operation of the institution, confront the inmate with an image of himself that is grotesque, absurd. A prisoner who refuses to internalize this image, who insists upon seeing other versions of himself, is in constant danger.

Somebody with a wry sense of humor had a field day naming the cluster of tiny streets bordering Western Penitentiary. Doerr, Refuge, Ketchum. When I reached the left turn at Doerr that would take me along the south wall of the prison to the parking-lot entrance, I still wasn't ready to go inside. I kept driving past the prison till the street I was on dead-ended. A U-turn in the lot of a chemical factory pointed me back toward the penitentiary and then for a few long minutes I sat in the car.

The city had vanished. Western Penitentiary was a million miles away. Taking a new route had been like reneging on my end of a bargain and now I had to pay the penalty. Certain magic words had not been chanted, the stone had not rolled away. I was displaced, out of time. Five days a week going about the business of earning a living, other people drove into the lot where I sat. Punching in and punching out. Doing their time in the shadow of the prison. The forty-foot-high stone walls did not exist for them. Caged men were a figment of someone's imagination, just as the workers parking in this lot each day were being imagined by me. How could one world reside so placidly next to the other? Men coming and going to their jobs, other men whose job was occupying the locked cells that created the prison. Ordinary men and prisoners, a factory and a penitentiary under the same gray sky. I couldn't move.

I heard myself in the factory cafeteria haranguing the workers:

Do you ever think about it? About that place over there? I mean when you drive by in the morning or when you're on your way home to your family or whatever? Do you see it? Do you ever wonder what's happening inside? What kind of men are locked up in there? Why are they inside and you outside? Can you imagine what happens when the lights go out at night? What do the prisoners think of you?

I'd lose my cool. Start shouting and pointing and get belligerent. People would be scared away. What kind of nut was I? Why was I hassling them? Go bug the prisoners. Preach to them. They're the bad guys.

Sitting alone in my mother's Chevette, the prison a half mile down the road, I turned off the motor so I could hear the factory humming and clanking within its low-slung brick walls behind my back. I was lost. The artificiality of *visiting* came down on me. I lived far away. Light-years away on a freezing planet, a planet empty except for the single solitary cell I inhabited. Visiting was illusion, deceit. I was separated from my brother by millions of stars. As distant as the employees of Chase Chemical Company who passed him every day on their way to work.

I focused on the ritual, the succession of things to be done in order to enter the prison. In my mind I passed through the iron gates of the official parking lot, I glanced at the stone walls, the river as I crossed the crowded lot to the visitors' annex. I climbed the steep concrete stairs. I faced the guard in his cage outside the waiting room, presented my identification, stated my brother's name and number, my relationship to him, wrote all that down on a sheet of mimeo paper, then found a seat in the dingy room, avoiding the blank faces of other visitors, frustration and anger building as I wait, wait, wait for the magic call that allows me down the steps, across a courtyard, up more steps, through steel doors and iron-barred doors into the lounge where my brother waits.

I saw it all happening, as it had happened many times before. Dreaming the process, the steps one by one, and then I could do it. Turn the key to start the engine. Begin the visit again.

During the half mile back down Preble Street I thought of death.

Entertained the silly idea that what was most frightening about dying was the inability to rehearse it. You only died once, so you couldn't anticipate what would be required of you. You couldn't tame death by practicing. You couldn't ease it step by step from the darkness of the unknown into the light. Visiting prison is like going to a funeral parlor. Both situations demand unnatural responses, impose a peculiar discipline on the visitor. The need to hold on wars with the need to let go, and the visitor is stuck in the middle, doing both, doing neither. You are mourning, bereaved but you pretend the shell in the coffin is somehow connected with the vital, breathing person you once knew. You pretend a life has not been stolen, snatched away forever. You submit to the unnatural setting controlled by faceless intermediaries, even though you understand the setting has been contrived not so much to allay your grief, your sense of loss but to profit from them, mock them, and mock the one you need to see.

In the half mile back to the prison as the walls loom higher and nearer I asked the question I always must when a visit is imminent: Is Rob still alive? The possibility of sudden, violent death hangs over my brother's head every minute of every day so when I finally reach the guard's cage and ask for P3468, my heart stands still and I'm filled with the numbing irony of wishing, of praying that the guard will nod his head and say, *Yes*, your brother's still inside.

After the solid steel door, before the barred, locked gate into the visiting area proper, each visitor must pass through a metal-detecting machine. The reason for such a security measure is clear; the extreme sensitivity of the machine is less easily explained. Unless the point is inflicting humiliation on visitors. Especially women visitors whose underclothes contain metal stays and braces, women who wear intimate jewelry they never remove from their bodies. Grandmothers whose wedding rings are imbedded in the flesh of their fingers. When the machine bleeps, everything it discovers must go. You say it's a wire in your bra, lady. Well, I'm sorry about that but you gotta take it off. Of course the women have a choice. They can strip off the offending garment or ornament, and don one of the dowdy smocks the state provides for such contingencies. Or they can go back home.

I dump wallet, watch, change and belt in a plastic tray, kick off my sandals because they have metal buckles, tiptoe barefoot through the needle's eye without incident. I wonder about my kids' orthodonture. The next time they come to visit Robby, what will the machine say about the metal braces on their teeth? What will the guards say? Whose responsibility will it be to inspect the kids' mouths for weapons? Will the boys feel like horses on sale? Have I taught Dan and Jake enough about their history so that they'll recall auction blocks and professional appraisers of human flesh? And the silver chain Judy has worn since Jamila's birth? The good-luck charm she believes kept them both alive those terrible weeks in the hospital and hasn't left her neck since?

But I'm alone this trip and I pass through. No sweat. Not like the time in an airport during the early seventies when paranoia about skyjacking was rampant and a lone black male, youngish, large, athletically built, casually dressed, "fit" the profile of an air pirate and I was pulled aside for special searching. Who conceived the profile, who determined its accuracy, its scientific, objective utility, who decided it was okay to body-search an individual who fit the profile, were matters not discussed in public and certainly not with me. Protesting too vehemently either the search or its validity could quickly become a crime in itself. If not an offense serious enough to get you arrested, at least grounds for barring you from your flight. A question as highfalutin as the constitutionality of this hit-and-miss harassment, these kangeroo courts instantly set up in airports across the nation, such a question from a youngish, largish, casually dressed, lone, black male would have closed the case, proven the appropriateness of the profile for netting not only skyjackers but loudmouthed, radical militants.

As I passed through the prison's metal detector I was recalling my adventure in Denver's Stapleton airport and remembering another time around the Christmas holidays when my sons were forced to unload their new cowboy pistols from our carry-on bags and stow them in the baggage hold, a precaution I thought was silly, even funny, until I watched a passenger who arrived behind us talk his way onto the plane with a .38 in his briefcase. He was an off-duty cop, like the moonlighting security guards policing the baggage-inspection area. A whispered conversation, a couple hearty laughs and winks among good ole boys, a pat on the shoulder, and this white guy and his pistol were on the plane. Meanwhile my whole family was forced to wait for special cardboard containers that would secure my kids' toy guns out of reach in the plane's belly. Yes. I was angry both times. The stifled, gut-deep rage that's American as apple pie. The black rage that makes you want to strike out and smash somebody's face because you know they have you by the throat, killing you by inches. You know you're being singled out, discriminated against simply because the person doing it to you has the power to get away with it and you're powerless to stop him. Not funny when it happens. But in retrospect what could be more hilarious than a black American outraged because his rights are denied? Where's he been? Who's kidding whom? Hasn't the poor soul heard what Supreme Court Chief Justice Roger Taney announced loud and clear as the law of the land, a law lodged in the heart of the country, a law civil rights legislation has yet to unseat: Blacks "have no rights which the white man was bound to respect."

Rephrase Justice Taney's dictum so it reads, "The weak have no rights that the strong are bound to respect." Its universal applicability, its continuing force as law in the workings of our society becomes clear. Inscribe it in a slightly different form over the entrance to Western Penitentiary—*Prisoners have no rights that the keepers are bound to respect*—and you've generated the motto of the prison. Lots of words and much blood have been spilled attempting to justify, destroy, or sustain democratic institutions in America. An unresolved paradox remains always at the core of the notion of majority rule. Minority rights exist only at the sufferance of the majority, and since the majority is ultimately governed by self-interest, the majority's self-interest determines any minority's fate. No rights that they are bound to respect. Certainly not as long as they're bound to self-interest, to the greatest good for the greatest number. The keepers run prisons with little or no regard for prisoners' rights because license to exercise absolute power has been granted by those who rule society.

When a convicted criminal enters prison, he is first stripped of the clothing that connects him to the outside world. Re-dressed in a prison uniform, subjected to prison discipline, the inmate undergoes an abrupt transformation of who and what he is. The prisoner is being integrated into a new world, new terms of existence. Among orthodox Jews, a father may say Kaddish for a living son or daughter who has committed some unforgivable transgression. In this rare circumstance, Kaddish, a prayer of mourning, is also a declaration of death. The child becomes as dead to the father, a nonperson, cut off absolutely from all contact, a shadow the father will not acknowledge, a ghost referred to in the past tense as one who once was. Everyday hundreds of prisoners experience a similar transition into a condition of nonexistence. Strangely, we have yet to name this declaration of civil death, this ritual that absolves us from responsibility for the prisoner's fate.

Although society declares to the prisoner you are no longer one of us, you are beyond the pale, the prisoner's body continues to breathe, his mind nags and races; he must be somewhere, something. He wants to know, as we all need to know: what am I? Into the vacuum society creates when it exiles the prisoner, step the keepers. In theory, their job is to guard incarcerated bodies, but because no one else speaks to the prisoners or for the prisoners, the keepers exercise an incredible power over their charges. Keepers can't pretend the inmates don't exist. They must create a landscape, an environment that secures the prisoners placed in their hands. As the keepers decide what time prisoners must awaken, when they may clean themselves, when they may eat, to whom they may speak, how they may wear their hair, which patches of ground they may march across and how long they may take crossing them, as the keepers constrict space and limit freedom, as the inmates are forced to conform to these mandates, an identity is fashioned for the prisoners. Guarding the inmates' bodies turns out to be a license for defining what a prisoner is. The tasks are complementary, in fact inseparable.

Prisoners are a unique minority; they exist in a political, ethical limbo via-à-vis free-world people. Out of sight, out of mind. Prisons segregate absolutely a troublesome minority from the majority. It's in the self-interest of the majority to suspend all ties to prisoners. A brutal but simple expedient for accomplishing this suspension is to lock up prisoners and charge the prisons with one task: keep these misfits away from us.

America's eight hundred prisons contain an "inmate nation" of nearly half a million souls. *Time* magazine in 1982 estimated that the prison population grows by 170 people each day, that it has doubled since 1970 and would double again by 1988. Approximately one out of six hundred Americans is in prison, a percentage surpassed only in the notoriously oppressive regimes of the Soviet Union and South Africa. Other sources declare that 2.5 million Americans are under some sort of correctional supervision (reform schools, jails, etc.) at a cost to the public of 4.8 billion dollars a year. The nation's prisons are hopelessly overcrowded. More cells are being constructed daily.

A careful reading of the literature of corrections reveals that the custodial function of prisons is paramount in the public eye. A recidivism rate of over 70 percent is stale news, but prison breaks make the front pages. Wardens and guards are fired for allowing their charges to escape. One escapee can make a whole prison system look bad, while the death of one or five or twenty inmates in a bloody riot protesting prison conditions is treated as an acceptable cost in maintaining institutional discipline and security. Whatever else prisons might or might not accomplish (moral rehabilitation, vocational training, education, punishment, deterrence) seldom arouses public concern so long as prisons keep the bad guys away. The length of prison sentences in most states has been steadily increasing in the past five years. In New Jersey, for instance, the average prison sentence grew by 40 percent between 1978 and 1982. Society's prescription for handling those adjudged criminals is becoming less and less ambiguous. Lock em up and throw away the key. Separation must be absolute. We don't care how you do it. The point is, we want these dangerous ones out of our hair and as long as you keep them out we won't bother you. The moral and ethical principles that bind society don't count inside prison. You, the custodians, formulate whatever rules, whatever system you require to keep the prisoners in captivity. You must stand between them and us. You are not a connection between the free world and the prison world but a chasm, a wall, a two-sided, unbreakable mirror. When we look at you we see ourselves. We see order and justice. Your uniforms, your rules reflect humane discipline. We see our faces, a necessarily severe aspect of our nature in the stern mask above your martial attire. When prisoners gaze into the reverse side of the mirror they should see the deformed aberrations they've become. Keepers are set in place to reflect and sustain this duality. In between the bright mirrors stretches an abyss.

My papers are in order, I've survived the gauntlet of minor annoyances and humiliations, so I'm allowed into the lounge where inmates and their visitors meet at Western Penitentiary. I have a minute or two before Robby pops in from his side of the mirror. He must undergo a strip search, bend over and spread the cheeks of his ass, before he enters and again when he leaves. The room is longish, rectangular, sleaze yellow. Vending machines line one wall. At the far end of the room, three small desk-height tables reserved for lawyers and their clients. A double row of benches and chairs set back to back extends through the center of the room, forming two aisles. Another row of seats runs the length of the third wall. A guard sitting behind a high, narrow, rostrum-like desk presides over the visitors' entrance to the lounge. Next to him an enclosed, inmate-supervised play corner for kids.

I take it all in too quickly, automatically. Like gulping a dose of nasty medicine to kill the taste. The room's so familiar it recedes immediately into the background. I remind myself, force myself to notice details. Is there anything different about the physical setting, have new signs been posted, has the furniture been rearranged, can I detect any mood, any threat in a quick survey of the room and its occupants? It's dangerous inside the prison walls to lose your edge, your precise awareness of what's happening, what's at stake. Awareness, consciousness, no matter how painful, are the only tools you have to work with. Your only advantage in the game the keepers have designed so they always win.

Robby hugs me, we clasp hands. My arm goes round his body and I hug him back. Our eyes meet. What won't be said, can't be said no matter how long we talk, how much I write, hovers in his eyes and mine. We know where we are, what's happening, how soon this tiny opening allowing us to touch will be slammed shut. All that in our eyes, and I can't take seeing it any longer than he can. The glance we exchange is swift, is full of fire, of unsayable rage and pain. Neither of us can hold it more than a split second. He sees in me what I see in him. The knowledge that this place is bad, worse than bad. That the terms under which we are meeting stink. That living under certain conditions is less than no life at all, and what we have to do, *ought* to do, is make our stand here, together. That dying with your hands on an enemy's throat is better than living under his boot. Just a flash. The simplest, purest solution asserting itself. I recognize what Rob is thinking. I know he knows what's rushing through my mind. Fight. Forget the games, the death by inches buying time. Fight till they kill us or let us go. If we die fighting, it will be a good day to die. The right day. The right way.

After that first contact, after that instant of threat and consolation and promise flickers out as fast as it came, my eyes drop to the vinyl-cushioned couches, rise again to the clutter of other prisoners and visitors. I force myself to pretend the eye conversation never took place, that Robby and I hadn't been talking about first things and last things and hadn't reached a crystal-clear understanding of what we must do. We'd lost the moment. The escape route closed down as he looked away or I looked away. We're going to deal with the visit now. We're going to talk, survive another day. I have to pretend the other didn't happen because if I don't, disappointment and shame will spoil the visit. And visits are all we have. All we're going to have for years and years, unless we choose the other way, the solution burning in Rob's eyes and mine before each visit begins.

The last iron gate, the last barred door. The visit proper doesn't begin until after we meet and touch and decide we'll do it their way one more time. Because the other way, the alternative is always there. I meet it every time. We know it's there and we consciously say, *No.* And the no lets everything else follow. Says yes to the visit. The words.

Whatever else the visit turns into, it begins as compromise, an acceptance of defeat. Maybe the rage, the urge to fight back doesn't rise from a truer, better self. Maybe what's denied is not the instinctual core of my being but an easily sidestepped, superficial layer of bravado, a ferocity I'd like to think is real but that winds up being no more than a Jonathan Jackson, George Jackson, Soledad-brother fantasy, a carryover from the old Wild West, shoot-em-up days as a kid. The Lone Ranger, Robin Hood, Zorro. Masked raiders attacking the bad guys' castle, rescuing trusty sidekicks in a swirl of swordplay, gunfire, thundering hooves. Maybe I needed to imagine myself in that role because I knew how far from the truth it was. Kidding myself so I could take the visits seriously, satisfy myself that I was doing all I could, doing better than nothing.

Point is, each visit's rooted in denial, compromise, a sinking feeling of failure. I'm letting Robby down, myself down, the team. . . . Always that to get through. The last gate. Sometimes it never swings all the way open on its hinges. A visit can be haunted by a sense of phoniness, hollowness. Who am I? Why am I here? Listening to my brother, answering him, but also fighting the voice that screams that none of this matters, none of this is worth shit. You missed your chance to put your money where your mouth is. A good day to die but you missed it. You let them win again. Humiliate you again. You're on your knees again, scrambling after scraps.

Sometimes we occupy one of the lawyer-client tables, but today a guard chases us away. Robby's had trouble with him before. I commit the guard's name to memory just in case. My personal shit list for close watching or revenge or whatever use it would serve if something suspicious happens to my brother. I consider making a fuss. After all, I'm a professional writer. Don't I have just as much right as a lawyer or social worker to the convenience of a table where I can set down the tools of my trade, where my brother and I can put a little distance between ourselves and the babble of twenty or thirty simultaneous conversations?

The guard's chest protrudes like there's compressed air instead of flesh inside the gray blouse of his uniform. A square head. Pale skin except on his cheeks, which are bluish and raw from razor burn. His mustache and short curly hair are meticulously groomed, too perfect to be real. The stylized hair of comic-book superheroes. A patch of blue darkness etched with symmetrical accent lines. His eyes avoid mine. He had spoken in a clipped, mechanical tone of voice. Not one man talking to another but a peremptory recital of rules droned at some abstraction in the middle distance where the guard's eyes focus while his lips move. I think, Nazi Gestapo Frankenstein robot motherfucker, but he's something worse. He's what he is and there's no way to get around that or for the moment get around him because he's entrenched in this noman's land and he is what he is and that's worse than any names I can call him. He's laying down the law and that's it. The law. No matter that all three tables are unoccupied. No matter that I tell him we've sat at them before. No matter that we'll vacate if and when lawyers need them. No matter that I might have a case, make a case that my profession, my status means something outside the walls. No matter, my pride and anger and barely concealed scorn. I move on. We obey because the guard's in power. Will remain in power when I have to leave and go about my business. Then he'll be free to take out on my brother whatever revenge he couldn't exact from me and my smart mouth. So I take low. Shake my head but stroll away (just enough nigger in my walk to tell the guard I know what he thinks of me but that I think infinitely less of him) toward the least crowded space in the row of benches against the wall.

Not much news to relate. Robby cares about family business and likes to keep up with who's doing what, when, how, etc., but he also treats the news objectively, cold-bloodedly. Family affairs have everything and nothing to do with him. He's in exile, powerless to influence what goes on outside the walls, so he maintains a studied detachment; he hears what I say and quickly mulls it over, buries the worrisome parts, grins at good news. When he comments on bad news it's usually a grunt, a nod, or a gesture with his hands that says all there is to say and says, A million words wouldn't make any difference, would they. Learning to isolate himself, to build walls within the walls enclosing him is a matter of survival. If he doesn't insulate himself against those things he can't change, if he can't discipline himself to ignore and forget, to narrow the range of his concerns to what he can immediately, practically effect, he'll go crazy. The one exception is freedom. Beneath whatever else Robby says or does or thinks, the dream of freedom pulses. The worst times, the lowest times are when the pulse seems extinguished. Like in the middle of the night, the hour of the wolf when even the joint is quiet and the earth stops spinning on its axis and he bursts from sleep, the deathly sleep that's the closest thing to mercy prison ever grants, starts from sleep and for a moment hears nothing. In the shadow of that absolute silence he can't imagine himself ever leaving prison alive. For hours, days, weeks the mood of that moment can oppress him. He needs every ounce of willpower he possesses to pick up the pieces of his life, to animate them again with the hope that one day the arbitrary, bitter, little routines he manufactures to sustain himself will make sense because one day he'll be free.

I arrange my pens and yellow pad atop the table. But before we begin working on the book I tell Robby my sawing dream.

I am a man, myself but not myself. The man wakes up and can't see the stars. The smell of death surrounds him. Fifteen hundred other men sleep in the honeycomb of steel that is his home forever. The fitful stirrings, clattering bars, groaning, the sudden outcries of fear, rage, madness, and God knows what else are finally over at this hour of the night or morning as he lies in his cell listening to other men sleep. The monotonous sawing sound reminds him of the funny papers, the little cloud containing saw and log drawn above a character's head so you can see the sound of sleeping. Only the man doesn't see logs floating above the prisoners' heads. As he listens and shuts his eyes and gets as close to praying as he ever does anymore, praying for sleep, for blessed oblivion, the cartoon he imagines behind his closed eyes is himself sawing away the parts of his own body. Doggedly, without passion or haste, drawing a dull saw up and back, up and back through his limbs. Slices drop away on the concrete floor. The man is cutting himself to pieces, there is less of him every time he saws through a section. He is lopping off his own flesh and blood but works methodically, concentrating on the up-and-back motion of the saw. When there's nothing left, he'll be finished. He seems almost bored, almost asleep, ready to snore like the saw's snoring as it chews through his body.

Robby shakes his head and starts to say something but doesn't, and we both leave the dream alone. Pass on to the book, the tasks still to be accomplished.

Robby had said he liked what he'd seen of the first draft. Liked it fine, but something was missing. Trouble was, he hadn't been able to name the missing ingredient. I couldn't either but I knew I had to try and supply it. By the book's conclusion I wanted a whole, rounded portrait of my brother. I'd envisioned a climactic scene in the final section, an epiphany that would reveal Robby's character in a powerful burst of light and truth. As the first draft evolved, I seemed to settle for much less. One early reader had complained of a "sense of frustration . . . By the end of the book I want to know more about Robby than I actually know. I know a lot of facts about his life but most of his inner self escapes me." On target or not, the reaction of this early reader, coupled with Robby's feeling that something crucial was lacking, had destroyed any complacency I had about the book's progress. I reread Robby's letters, returned to the books and articles that had informed my research into prisons and prisoners. I realized no apotheosis of Robby's character could occur in the final section because none had transpired in my dealings with my brother. The first draft had failed because it attempted to impose a dramatic shape on a relationship, on events and people too close to me to see in terms of beginning, middle, and end. My brother was in prison. A thousand books would not reduce his sentence one day. And the only denouement that might make sense of his story would be his release from prison. I'd been hoping to be a catalyst for change in the world upon which the book could conceivably have no effect at all. I'd been waiting to record dramatic, external changes in Robby's circumstances when what I should have been attuned to were the inner changes, his slow, internal adjustment day by day to an unbearable situation. The book was no powerful engine being constructed to set my brother free; it was dream, wish, song.

No, I could not create a man whose qualities were self-evident cause for returning him to the world of free people. Prison had changed my brother, not broken him, and therein lay the story. The changes were subtle, incremental; bit by bit he had been piecing himself together. He had not become a model human being with a cure for cancer at his fingertips if only the parole board would just give him a chance, turn him loose again on the streets of Homewood. The character traits that landed Robby in prison are the same ones that have allowed him to survive with dignity, and pain and a sense of himself as infinitely better than the soulless drone prison demands he become. Robby knows his core is intact; his optimism, his intelligence, his capacity for love, his pride, his dream of making it big, becoming somebody special. And though these same qualities helped get him in trouble and could derail him again, I'm happy they are still there. I rejoice with him.

The problem with the first draft was my fear. I didn't let Robby speak for himself enough. I didn't have enough confidence in his words, his vision, his insights. I wanted to clean him up. Manufacture compelling before-and-after images. Which meant I made the bad too bad and good too good. I knew what I wanted; so, for fear I might not get what I needed, I didn't listen carefully, probe deeply enough. As I tried his story again I began to recognize patterns, a certain consistency in his responses, a basic impetuous honesty that made him see himself and his world with unflinching clarity. He never stopped asking questions. He never allowed answers to stop him. The worst things he did followed from the same impulse as the best. He could be unbelievably dumb, corrupt, selfish, and destructive but those qualities could keep him down no more than his hope, optimism, his refusal to accept a dull, inferior portion could buoy him above the hell that engulfed black boys in the Homewood streets.

Robby watched it all. Ups and downs. Rises and falls. What was consistent was the watching, the consciousness, the vision in which he saw himself as counting, as being worth saving at any cost. If he had lost that vision, if he loses it now, then we will all matter a little less.

To repair the flawed first draft I had asked for more from Robby. He'd responded sporadically with poems, anecdotes, meditations on his time behind bars. What he was giving me helped me turn a corner. I was closer to him. I was beginning to understand what had been missing in the first version of his story. I was learning to respect my brother's touch, his vision. Learning what was at stake in this give-and-take between us, initiated by the idea of a book.

A letter from Robby had added this coda to Garth's story, the story he thought might be one place to begin telling his own:

> After Garth's funeral, me, Mike, and Cecil, our ladies, and Garth's lady sat in Mike's car and waited for all the other cars to leave. We weren't doing any talking, just crying and sniffling. It was raining outside and the silence was broken only by the pitter-patter of the rain on the car. Now I was always the oldest of our crew and Garth had always been my little brother though always taller. So when Mike finally started up the car the radio came on and a song by the group War was on the box. The name of the song was "Me and Baby Brother" and the chorus goes: "Me and baby brother used to run together. . . . Running over one another headed for the corner." It was like it was just for me. I sat there in the backseat with tears just running down my face.

His new girl friend Leslie claims Robby lives through the words of songs and movies. Robby admits maybe it's true. He's sent me the lyrics of a Sly and the Family Stone jam, "Family Affair." The song was popular at about the time Robby was breaking up with his first wife, Geraldine. For him the song says everything there is to say about that period in his life. Part of the magic's in the words, the line-by-line correspondence between what was happening to him and the situations and people the song described:

> *Newlyweds a year ago but they're still*
> *Checking each other*
> *Nobody wants to blow*
> *Nobody wants to be left out*
> *You can't leave cause your heart is there. . . .*

But another part was the music itself, what transfigures the personal, the unique with universals of rhythm, tone, and harmony, what must always remain unspoken because words can't keep up with the flood of feeling, of experience music releases.

The music Robby loves is simple; the lyrics often seem sentimental, banal. Though rhythm and blues and rock 'n' roll are rooted in traditional African music, the soul sounds Robby listened to in the sixties had been heavily commercialized, exploited by whites. Fortunes were made by whites who produced, performed, wrote, and distributed this so-called black music. About the only thing whites didn't do to black music was destroy it. Miraculously, the best black singers and musicians transcended the destructive incursions on their turf. Afro-American musical styles passed through one more crucible and emerged on the other side modified externally but intact at the core. Robby could see himself, recognize his world in the music called soul.

Over 125 years before Robby discovered visions of himself reflected in "Family Affair," young Frederick Douglass learned in the music of fellow slaves truths about his life, about the ordeal of slavery and the capacity of the spirit to rise above it, truths that were articulated in the form of strange chants, cries, percussive clapping and stomping, call-and-response cadences created by black field hands as they marched from one back-breaking job to another. "Their songs still follow me," Douglass later wrote; and certain songs continue to haunt my brother. Simple songs. Lyrics as uncomplicated, transparent as the poetry of the gospels and spirituals we sang in Homewood A.M.E. Zion church: *Let my people go. Farther along we'll understand why. Amazing Grace. How sweet the sound. One bright morning. His eye is on the sparrow so I know He watches me.*

The messages are simple. The mysteries they enfold are not. What Robby hears is the sound of what he has been, where he has been, the people he traveled with, the ones here, the ones there, the ones gone forever. The best, the authentic black music does not unravel the mysteries, but recalls them, gives them a particular form, a specific setting, attaches the mysteries to familiar words and ideas. Simple lyrics of certain songs follow us, haunt us because the words floating in the music are a way of eavesdropping on the mysteries, of remembering the importance of who we are but also experiencing the immensity of Great Time and Great Space, the Infinite always at play around the edges of our lives.

You are my sunshine, my only sunshine. You make me happy when skies are gray. Our grandfather John French loved that song. Hummed it, crooned it high on Dago Red, beat out its rhythm on his knee, a table's edge, the bottom of a pot. *Froggy went a-courtin'* was another favorite, and we'd ride like Froggy jiggedy-jig, jiggedy-jig on Daddy John's thigh while he sang. Those songs had survived. John French found them and stored them and toted them on his journey from Culpepper, Virginia, to Pittsburgh, Pennsylvania, the place where we began to know him as our mother's father. He saved those songs and they documented his survival. All of that hovered in the words and music when he passed them on to us.

Here are some more of the lines Robby remembered from "Family Affair":

> One child grows up to be somebody
> who just loves to learn.
> And the other child grows up to be
> somebody who just loves to burn
> Mom loves the both of them
> You see it in the blood
> Both kids are good to Mom
> Blood thicker than the mud . . .
> It's a family affair.

What do these words tell me about my brother? Why did he share them with me? One reason may be his dissatisfaction with the picture of him I'd drawn in the first draft of this book. There will necessarily be distance, vast discrepancy between any image I create and the mystery of all my brother is, was, can be. We both know that. And he'll never be satisfied, but he's giving me the benefit of the doubt. Not complaining overtly, but reminding me that there's more, much, much more to know, to learn. He's giving me a song, holding open a door on a world I can never enter. Robby can't carry me over to the other side, but he can crack the door and I can listen.

Robby refuses to be beaten down. Sly said in another song that everybody wants to be a star. That wish contains the best of us and the worst. The thrust of ego and selfishness, the striving to be better than we are. If Robby fell because the only stardom he could reasonably seek was stardom in crime, then that's wrong. It's wrong not because Robby wanted more but because society closed off every chance of getting more, except through crime. So I'm glad to see Robby's best (worst) parts have survived. Can't have one without the other.

I let Robby know I've rewritten the book, virtually from start to finish. Plenty of blurred, gray space, lots of unfilled gaps and unanswered questions and people to interview, but the overall design is clearer now. I'm trying to explain to Robby how I feel released rather than constrained by the new pattern beginning to emerge. The breakthrough came when I started to hear what was constant, persistent beneath the changes in his life. The book will work if the reader participates, begins to grasp what I have. I hadn't been listening closely enough, so I missed the story announcing itself. When I caught on, there I was, my listening, waiting self part of the story, listening, waiting for me.

Yet I remained apprehensive about the prison section of the book. Robby wouldn't be able to help me as much in this last section as he had with the others. The method we'd evolved was this: Robby would tell his stories. I'd listen, take notes, reconstruct the episodes after I'd allowed them time to sink in, then check my version with Rob to determine if it sounded right to him. Letters and talk about what I'd written would continue until we were both satisfied. We'd had lots of practice performing that operation and I was beginning to feel a measure of confidence in the results it eventually produced. "Doing Time" was a different matter. The book would end with this section. Since I was writing the book, one way or another I'd be on center stage. Not only would the prison section have to pull together many loose ends, but new material had to surface and be resolved. Aside from logical and aesthetic considerations, finishing the book as object, completing the performance, there was the business of both rendering and closing down the special relationship between my brother and myself that writing the book had precipitated. All the questions I'd decided to finesse or sidestep or just shrug off in order to get on with writing would now return, some in the form of issues to be addressed in concluding the book, some as practical dilemmas in the world outside the book, the world that had continued to chug along while I wrote.

Robby was still a prisoner. He was inside and I was outside. Success, fame, ten million readers wouldn't change that. The book, whether it flopped or became a best-seller, would belong to the world beyond the prison walls. Ironically, it would validate the power of the walls, confirm the distance between what transpired inside and outside. Robby's story would be "out there," but he'd still be locked up. Despite my attempts to identify with my brother, to reach him and share his troubles, the fact was, I remained on the outside. With the book. Though I never intended to steal his story, to appropriate it or exploit it, in a sense that's what would happen once the book was published.

His story would be out there in a world that ignored his existence. It could be put to whatever uses people chose. Of course I was hoping Robby would benefit from a book written about him, but the possible benefits did not alter the fact that imprisonment profoundly alienated him from the finished product of our collaboration.

Simple things like sharing financial profits could be handled; but how could I insure a return on the emotional investment my brother had made? Once I'd gotten the book I'd come for, would I be able to sustain the bond that had grown between us? Would I continue to listen with the same attention to his stories? Would he still possess a story? Much of what he'd entrusted to me had nothing to do with putting a book together. Had I identified with him because I discovered that was the best way to write the book? Would the identification I'd achieved become a burden, too intense, too pressurized to survive once the book was completed? Was the whole thing between us about a book or had something finer, truer been created? And even if a finer, truer thing had come into being, would it be shattered by the noisy explosion (or dull thud) of the book's appearance in the world beyond the prison walls?

Some of these questions could be asked outright. Others were too intimidating, too close to the bone to raise with my brother. Yet we had to deal with all of them. In the world and in the prison section. The book, if there was to be a book, must end, must become in some senses an artifact. I wanted to finish it but I didn't want to let it go. I might be losing much more than a book.

The fears I could put into words I tried to share with Robby. He nodded, clenched and unclenched his big hands, smiled at the funny parts, the blackly comic pratfalls and cul de sacs neither of us nor anybody in the world can avoid. Yeah, shit's gon hit the fan. Yeah, sounds like it might get rough . . . but then again . . . what can you do but do? Many of my worries clearly were not his. I was the writer, that was *my* kitchen, *my* heat. He'd thought about some of the stuff worrying me but I could tell he hadn't spent lots of time fretting over it. And wouldn't. Many of the troubles I anticipated were too far down the line to tease out Robby's concern. In prison he had learned to walk a very fine line. On one side of the line was the minute-by-minute, day-by-day struggle for survival to which he must devote his undivided attention. On the other side his vision of something better, a life outside the walls, an existence he could conceive only if he allowed himself the luxury of imagination, of formulating plans in a future divorced from his present circumstances. The line was thin, was perilous because any energy he squandered on envisioning the future was time away, a lapse in the eternal vigilance he must maintain to stay alive in his cage. Yet the struggle to survive, the heightened awareness he must sustain to get through each moment, each day made no sense unless his efforts were buying something other than more chunks of prison routine. And plans for the future were pipe dreams unless he could convince himself he possessed the stamina and determination to make it step by step through the withering prison regimen. These options, realities, consequences defined the straight and narrow path Robby was forced to tread. Like Orpheus ascending from Hades or Ulysses chained to the mast or a runaway slave abandoning his family and fleeing toward the North Star, my brother knew the only way he might get what he desperately wanted was to turn his back on it, pretend it didn't exist.

Walking the line, leaning neither too far to the left nor too far to the right, balancing, always balancing the pulls of heart and head in one direction against the tugs wrenching him in the other—that was Robby's unbearable burden, made more unbearable because to escape it all he had to do was surrender, tilt one way or the other, and let the weight on his shoulders drag him down.

The source of my brother's strength was a mystery to me. When I put myself in his shoes, tried to imagine how I'd cope if I were sentenced to life imprisonment, I couldn't conceive of any place inside myself from which I could draw the courage and dignity he displayed. In prison Robby had achieved an inner calm, a degree of self-sufficiency and self-reliance never apparent when he was running the streets. I didn't know many people, inside or out, who carried themselves the way he did now. Like my mother, he'd grown accustomed to what was unbearable, had named it, tamed it. He'd fallen, but he'd found the strength to rise again. Inch by inch, hand over hand, he'd pulled himself up on a vine he'd never known was there, a vine still invisible to me. I knew the vine was real because I'd watched my brother grasp it, because I could feel its absence in the untested air when I thought of myself in his situation. To discover the source of my brother's strength I found myself comparing what I'd accomplished outside the walls with what he'd managed inside. The comparison made me uncomfortable.

I didn't envy my brother. I'd learned enough about the hell of prison life not to mistake what I was feeling for envy. No, I wouldn't trade my problems for his. I'd take my chances on the outside. Yet something like envy was stirring. Worse than envy. The ancient insatiability of ego kicking up. Why hadn't I ever been able to acknowledge a talent, success, or capacity in another person without feeling that person's accomplishment either diminished me or pointed to some crucial deficiency in my constitution? What compound of greed, insecurity, and anger forced me always to compare, compete? Why couldn't I just leave myself out of it and celebrate Robby's willpower, his grace under pressure? Why couldn't I simply applaud and be grateful for whatever transformation of self he'd performed? Were my visits to prison about freeing him or freeing myself from the doubt that perhaps, after all, in spite of it all, maybe my brother has done more with his life than I've done with mine. Maybe he's the better man and maybe the only way I can face that truth about him, about myself, is to demystify the secret of his survival. Maybe I'm inside West Pen to warm myself by his fire, to steal it. Perhaps in my heart of hearts or, better, my ego of egos, I don't really want to tear down the walls, but tear my brother down, bring him back to my level, to the soft, uncertain ground where my feet are planted.

If somebody has sung the praises of a book or movie, I go in looking for flaws, weaknesses. No matter how good these books or movies, my pleasure is never unalloyed because I'm searching for the bad parts, groping for them even when they're not there; so I usually come away satisfied by my dissatisfaction. I'm stuck with a belief that nothing can stand too close an examination. The times when I experience the world as joy, as song, some part of me insists even in the midst of the joy, the song, that these moments will pass and nothing, nothing promises they will ever come again. My world is fallen. It's best to be suspicious, not to trust anything, anyone too far. Including myself. Especially the treacherous, layered reality of being whatever I think I am at a given moment. It's a fallen world. My brother is rising from the ashes but because he is my brother, another fall is as certain as this rising and my particular burden is to see both always. I can't help it.

Does what he's achieved in the narrow confines of a cell mock the cage I call freedom? What would I do in his place? How would I act? Are the walls between us permanent? Do we need them, want them? Is there a better place without barred windows and steel doors and locked cells where there's room for both of us, all of us?

What it comes down to is saying yes. Yes to the blood making us brothers. Blood bonding us, constraining us to the unspoken faith that I'm trying to do my best and he's trying to do his best but nothing we do can insure the worst won't happen so we keep at it, as best we can, doing the book and hoping it will turn out okay.

He's been thinking a lot about the time on the road, the three months as a fugitive when he and his partners crisscrossed the country, playing hide and seek with the law. He's tried to write some of it down but he's been too busy. Too much's been happening. School. He'll graduate in January. A little ceremony for the few guys who made it all the way through the program. An associate degree in engineering technology and three certificates. Rough. Real rough. The math he'd never had in high school. The slow grind of study. Hours relearning to be a student. Learning to take the whole business seriously while you hear the madness of the prison constantly boiling outside your cell. But I'm gon get it, Bruh. Few more weeks. These last exams kicking my ass but I'm gon get it. Most the fellows dropped out. Only three of us completed the program. It'll look good on my record, too. But I ain't had time to do nothing else. Them books you sent. I really enjoy reading them but lately I ain't been doing nothing but studying.

· · ·

It's funny cause I really want to put some of the stuff about running on paper. Got it all right here in my head. I can see it, I can say it to myself but when I sit down with a piece of paper in front of me I can't write a word. Doesn't seem right. Don't know where to start. But I been thinking lots about it. Been over it in my mind and it won't be that hard to tell you. Maybe it's just being so busy. School. And my job in the hospital. And this new lady, man. She's really on my mind. What can I tell you? Like you mize well say I'm in love. Sounds funny, don't it? Being in here and talking about falling in love. Talking about loving some lady. It happens though. Even in this fucked-up place, even to your fucked-up brother.

Don't laugh. I see you trying not to laugh. Your baby brother, Rob, the ladies' man. I see what you're thinking. You know I always been innerested in the ladies. Love them to death. And they been liking me back, too. Ever since I was little. So what can I say? I can't change. And the ladies still be liking me so I'm subject to falling in love.

Losing Tanya had me real down. Down as I ever been in here. Took me a long time to get her to see she was beautiful. Had to keep telling her she was somebody special. Teach her to see what I already could see. Wrote her poems. Got her reading some the books I was into back then. She took a new name. Atiya. I could see it happening, see her growing stronger, and it made me happy. Ain't nothing never made me more happy. Like she started blooming. Coming out her shell. She really was a different person. For a long time Tia couldn't see what I saw. She been lied to so much she believed that blond-hair, blue-eyed shit. She look in the mirror couldn't see nothing but nappy hair, glasses, and ugly. Took a long time but Tia started changing, getting stronger. Seeing her change made me happy, but it worried me, too. I knew one day she wouldn't need me to lean on.

It had to happen. She'd see how good she was and then she'd have to go off on her own. You know what I mean? Try out her wings. I knew it. And I didn't want to stand in her way. But then I started losing her and I wasn't ready. Tore me up when things started to go bad between us. Visits wasn't so regular. Not answering my letters. Something missing when she did come to see me. Little ways she had of looking away, looking down. And when we be talking she didn't bring up stuff like she used to. All them plans we had. Like she forgot about em. Wasn't *us* and *we* and what *we* gon be doing together. She changed jobs. Was into seeing new people I didn't know. What we had wasn't going nowhere. Wasn't nowhere for it to go with me locked up in here. She knew that and I knew that. But we been through so much together neither of us could say out loud what we both be thinking. You know. Like the Gladys Knight and the Pips jam: "Neither One of Us Want to Be the First One to Say Good-bye." That's the way it was. Saw it coming a long way off. Wasn't no way it wasn't gon happen. Still, when it hit me, I wasn't ready. Couldn't handle it. Like a crazy man for a while.

Hey, Sister

I see you there behind your mask
    Of powder and your store-bought hair
I see a light that shines as a star
    That comes from over there
That place we were before we
    Came over here
I feel the warmth that still comes from you
    Though your emotions are freezing in white snow
Sister you can be a leader too
    Wipe away your false colors
Wear your Blackness Queen.

My Woman

My Woman, Woman of my soul
You are the essence of true love
I fall asleep at night searching for you
And awaken in the morning feeling
You were almost there

My Woman, Woman of my life
I long for the soft swell of your belly
The sweet aroma of your body
The warm press of your thighs
I long to sleep with you every night
Until life is nigh and re-creation is ours

My Woman, Woman of my heart
It is your love and trust
That makes me truly man
It is your love and devotion
That makes me the envy of every man

My Woman, Woman of my Blackness
You are the beginning of my family

The ending of loneliness and disillusion
I am you, you are me—together
WE ARE UNIVERSAL

Valentine's Greeting

. . . Loving you is not just once a year
Loving you is always knowing you're near
So I'll say this now and in every way
I give you all my love, this Valentine's day.

Atiya

You are me
You are the life of me
You are my guarantee for life
It is you who must preserve what I build

Protector of my haven
YOU
Overseer of my future
I pledge Love

My brown glow, my sunswept vision
Maker of my smiles, comforter of my frowns
You are my belief in forever
Forever is loving you for only a day

I found in you my reason for being black and a man
My golden lady with you I have realized my destined plan
Stay inside me pumpkin and together we
Will swell up and explode into new life
Let me stay inside you sunlight and I will
Protect our haven, your heart as long as
I breathe life.

Spirits

Call me louder, I still can't hear
Can't hear you say
'Husband come home'
I lay awake at night listening in the darkness
Call LOUDER

If I could hear you
I know I would come
My spirit running ahead of me
Jubilant at returning to its love haven
HOLLER

Say 'Husband come home'
Not with word
Words are meaningless tools
To the love spirit
We must holler both together
Our spirits will burst free and unite

Let's do it!
We can do it!
Try! Do it!
Do it
NOW
COME! HOME!

She was gone. I'd lost my Tia. My wife, my fine black woman. When it
hit me I just about went down for the count, Bruh. Shit. Talk about a
lonely, sorrowful dude. She was gone. And she was all I had. I mean
youall were still out there. Mom and you and the family. But that's different. That ain't the same as having your woman. She been with me
so long. We been through so much. The trial. Appeals. She been the
one standing by me every time I got disappointed. Every time the man
be telling me you ain't worth shit, ain't nothing about you worth saving,

Tia was there beside me, crying wit me. Wouldna made it without her. I owe her so much. Always will. Soon's I got my head together I couldn't stay mad with her. She did what she had to do. I knew all along the day would come when she'd believe me, when she'd believe in her own self and she'd have to try her own wings. So I ain't bitter now. But I was hurt. And mad, too, for a while. You know how you 'get. Your whole world starts to crumbling and seems like ain't nothing you can do but hit back.

I was crazy for a while. And they always watching you in here. Remember how Mom used to scare us into being good around Christmastime. You know how she always be saying Santa Claus is watching. He sees you doing wrong and he's not nice to bad little boys and girls. You remember? Got to be a real pain in the ass. That Jolly Ole St. Nicholas ass punk looking over your shoulder all the time, getting in your business. Sees you when you sleeping. Sees you when you wake. Better be good for goodness' sake. That's how it is here. They know when something's bothering you. When you're down. That's when they come round and fuck wit you. Play with your head. It's dangerous then. They can mess with your mind and, believe me, they will try. They're good at that shit. Put you in a world of trouble. Been round here long enough to see it happen to plenty other guys.

Don't take much to set somebody off when they down. See, you be hurting already. Don't be giving a fuck about nothing and you ready to climb the goddamn walls anyway and one them guards come over and say something. Don't have to be much. You ready to explode anyway so he don't have to say much. Just a word sometimes or that nasty cracker tone of voice will set somebody off and *Boom*. He's gone. He's messed up real good before he even knows what he done. Real heavy-duty trouble. Good time gone. Probation gone. Ninety days in the hole. Seen it happen to other guys so when I felt myself slipping, I started saying to myself just what I been saying to you. Watch out. Be careful. Don't let nobody see you down.

It was good. Real good between me and Tia. For both of us. She gave me everything a woman can give a man. Stuck by me seven long, hard years. She came down here to the joint when nobody else would. We helped each other. But then what had to happen happened, so wasn't no point in crying over spilled milk. Told myself, Don't be bitter. Talked to myself till I was blue in the face. It wasn't easy. I was hurt bad. But Tia was gone and that was that so I had to get my own shit together. Couldn't let them clowns see I was tore up. They'd start hanging round like vultures.

Wrote her a letter or two. Wrote one to you, I think, crying the blues. Finally I started to get it together. Stop feeling sorry for myself. I mean I could see the big picture. What I done for Tia. What she done for me. Why she had to go.

I'm still coming round. Ain't there yet but I'm getting my feet back on the ground. I started feeling glad almost. Feeling free. Like there were all these months we both knew something bad had to happen. Visits got to be something I didn't really look forward to. Too much pressure. The whole time I'm seeing her I'm kinda choked up and saying all kinds of bullshit but what I really need to say. Looking back now I know I said things to try to hurt Tia. Make her feel bad as I was feeling. Pushing her away cause I knew I was losing her anyway. Got to be a real drag. What we had was too good to end ugly, so when I finally could say to myself, *She's gone. It's over*, I felt kind of relieved; not glad, but free in a way to get on with whatever's coming next.

And next is this lady I think I'm in love wit. The one got my nose open I got to talk to you about. What time is it? I know you want to hear about the road but I got to talk to somebody bout this other thing. It's something else, Bruh. We got time, ain't we? We got another hour and fifteen minutes.

She's a pretty thing. Light-skinned like Mom, only she got green eyes. Big pretty green eyes, man. Built kind of slim. About medium height. Come up to bout here on me. Little taller than Judy. Kinda Judy's shape too, now I think about it. Slim but not too slim in the right places. Curly-headed. That kind of light brown almost reddish hair in a nice neat fro. Freckles on her face. A fox. Stone fox. She been pretty all her life but that been her downfall, too. She don't like being pretty no more. She been hurt behind it too much. She's all alone in the world. Orphan long as she can remember. Lived with some her people way back when she was a little girl. An aunt and uncle or something cause her mama dead and daddy long gone. That's all the family she remembers, that aunt and uncle or whoever they was, and she don't want to remember too much about them. She's just a little kid and the old dude, he spozed to be taking care of her. Well, you know, he start to getting after her. Messing with her. And the aunt she finds out. Locks Leslie in the closet like it was Leslie did wrong. Leslie don't like to talk about it but she been laying it out to me. Just a kid, nobody to turn to, and the old dude's after her and the aunt hates her. Locks her up. Burns her with a iron. She got the marks today. Can you see something like that? It's hard to believe after coming up like we did with nothing but love all around. Burning a kid cause some old, hard-leg nigger's messing wit her. Them people must been crazy, man. But that's the way it was. It's the hand Leslie got dealt.

Wherever she goes, the first thing happens is some man in the house after her drawers. Then the women hate her. She's out in the street again. Nobody to turn to. She been in foster homes and state homes and places like that all her life. I tease her, call her Little Orphan Annie sometimes, but it sure ain't no joke. When she first started telling me about her life she couldn't get out ten words before tears is running down her cheek. Told her, Stop. Ain't no need talking bout none that. But she said she ain't never told it to nobody and she wanted me to listen. She'd mop them green eyes and say, Listen. So I did. And it's stone ugly. One bad thing after another. You know like in a orphan home then a foster home then juvenile court. Black girls whip her ass cause she's white. White ones ganging her cause she's a nigger. Knocked up two or three times. She's so young she don't really know nothing bout taking care herself. Nobody ain't told her nothing. And the dudes don't give a fuck. They just coming on strong and sweet-talk and bullshit and you so sweet pretty baby next thing she know she pregnant. And she only thirteen or fourteen years old.

Just a matter of time till she's into dope and selling pussy and stealing. Still a juvenile so she don't do no heavy time. They put her away then she on the street again in a few months. Tried to make her a ward of the state and do cause she ain't got no people and nobody wants her, but she says it's better in the streets than in them state homes. People after her in the homes. Fine little green-eyed, white-skinned colored girl. Hey, now. Ima get me some of that. Same old shit inside or outside. Least on the outside she could make a little money. Have some freedom. So she's a runaway. Gets in more trouble behind that. Soon as she's eighteen, they can't hold her no more so she's out in the street. Been there ever since.

Met her when she come to visit one the brothers. She's living with the guy's old lady. Watches the kids and cooking and cleaning for rent.

She got a place to sleep and she's helping out cause Yusef's old lady working every day and somebody needs to take care the kids. Leslie ain't got no privacy or money or nothing but she's probably in the best situation she ever been in. Nobody after her. Playing mama to Yusef's kids.

She likes kids. Says she knows she spoils em but things been so rough for her when she was little she can't help it. Only thing was dope. She had to have it. She was stealing, doing a little light hustling to get dope money. Wasn't exactly a junkie but she was steady into getting high so it just a matter of time before she got busted or got hooked bad. Yusef's old lady knew about the dope. But Leslie's cool round the kids. She loves the kids and it's a good thing her being there while Yusef's in the joint so they ain't said nothing to Leslie. But Yusef knew and he's my man so he hipped me after I started hitting on Leslie. Didn't have to tell me nothing, really. Been round that shit long enough to know. Anyway she come with Yusef's old lady and his kids first time. Tia and me in the lounge, too. I pinned this fine chick over by the corner where the kids be playing. No doubt about it. She's checking me out. She's cool but I know she's scoping me. Paying attention to what I'm doing. How I carry myself. I goes over to Yusef to get a light. Curious, you know. Not a word but them green eyes steady telling me tales.

Didn't pay it no mind at first. Just feeling good cause this fine lady digging me. Then she sent a message. Yusef knows me and Tia having trouble. He seen the crying and arguing so he says Leslie wants to know if she could come and visit me sometime. Tia ain't been using half the visits and nobody else but Mom comes down here so I says, Yeah. Come on. That's how it started.

One thing led to another. Made up my mind to help her. First thing had to be getting her off that dope. Hipped her to my man Larry and he gave her some pills help get her straight. Then we started serious talking. Who she was. What she really wanted in life. How she could get it.

Told her she could do whatever she wanted to if she set her mind on it. See, fighting the dope was the first step. I told her how and helped her get the pills and she come through and did something she didn't think she could do. She starts to believing in me. Listening to me. But it's slow work. She been beat down. She ain't never thought about things the way I'm trying to make her think. And she ain't never met nobody like me. Somebody trying to help her. Somebody trying to do something for her and ain't shucking and jiving. Just telling her the truth. No bullshit. I wasn't asking for nothing in return. I'm in her corner and that's new to her. A man telling the truth. A man caring bout her. She needed that bad. Didn't know how much she needed it, how much she been missing it all her life till she met me and we started rapping.

Don't take long before we tight. Real tight. Chick woulda gone out and jumped off Highland Park bridge if I told her to. Yeah. She started depending on me. Leaning on me. And I'm steady rapping. Trying to set her on her own two feet. Believe in her own self. She come a long way. She's off dope and staying out the street but it's hard. No money. No time to herself, really. And she don't see no man but me. She's still hating men and hating herself for being pretty. It's a crying shame. A girl like that with so much going. She's smart, John. Smart as a whip. And good-looking. But she been in a bind since day one. She ain't but twenty now and she done been through hell. She was just about dead. A rotten life, man. Miserable. Makes me wonder. Why's anybody put on earth to live a life like that?

But Leslie got a chance now. Maybe she can start over. Ima do everything in my power to help her cause I'm digging her to death, Bruh. She wants to marry me.

■ ■ ■

Robby's smiling. Grinning at himself. He can barely believe what he's saying. His good luck. Fortune smiling on him so he can't help smiling back even though none of it makes any sense. He's a little embarrassed. After all, he's caged. His sentence is life. The bars are real. The romance he's describing has found a way around all that. He's tickled because he knows he shouldn't even entertain notions of love and marriage, let alone expect such goodies to actually fall in his lap. He's getting away with something and can't help grinning. Rob's amazed because something's happening that ain't spozed to happen. No way it's spozed to happen. Prisons are organized to prevent it. He's a man in love with a woman, being loved in return. The gates remain locked but for the moment he's holding the key in his hand.

■ ■ ■

Hope you can meet her. You'll dig Leslie. She's had it real rough but she's sweet. And shy. Been after her to go meet Mommy but she's scared. She been burned so much she's fraid of people. She thinks they take one look and know everything about her. Think she's nasty. That's why them guys could sweet-talk her. She's shamed of herself so she be needing people to say something nice. Then she try to be nice to them. Dudes just use her up and get a hat. She's ready to die then. Ain't nothing left.

But she got a chance now. We got a chance. One thing, though. What I wanted to talk to you about. I got this problem. See, Leslie thinks I'm coming out the joint in a year or so.

Yeah. She believes that. Yusef told her that bullshit before she visited me the first time. She asked him all kinda questions about me and well, you know . . . Yusef built me up. He's my man, but the cat's known to exaggerate. Tell big, fat lies is what I'm saying. Put me in a bind. Had to say to Leslie, Hold on, baby. Don't know what Yusef been laying on you but I'm just Robby. Ain't no superman or supercon or superstud or nothing like that. Just Robby.

But the part about my sentence. Didn't even know Yusef told her a lie about how long I got to be in here. We's talking one day and she's saying something about me finding a job and saving money and it don't sound right. What ain't right is she got me back on the street working in a year or so and ain't nothing like that in the cards. Six, seven years . . . Maybe. If everything goes alright. If I live that long. If they don't decide to take me off. So I know she's mixed up but I let it slide. Don't seem no big thing at the time. Just getting to know her and do and I don't want to scare the chick away, so shit. If she wants to believe I'll be outa here tomorrow, let her believe it.

I let it slide but then things start getting serious. I'm her man. Tia's out the picture now so ain't no sneaking round and shucking now. Leslie's the one and I'm her man. She's starting to count on me being with her on the outside real soon. Talking bout a year's a long time to wait but she can hold on. Then I try and tell her. Look here. Ain't nothing certain, babe. This is the slammer and it's mean in here. The man ain't gon turn me loose less he wants to. They got a million ways to keep me in here. Anything can happen is what I try to make her understand. Can do my time and get put in a trick and there's more time to do. Can't count on no year. Can't count on nothing.

Well, her face drops. Her lips is trembling and she's scared. She's scared and I'm just talking bout adding a year to the year she's figuring.

She commence to coming apart right there in front my eyes. Thought she'd come a long way but she was ready to lose it all in a minute.

Ain't never seen nobody change that quick. The dope, the hustling, all them bad times back in her eyes like she's looking at a ghost or something. She can't take it. She's still too weak. Everything I been building up starts to crumbling right there in front my face, man. I got scared. Didn't say no more about time. Neither one of us can talk. She don't look at me for a couple minutes. We just sitting on one these funky benches like two dummies till she get herself together. She looks me dead in the eye then. Looks through me to my heart. She's a little girl again. Says, Robby I love you. Says, I'll wait. Two years if it gotta be two. They can't keep you from me forever. If they keep you in here past your time, I'll wait.

Now I'm just about dying. I know I got to tell this lady exactly where it's at. But I can't. Can't do it to her. Yusef done fed her a fat, juicy lie and it's wrong but I just can't hurt her no more. She ain't ready.

Brought the whole thing up another time. It just kept worrying me. Messing wit my sleep and everything else. Bothering me cause here I was playing with her just like all them other dudes. Wasn't no way Ima be out the joint in no one or two or three or Lord knows how many years. Had to tell her that cause that was the stone truth. Had to be straight wit her or I was just gon hurt her again like all them other guys. She was depending on me to tell her the truth.

Anyway, I tried another time to bring it up. You know. Tipping up real easy on the whole bit. Spoze this and spoze that . . . spoze you had to wait ten years, twenty years. How you think people handle ten years? Plenty guys in here doing big time like that. Just spozing. Just something to rap about. Like I was curious about how a guy's old lady keep coming back to this place five, ten years. Wondering how they do it. Cause some do. You know. Just questions-in-my-mind kind of thing so she don't panic.

Just spozing—but she don't want to hear it. In no way, shape, or form. She said it's too terrible to think about. Why'd I even want to talk about something so terrible? She said she knew what she'd do. She said she'd kill herself if they took away the man she loved.

She started getting trembly again but when she said she'd kill herself she meant it. She been hurt bad. She been beat down but Leslie got a hard streak. Got to have one or she wouldn't be alive today. She did what she had to do. She been in places and into things I don't know if I coulda handled. And I'm a grown man. And she was just a kid. So she got something sure nuff hard inside. She don't play. Soft and sweet but she can get down when it's gittin-down time. When she said she'd kill herself, that's just what she meant. She tried it a couple times before. Wasn't her fault she ain't dead. Hard and soft. A strange lady, Bruh. A whole lot to her. But I knew she wasn't ready to find out I got a life sentence. She can't deal with it. And I ain't been able to deal wit telling her.

So it gets worse every day. Harder. We more and more in love but that thing's between us getting deeper and deeper. I can't hurt her. Can't watch her coming apart again. She might leave here and do something crazy and I can't handle that. I'm in a bind. Damned if I do. Damned if I don't. I been needing somebody to talk to bout this stuff. It's messing wit my sleep, my studies. I know I got to tell her. Swear to myself I'll tell her next time she comes. Then she's sitting beside me looking good and I just can't do it. Like I got iron on my tongue. Then I try to write a letter, but the pencil just sits there in my hand. Keep seeing her face and thinking how good she makes me feel and I'm scared of losing her. Cause I love that lady and she loves me and I'm scared of hurting her but I'm more scared of losing her, so I don't say nothing.

She's depending on me for the truth. That's what makes it so bad. Makes me just like them jive dudes she been dealing wit all her life. The ones been hurting her. Spozed to be her man and saving her and getting her straight but I'm lying to her. I know it but I can't do nothing about it.

• • •

What can I say to my brother? Yes. I know exactly where you're coming from. Matter of fact I was in the same place recently. Dealing with the same dilemma. Living a lie. Damned if I came clean, damned if I didn't. Should I tell him I failed Judy more drastically than he's failing Leslie? Say, Yes. I understand because I'm in love but I've also tainted the waters. I've hurt my woman doubly by doing wrong then holding back the truth. My betrayal was worse than my brother's because I initiated the deceit, the lies. I didn't get trapped by somebody else's lie. I was responsible for the whole, rotten mess. Nobody to blame but myself when I saw in Judy's eyes the depths of the trust I had violated, the depth of the pain that would fill her eyes if I told her the truth.

Judy had counted on me, not leaning like your Leslie but just as vulnerable in her own way. Judy's been lucky. Loved and supported all her life. Born into a financially secure family. She's gifted with the good looks and intelligence you've discovered in your woman, and Judy's white in the only way that matters in our America, certified white through and through so she's never had to face the horrors Leslie's white exterior brought down on her. Judy stands on her own two feet. Part of the beauty of living with her has been my gradual, inch-by-inch recognition—with years sometimes between the inches—of who she is, of her need to be who she is in tandem rather than behind or above or below what I am. But none of that helped. The rug can be pulled out from under two feet as easily as one and Judy's had less practice than Leslie at falling.

I could say to Robby: Yes. We're brothers sure enough. And I do say: Tell Leslie the truth. Right away. Don't let it slide a day longer. Things only get more complicated the longer you wait. Nothing gets better. Time passes and you can get busy with something, you can distract yourself and pretend things will sort themselves out, but that's bullshit. All you insure by putting off the moment when you tell the truth, the whole truth, is that things will get worse. The hurt you inflict deepens. Your inner turmoil grows more disruptive, bitter. Waiting opens the possibility of losing control, of allowing what you won't disclose to come to light in another fashion. And that's fatal. You lose once and for all the small consolation that a voluntary confession might have brought. You're a thief caught in the act and nothing you say can change that.

I let Robby know I'm speaking from experience and that's why I'm preaching at him. I'm telling him to act in a way I didn't. I didn't confess. I got caught cheating. So I'm a witness. I can authenticate the terrible cost of holding back the truth by describing the chaos of my life, the troubles I must return to when I pass out of the prison walls. Procrastinating, rationalizing, letting things sort themselves out, waiting for a mythical "right time" when telling the truth won't exact too awful a price—that had been my way. And the shit had sure nuff hit the fan.

Brothers. Robby says he knows I'm right. He says he's come to the same conclusions and knows what he should do but he just can't quite bring himself to say what has to be said to his woman.

I needed to talk to somebody, man. Needed to hear somebody say the things I been saying to myself all along. I know you're right, Bruh. And I'm sorry you having trouble at home. I hear you talking and I know what's right.

But if she did something bad to herself. If I lost her, man . . .

We can't get any further. It's a familiar place. A treacherous convergence of selfishness and caring for another and ego and wanting to be bigger, better than you are and valuing the truth and profiting from untruth and wishing for the best and dreading the worst; a welter of conflicting emotions, a nexus of irresolution and despair, of self-pity and self-disgust, desire and guilt. A place immediately recognized. A hard place because you can't go forward and you can't back off. It's hard and familiar because I've been there before. I realize this predicament has something to do with who I am and how I live, choices made long ago. My limits are clearly reflected by the nature of the dilemma. Like here is my arm and it's such-and-such a length and it's my arm and always will be the length it is and that shelf I've never been able to reach will continue to elude me. No point in straining nor complaining. I'm never going to get at whatever it is up there on that shelf I can't reach. No ladder in the world will lift me one inch closer.

We walk to the vending machines. Feels good to stretch. Time goes fast when my brother and I talk. I forget how long I've been sitting listening, till I rise out of my seat. My body moans, Whoa. Take it easy now. Easy, easy does it. Much cracking of joints, muscles creaking, and joints popping—a clatter I think everybody within ten feet must hear. Even when I was in super shape playing college basketball, my muscles were stiff as boards before and after practice. It's always taken me a long time to limber up. Lots of days touching my toes without bending my knees is out of the question. An aging jock's hobble stylizes my first three or four steps up and away from a chair if I've been sitting any length of time.

The rule is only visitors may drop coins into the vending machines. Money may not be passed to a prisoner; visitors must take the prisoner's order, pull the knobs, and push the buttons, while the prisoner stands aside like a bewildered child or a mental defective. If the rules didn't make the process so blatantly humiliating, I think Robby might eat and drink more. As it is, he usually asks for a soft drink, sometimes an apple. Except when the kids come and then it's a party. They compete for quarters and the chance to buy Robby junk food so they can gobble it with him. When it's a game like that, Robby orders everything and the kids troop back and forth to the machines till the coins give out or the squabbling gets too loud or one of the adults gets tired of the traffic and hisses, Sit down, youall, that's enough.

Once or twice Robby's broken the rule. Taken change from me, inserted it, extracted the selection all by himself. Today, with the guard already in our face about the table and the history of ugliness between him and Robby, I do the purchasing while my brother stands by, the image of dependency and helplessness. The situation's awkward for both of us. What should Robby do with his hands while I manipulate the machine for him? How should he reach for the paper cup of orange soda? What should he say when I pass it to him? Are the few swallows of sweet, bubbly orange yuck worth all the trouble? I tell Rob to watch me closely so one day when he grows up he can work the machine on his own. He shakes his head, attempts to smile, but it's sickly sweet as the pop. He's just trying to be nice to me. Joking doesn't take away the sting, make this business any less of a slap in the face. But he appreciates the fact that I try. It lets him know I know what's happening and we cross the lounge back to our seats.

The room's crowded now and noisier. I try to ignore other visitors, grant them the privacy I'm seeking with my brother when we sit down again on the little bit of turf we've claimed: two vinyl-cushioned seats with a low, eighteen-inch-square table between us. Some prisoners and their guests form huddles, some couples cling as long and hard as the rules allow, other groups sit three or four in a row, eyes front as if they're staring at a movie on the far wall. Their lips move but what they say is lost in the general din unless your face is a foot from theirs. In this coffin-shaped room filled with chairs and benches, there's no place to hide. People position themselves in various ways to steal a little privacy but nothing shuts out the strangers crowded into this space we all must share.

Many more black faces than white. Most prisoners and the majority of their visitors appear to be under thirty. Lots of little kids. From time to time explosions of noise. A prisoner yells across the room for a cigarette or to greet another prisoner's familiar guests. A racket of hand slapping, exclamations of surprise, happiness and *Oh, my God* when someone spots a person he or she had never expected to find in this place.

Prisoners wear sky-blue tunics and string-tied trousers a darker shade of blue. Most are extremely fit. Lean, muscular, the pared-down, honed bodies of athletes beneath their baggy uniforms. Robby does one thousand push-ups daily in his cell. Took him six months to work up to the magic number. He also runs five or six miles a day in the prison yard. Staying in shape is more than recreation. It's a necessity for survival. He's told me I'm his measuring rod. Since I'm ten years older than Robby, he derives a little comfort from the fact that I still play basketball. He can imagine himself ten years down the road. If he stays in shape until he gets out, even if it's not for another seven or eight years, he can at least look forward to having something left of his body. He sounds almost grateful when he says, You're holding up pretty good. You don't look that old and you're forty-one, right? Ten years before I'm that old. Maybe it won't be so bad. He's teasing too. Makes it clear he appreciates the odds I'm fighting. An old guy trying to sustain a young man's body. Well, he lets me know I'm doing alright. For an old dude.

Robby's played lots of basketball since he's been in prison. Gotten serious about it. Serious enough to break his nose and strain ligaments and be confined to a wheelchair last spring. He has a ballplayer's long feet and hands. When he was a kid I tried a couple times to teach him a little bit about the game. He possessed all the requisite natural talent. Quickness, good spring in his legs, coordination, foot speed. On the other hand, he had no inclination to learn the basics, no desire to invest time and energy improving his skills. He played occasionally but didn't have an accurate shot or a sense of the total game. Basketball for him was half-court playground messing around, but every now and then he'd expose hints of unusual ability: a rebound snapped down from rim level, two or three breakaway strides carrying him past everybody else, a twisting, turning off-balance move to the hoop and a shot ricocheting off the board that shouldn't go in but does. Never could get Rob to concentrate on fundamentals because his mind was on those games you play with people who have soft legs. I wonder how well he plays now. If he's gotten his game together enough to compete on playground courts like Mellon Park where the real devils hang out.

Playing basketball together, walking together along an ocean beach under a clear blue sky, a hot sun, waves pounding, not a soul in sight for miles. We must have done these things before because they're sharply etched on my senses. The slap of the ball on concrete, the good sweat oiling face and arms, people sitting along the cyclone fence signifying, the rattle of the whole backboard shaking when somebody jams, salt taste on my lips, surf boiling, seamless blue arching over everything.

I'd never spoken to my brother about walking along a beach or playing ball together. It would be too painful. I'd have to admit they weren't scenes recalled from a life we'd shared in some better, cleaner world. I couldn't spell out the reality of these moments without also revealing the yearning, the aching sense of loss that permeated them.

Robby's son, Omar, inherited his Daddy's long feet and hands. My brother's first marriage, the one that produced Omar, seems to have occurred several lifetimes ago. A healthy, handsome son, a good, loving wife, the sort of family unit and simple, everyday life Robby dreams of now, were once within his grasp. But it all came too soon. He wasn't ready. He blew it. Not alone, of course. Society cooperated. Robby's chance for a normal life was as illusory as most citizens' chances to be elected to office or run a corporation. If "normal" implies a decent job, an opportunity to receive at least minimal pay-off for years of drudgery, delayed gratification, then for Robby and 75 percent of young black males growing up in the 1960s, "normal" was the exception rather than the rule. Robby was smart enough to see there was no light at the end of the long tunnel of hard work (if and when you could get it) and respectability. He was stubborn, aggressive, and prickly enough not to allow anyone to bully him into the tunnel. He chose the bright lights winking right in front of his face, just beyond his fingertips. For him and most of his buddies, "normal" was poverty, drugs, street crime, Vietnam, or prison.

I'd promised to bring Omar on one of my visits. Robby's first wife, Geraldine, had remarried. Robby was part of an ugly past Geraldine would just as soon forget and have Omar forget as well. Robby hadn't been there when she needed him. She'd struggled to make ends meet for her and her child. She was in no mood to share Omar now, just because Robby claimed to need him. And there was the problem of Omar's relationship to his new father, the split allegiance and fuzzy lines of authority, the shadow over Om's new life cast by the man in prison who was also his daddy. Understandably, Geraldine wanted to minimize potential trouble, protect her new life. She'd have to be convinced Om was ready and Robby was ready, so getting Omar to visit the prison was a complicated business. I hadn't yet made good on my promise and felt guilty, and promised again, after I finished telling my brother all the news of his son, to try to bring Omar next time.

I didn't tell Robby it wasn't so much a question of running up against complications as it was my failure to keep in mind the urgency of his request. I didn't forget my brother's need to see his son. A more embracing, profound forgetfulness was involved. A forgetfulness that had operated for years. In order to live with myself and manage my life in the intervals between visits I had learned to shut my brother out of my mind. I could deal with his plight only by brutal compartmentalization. I allowed the prison walls to perform their duty. Life goes on. . . . Shubby do. Shubby do. Mine couldn't if I brought the prison world back out into the streets with me. I forced myself to forget, become as deaf and dumb as the blocks of stone walling him away.

It was a trick I'd learned early on. A survival mechanism as old as slavery. If you're born black in America you must quickly teach yourself to recognize the invisible barriers disciplining the space in which you may move. This seventh sense you must activate is imperative for survival and sanity. Nothing is what it seems. You must always take second readings, decode appearances, pick out the obstructions erected to keep you in your place. Then work around them. What begins as a pragmatic reaction to race prejudice gradually acquires the force of an instinctive response. A special way of seeing becomes second nature. You ignore the visible landscape. It has nothing to do with you; it will never change, so you learn a kind of systematic skepticism, a stoicism, and, if you're lucky, ironic detachment. I can't get to the mountain and the mountain ain't hardly coming to me no matter how long I sit here and holler, so mize well do what I got to do right here on level ground and leave the mountain to them folks think they own it.

You chop your world into manageable segments. You segregate yourself within the safety zones white people have not littered with barricades and land mines. Compartmentalization begins with your black skin, with your acknowledgment of racial identity, and becomes both a way of seeing and being seen. Blackness is a retreat to the security of primal night. Blackness connects me with my brother but also separates us absolutely, each one alert, trembling behind the vulnerable wall of our dark skins.

Gradually, I'm teaching myself to decompartmentalize. This book is part of the unlearning of my first response to my brother's imprisonment. In spite of good intentions, I constantly backslide. In large matters, like arranging for Omar to accompany me on a visit, or small, neglecting to relay somebody's greeting to my brother or a hello from Robby to some friend on the outside, I'll revert to my old ways. My oversights embarrass me, shake me up, because I'm reminded that in crucial ways my brother still doesn't exist for me in the intervals between visits. The walls become higher, thicker, unbreachable when I allow myself to be part of the conspiracy.

When you're in the prison visiting lounge, you never know who you might run into. It's like returning to Homewood. I'd been away from my old neighborhood over twenty years, beginning in 1959 when I left Pittsburgh to play basketball at the University of Pennsylvania in Philadelphia. Since then Homewood has been a place to visit, with visits sometimes separated by years. The visits have been more regular lately, a day or two at a time twice a year, usually at my mother's house, visits taken up with family business and family socializing; so I'd lost touch with high school friends, the people in the neighborhood where I'd grown up. My parents had twice moved to other sections of Pittsburgh—East Liberty, Shadyside—before they finally separated, so my only constant link to Homewood has been my grandmother's house on Finance Street.

I'd never called my grandmother, Freeda French, anything but "Freed." The house on Finance was always known by the kids in the family as "Freed's." Finance Street parallels the railroad tracks that form the southern boundary of Homewood. I'd logged many hours on my knees, leaning on the backrest of Freed's overstuffed couch in front of the living-room window, gazing up the hillside at the trains passing through the sky of Homewood. Following the railroad tracks to Homewood Avenue would take me to Westinghouse Park, where there were swings, trees, open green space, and later a swimming pool, basketball courts, a ball field, and girls. I learned to daydream through Freed's big window. Learned to play basketball during summers on the tiny, enclosed cement court adjacent to the pool I was never allowed to go swimming in because my mother believed people caught TB from the questionable water.

Walking down a Homewood street or more likely riding through in a car, I had the habit of looking for people I knew. Faces I'd think I recognized usually turned out to be somebody else. Faces just *seemed* familiar. On closer inspection, after the obligatory wave and the mutual checking out, I'd have to admit it wasn't Reggie or Punkin Mallory or Brother Allen or Bobbi Jackson. Took me years to figure out what I was doing wrong. When I'd take my wife and kids to Freed's, I was looking for the Homewood I'd left twenty years before. Vaguely familiar faces I'd glimpse in the streets probably belonged to the sons and daughters of my old crowd. All along I'd been skipping a generation, acting as if time stood still in Homewood.

My grandmother's been dead ten years but when we exit the parkway and turn onto Braddock Avenue, and Braddock intersects Finance just after the low train bridge, I think: Freed's, and she's sitting in her rocker beside the mantelpiece, her glasses slipped down to the wings of her nose, her long, bony fingers worrying an edge of the sweater draping her thin shoulders. Loose wisps of gray escape the neat thickness of her hair, parted in the middle and piled atop her head. She'll sound as if she's beginning to cry when she says *Spanky*, the old nickname she's never stopped calling me. The first time she sighs *Spanky* is when the journey of three hundred miles from Philadelphia or seven hundred miles from Iowa City or three thousand miles across an ocean really ends, when I'm really home again. I can't wait to see her, to see the smile break across her features and hear what first sounded like crying become crinkly laughter. She'll seem frighteningly old and distant behind the blank moons of her glasses, till I find her eyes. I anticipate the cold bump of the metal rims against my cheek when I bend down to kiss her. Memories of time collapsing, of being a kid at the window, of running away to play college ball, of losing Homewood and finding it again race through my mind in the instant it takes to locate the bent Finance Street sign out the car window. I tell myself: Don't turn here. Keep straight on Braddock to the traffic lights on Bennett. Freed's not here anymore.

The prison lounge is like returning to Homewood because you never know who you'll see, who will pop up and in what disguise. Like Homewood because you must teach yourself to read faces, decipher them, keep in mind how long you've been away. You must remember that the present moment is a tightrope you're negotiating and an unexpected face can terminate your act abruptly. You lose the illusion that *now* is anything more than the thinnest strand stretched over the immensity of what you were and always must be.

In the visiting lounge two or three years ago I'd asked Robby who that guy was. The old white guy over there with the priest.

That's Murphy, man.

Does he have a nickname? Does anybody call him Reds?

Don't nobody like him or talk that much to him. Might be Reds for all I know. He's Murphy to me. Used to be a cop. Lucky ain't nobody killed him. Cops ain't too popular in the joint. You know what I mean. Lotta guys in here love to get they hands on a cop. Wouldn't think no more of offing a cop than stepping on a roach. Once a cop, always a cop. All of em snitches. But old Murphy been here a long time. Don't nobody bother him much no more. He's just another con now.

It had to be Reds. The elongated, pale face. Big hands. His thick body softer now, going to fat, but that aggressive forward hunch still in his shoulders. *Tyrannosaurus rex.* Arms short for his body, hanging limp but bent at the elbows, coiled, ready to receive a pass or snap into position for a two-hand set shot.

Reds was nearly bald except for a few strands of thin, reddish hair combed back over the steep crown of his skull. Like my grandmother, Reds had called me Spanky, my Homewood name. He had played highschool ball against Maurice Stokes and Ed Fleming, legendary Homewood heroes who'd gone on from Westinghouse High to college, then the NBA. To hear Reds tell it, he was better than both of them. They were good, strong kids, but raw. He could shoot and pass rings around them. His team won every match against Westinghouse when Reds was big gun at Central Catholic.

Real shootouts when the public school champs played the Catholic league winners for the city title. Stokes and Fleming were tough, real tough, but Reds didn't mind admitting he was the best. If he'd gotten a chance at college ball like they did, no telling how far he'd have gone. But it wasn't in the cards.

Reds was one of the kings of the playground, an aging king but still on top when at thirteen or so I first had ventured away from my home court—a single wooden backboard on a pole in Liberty Elementary School's dirt left field—to Mellon Park, where good players from all over the city congregated. For some reason Reds liked me. Maybe he remembered me, even younger, watching the games in Westinghouse Park. I remembered him. He was one of the few white players there, and maybe I reminded him of those summer days in Homewood, of the wide-eyed peanut gallery that always gathered to watch the big guys play. Whatever, he took me under his wing. Made sure I got a chance to play every now and then in less high-powered Mellon games. He also guaranteed my safe passage through the white neighborhoods I had to cross walking to and from Mellon Park. *Spanky's okay. He's a good kid.* That was all Reds had to say.

Reds wasn't a cop then. He drove a bread truck for National Biscuit Company. Coincidentally, Nabisco sponsored my favorite radio show: "Straight Arrow." I'd always identified with Indians more than cowboys, and the song that began each "Straight Arrow" episode—

> *. . . N - A - B - I - S - C - O*
> *Nabisco is the name to know*
> *For a breakfast you can't beat*
> *Eat Nabisco shredded wheat. . . .*

—was a magic formula that transmogrified me into one of my Indian heroes.

Not that the white kids in the neighborhoods bordering Mellon Park posed any actual danger to life or limb. More a matter of harassment. Nigger this and nigger that and maybe a stone or two at your feet kicking dust off the asphalt, or a gang of six or seven kids with nothing better to do than block the sidewalk so I'd have to go around them and worry for the next fifty yards or so whether they'd decide to chase me or not.

Reds looked out for me. Then, over the years, as I grew bigger and stronger, Reds gradually became less of a fixture at Mellon. His skills declined. The deadly two-hand, over-the-head set shot that began when he slid one foot behind the other, stopped being automatic. His leaning jumper, which had always looked awkward because it was propelled with two hands like his set shot, dated Reds. Young skywalkers grinned and swatted it back in his face.

When Reds sprinted or touched down after the jumper, you could hear coins crashing in the deep front pockets of his chinos. The jingle-jangle was out of place; Reds sounded as if he didn't belong on the court, as if he were just passing through on his way to work. I remember wondering why he always carried pocketfuls of change, remember the shock of seeing his pale white thighs when he turned up one scorching Sunday afternoon in Bermuda shorts.

As a new generation of ballplayers—blacks from Homewood, East Liberty, and the Hill, whites from Point Breeze, Morningside, and the suburbs—rose up, I battled them on even terms. My rep was established and I didn't need Reds or anybody else. Reds would show up occasionally, a faded star in the background still spinning stories about the time he outscored Stokes and Fleming combined. He took his turn with everybody else rehearsing his glory days and drinking sweet wine in the weeds behind the cyclone fence that surrounded the court. Reds wasn't a wino; but winos, hangers-on, and players sitting in the shade waiting for winners—when you could find shade at Mellon—were his audience.

I always greeted Reds, but as I became a king in my own right, we had less and less to say to each other. I began avoiding him when I could. He'd embarrass me, the way he'd holler Spanky. I didn't like it, but let it slide. Reds was Reds and always would be. To him I'd always be Spanky, always be a kid who needed his running commentary on passes I should have made and shots I shouldn't have taken.

Playing Big Five and Ivy League ball in Penn's Palestra kept me busy and sometimes happy. But college basketball lacked the spontaneity, the free-form improvisation and electricity of the playground game. Remember the early sixties before Texas Western's all-black five defeated Adolph Rupp's lily-white Kentuckians. Most coaches designed offenses more suitable for corn-fed, Big Ten linemen than for the high-flying whippets and greyhounds the city game was beginning to breed. "Playground move" was synonymous with bad move. Not *bad* move, but something undisciplined, selfish, possibly immoral. Twenty years later, coaches are attempting to systematize and teach the essence of the game invented on the playgrounds.

At Penn I became a better player, but I paid a steep price for that and other cultural improvements. Teachers, coaches, nearly everyone important in the white university environment, urged me to bury my past. I learned to stake too much of who I was on what I would become, lived for the day I could look back, look down on Reds and everybody else in Mellon Park, in Homewood.

If Reds was around Mellon when I returned home from college to play during summer vacations, I can't recall. On the court I wouldn't have answered to Spanky. That I do know. I resented any reference to my punkhood when I had to be protected from punks. The past was incriminating. The past was skinny legs, a silly nickname, a pickaninny potbelly that wouldn't go away till I was fifteen.

Yet Mellon Park continued to be a special place in my imagination. When I balked at the regimen, the monotony, the blue-collar ethic of practice, practice, practice, the prospect of beating Princeton or Yale was seldom incentive enough to inspire more effort. To keep hustling in practice and school, I'd imagine how lame I'd sound trying to explain to the older guys from the playground—men like Delton and Smitty, Reds and Rudy and George Brown—why I blew the chance they never had. I'd anticipate the golden summers at Mellon, the chance to show off my new skills and prove I hadn't forgotten the old ones, the only ones that mattered in my heart of hearts.

Mellon remains a magnet on summer weekends for Pittsburgh's high school, college, pro and playground royalty. The court's run down now. Scarred backboards, rims bent and loose, two cracks in the asphalt just beyond one foul line so driving down the lane is like walking up steps. Neglected, going to seed, the buckling, gray rectangle is a microcosm of the potholed city. Tradition and location conspire to preserve Mellon's uniqueness. Over the years Pittsburgh's best have always played at Mellon. And since the park's not really in anybody's neighborhood it's a no-man's land, the perfect place for a battlefield, one of the only inner-city basketball courts where white and black players confront one another.

At Mellon a few summers ago I learned what it felt like to be a ghost. A bunch of older guys (I had ten or fifteen years on most of them) were waiting for winners and reminiscing about Mellon's good ole days. I listened to them talk about this dude went to Peabody High. He was bad, yeah. Played in college. Won some kind of scholarship or something. Had a nice game. What was his name? I said my name, and one or two nodded. Yeah . . . yeah. That's the dude. He could shoot the ball.

When Robby had said Reds was a cop, a memory had been tripped, but I couldn't contextualize it. Maybe I was creating it after the fact, but I saw Reds in his city cop uniform, two-tone blue like the prisoners wear. He sports shiny boots, a Sam Brown belt across his chest, a holster and cartridge belt slung gunfighter-low on his hip. The leather squeaks. It's Reds's face under the polished black visor of the cap but somehow different, ominous, even though he's smiling and basking in all the attention his uniform gets, out of place in Mellon Park.

I was trying to explain Reds to my brother. The problem was, I wasn't sure myself. Years and years since I'd thought of Reds in any connection, then suddenly there he was across the visitors' lounge, his long torso and big head, the bow of his belly, his hands still poised and ready for a pass.

What's he in for?

Chopped his wife up in little pieces.

He used to look out for me at Mellon.

Say he caught her with another dude. Went crazy and wasted his old lady.

Reds passed by later. He shook my hand. *Spanky*. Nodded at my brother. An incredulous look, a few mumbled words; but he was remembering everything, and everything was too much. Neither of us wanted to linger, or to deal with it, so off he went again with the priest and an older woman, his sister, mother, cousin, whoever.

Robby told me during a subsequent visit that Reds had bragged about how tight he was with the Widemans. And Widemans included my brother, so Reds figured he had gained an in with the black guys among whom Robby was a leader. Reds traded on that association, boasting, carrying himself a little taller, straighter, bumming cigarettes till he carried it a bit too far, got too familiar, and Robby had to tell him cool it. A strange sort of payback, a false neatness rounding off my relationship to Reds. For a month or two, I had been Reds's safe passage through one black corner of Western Penitentiary.

So you never know who will pop up. Where a name, a face will take you. How much of your unguarded, unexposed, unused past you'll suddenly have to make sense of.

When I lay in my cell hurting, swept with a grief that after years of this tormented existence has turned to melancholy, I look at the wall and the shadow from the light coming in between the bars on my door, and it wiggles and ripples along with the flow of the river that passes outside the walls of my tomb. It hurts most on spring and summer nights after seeing Leslie and still having the warmth and smell of her body on my mind. At times like these the life rhythm of the river's ripple in the wall's shadow brings a burning in my eyes and the taste of salt on my cheeks.

I'd asked Robby to write out a schedule of a typical day, an hour-by-hour log that would familiarize me with the prison routine. At what hour did the prisoners' day begin? When were mealtimes, work times, free periods in the yard? Was it like high school? Did bells or P.A. announcements punctuate the prison day? Were all lights in the range extinguished at a certain hour or were prisoners allowed reading privileges in their cells? I needed that kind of concrete, mundane information so I could walk through a day with Robby on paper. He hadn't forgotten about my request, but he hadn't gotten around to it yet either.

. . .

I started it, man. Won't be hard to do. But what with school and work and everything, I just can't seem to get nothing done. I got the time, in a way. That's all I do got in here is time. But it's funny. You know. Like you'd think you could get a whole lot done in the joint. Time's what you got, like I say. Tons of time. Time on top of time. You wake up in the morning and you think about the fact the day's just starting and you got to get through the whole thing, you got all them hours and hours till you drop off to sleep. Damn. It makes mornings miserable. People's evil in the morning. Like you open your eyes and *boom*. The whole bag of shit slams down on your shoulders. You in the joint. It's another day just like the last miserable day and you still in the joint and ain't nothing you can do about it. Not today. Not tomorrow.

But you ain't really got no time be worrying bout tomorrow when you wake up in the morning. See cause you got today staring you in the face and today's a bitch. Like what the fuck am I doing in here? Why me? How the hell Ima make it through all them hours till I'm sleep again?

Don't nobody say nothing in the mornings. Everybody stone evil. Look at a dude cross-ways he's liable to flip out. Try and kill you wit a spoon. During breakfast cats be staring down in they bowls. Like if they could get down in there with the shit that's where they'd be. Even the guards don't fuck wit nobody in the morning. Half the time I don't know what I be eating. I'd skip breakfast if I was allowed. Food's nasty. Niggers be evil and funky. A new day's starting and nobody don't like it. Nobod; don't want to be here. It's real quiet in the mess hall but everybody screaming inside. That's how it is. Sometime it be noon before I'm ready to talk to anybody. Hear the goddamn bell first thing in the morning, I want to die. Want to turn over and go back to sleep and stay sleep.

You got time but you can't do nothing wit it. I mean there's twenty-four hours to a day in here just like out in the world. You ain't booked up or nothing for most of them so you'd think you could take care of business, but ain't hardly no business gets taken care of in the joint.

Cause it ain't really your time. Don't know how many evenings I sat down to write you or write somebody else and there ain't nothing to say. Can't write word one. It ain't like I ain't got time. I be itching to write all day. Writing letters in my mind while I'm doing other stuff. Can't wait to get back to my cell so I can write this hot letter but then I'm by myself and I sit down and ain't nothing to say. Ain't nothing worth saying cause ain't nothing happening, really. That's why it's good when you ask me a question or ask me to write about something specific. Sometimes that helps me get started.

Maybe it got something to do with being lonely. Being so fucked up inside you never feel like doing nothing. Being lonely's one the worst things about the joint. Probably *the* worst. Always a lot of fools and crazy people surrounding you so you ain't never alone but you always lonely. Longer I spend in here, the more I back away. Even back away from hangout time with the fellas on the range. I got to find my own space. Even if it's tiny. See, in your cell you ain't got nobody else to worry about but your ownself. It's one of the few safe places in here. Course people been offed in they cells. Ain't no place really safe, but least you can be alone, be in your cell with your own stink and your own little bit of stuff and your own thoughts and do. Cause outside your cell ain't nothing going on but the same ole shit. That's what gets to you after a while. Repetition. Same ole, same ole all the time. Same bullshit on the hangout corner. Same slop at breakfast. Same nasty guards. One day just like the other. Same simple cats doing the same dumb numbers. Day in and day out, every day. It gets to you. It surely does.

Longer you're in jail, the more you realize ain't nothing happening. Just the same ole foolishness every day. Junkies trying to get over, wolves chasing pussy, punks shaking they ass, gorillas beating on people, the guards writing people up cause the guards is mean and ain't got nothing better to do. See, it's all just games. People playing the same ole jive games and after a while you just get sick of it. You seen it all before so you start to backing away. Don't want to be round nobody.

That's about where I'm at. Like a hermit most the time. Do my job at the hospital then I want to get back to my cell. Got my schoolwork. Got my own thoughts to think. Guys say, Hey, Faruq. Where you been, man? Ain't seen you for days. But I don't want none of it. Naw, man. Everything's cool. You go on without me, man. I seen it all too many times before. Same bullshit. Same lies. Same games these fools be running on one another. It don't have nothing to do wit me no more. This ain't gon sound right but I'm telling you anyway. When I can be alone, the loneliness ain't so bad.

Your brother's becoming a hermit. Me. The one they used to call Peter Pan the Fun Time Man cause I said I ain't never growing up. Just party, party all the time.

Younger guys think something's wrong wit me now. They don't understand. I try to explain but it ain't no use. They got to find out for theyselves. Like I did. Mommy always said a hard head makes for a soft behind. But I had to find out on my own. Most the young guys in here never will get hip. They get hooked up in the games and they gone. They lost and don't know it. When I first came in here I seen guys into a hermit bag. Some the older dudes been here a long time. I couldn't understand it, neither. But now I do.

Me and Cecil still tight. He's a Muslim now. Ghafoor's his new name. Ghafoor's still my man. And I still got the Juma. That's our church. Ain't active as I once was. Warden called it sending away troublemakers, but what he really be doing was breaking up the Muslims. Mike's gone and a lot of the other brothers from our group. New guys from the other end. That's what we call Philly, the other end, brothers from Graterford and Huntingdon they kinda took over the Sunni Juma. It's different now. To me they trying to be what Arabs was fourteen hundred years ago. Being a Arab's not what I want to be. They too heavy on rules and regulations, the little nickel-dime shit that don't really mean nothing. We got enough rules and regulations. Don't need no brothers acting like they guards, telling me what to do. You wouldn't believe how silly it can get. Like you on trial again. Is you smoking, Brother Faruq? How many times you pray last week, brother? People hung up on the rules. They stagnant to the point where they won't change no more.

So I'm backed off the Muslim thing too. Least the organized part of it. Meetings and do. I still pray. Get strength from my prayers. I'll always pray.

Seems to me every religion does the same thing. They all got a bunch of rules to put people in line and then when they got em in line they take advantage. I can't buy that and that's the way they all seem to work. Muslim ain't no exception. But I learned to pray as a Muslim. So I'll keep on doing it that way. Need my prayers.

Ima get that schedule written up. Most my time away from my cell is in the hospital. My schedule's kind of different from most people's behind me working there. I like my job. Get to be around the nurses, for one thing. You know I dig that. Being around anybody who ain't locked up is a real pleasure, don't care who it is. It's nice too cause in the hospital ain't no guards in my face all day. Sometimes I carry the meals up to the hospital so I can eat in there too. Food ain't no different but it sure do taste better when you ain't sitting with them nuts in the mess hall.

Superstar nuts is in the hospital. Administration calls it a hospital but part of what it is is a mental ward. We call it Fairview West. Fairview's the state hospital where they send certified crazies, so somebody named our little unit Fairview West. They call it the Bug Center too. That's what most the men call it. The Bug Center. Everybody in here's a little bit crazy, including your brother, but they keep the real radical nuts in the hospital.

You ask the administration, they'll tell you ain't no psychiatric ward. Don't need no psychiatric ward cause ain't no psychos in West Pen, right? Psychos get tested out the population. But I know better. I'm in the hospital every day taking care of the nuts.

You got to go through two locked doors to get in. Everything's metal in the nut ward so the nuts can't tear it up. Iron beds, iron toilets. Five beds in there. Ain't but about two feet apart. Don't really matter cause the patients is handcuffed and shackled and chained to they beds at night. Daytime too, if they need it. They ain't hardly going nowhere. Bars and locks on both doors, like I said. Nurses be complaining anyway. They scared. Ain't no guards stationed in the hospital. Being a guard is part of my job. I got to keep the nuts in line. Nurses depend on me. That's why we tight. There's a story bout this dude got paroled cause he saved one the nurses when a nut attacked her. I'll look at one real hard sometimes when a nurse is working the ward and I'll be thinking, Why don't you grab her, sucker? Just grab her a little bit so she screams and I can knock you out and get my ticket out of here.

See, ain't no guards cause the administration claims ain't no psychiatric ward. Don't need guards if ain't no dangerous crazies. Matter of fact, most the dudes come in ain't really that dangerous. Weird, stone crazy, but most them just pitiful. They need help. I mean, one cat he start to jack off every time a nurse passes. Pull out his Johnson and wave it around and talk nasty. Another one a nigger hater. Cuss you like a dog. Black this and nigger that. Spit at you when you trying to do for him. Felt like busting his chops many a time but you get used to the way they be acting. They can't help it. It's pitiful, really, cause they be needing help and ain't nothing nobody round here can do for them. Just keep em chained up like animals in that funky ward.

Nurses won't go in less they have to. Then it's only wit me or one the other dudes works in the hospital. The main ward's one big room holds thirty beds, then there's a separate ward for women and one for the nuts. Nurses got enough to do anyway so most the time it's just a question of medication, pumping Thorazine in the crazies to keep em quiet. When they been quiet a day or so, you turn em loose back in the population. That's how it goes.

Doctor visits every day and writes up prescriptions and checks out the patients but he ain't no psychiatrist. What surprised me most when I first started working in the hospital was how many guys wind up in the Bug Center. Different dudes every day. The turnover's something else. Might be ten, fifteen different inmates through there in a week. Stay a couple days then another one's in the bed. All five beds is always filled. People rotating in and rotating out. It's a damn circus. We got our regulars turn up every month or so. How do you do. Welcome back and all that. But new ones too. Goes to show you how many dudes in the joint ain't wrapped too tight. Cause like I said, it's only the radical nuts get sent to the Bug Center. And one gets transferred just about every day.

You see what I'm getting at. A good percentage of the population rolls through there but the administration keeps on saying ain't no crazies nor crazy ward so nobody gets no treatment, no help. It's a crying shame.

This one young white dude they jerked off the range. From New Kensington. Only been in a week or two. A nice-looking, clean-cut dude. He didn't even know he was in jail. He been into something but it wasn't just a matter of being high. This dude was stone out his mind. Screaming and crying and carrying on. Begging people not to hurt him. He thought monsters was after him. Kept screaming monsters was after him. Gon eat him up. Monsters and God. God was hooked up in it too. Dude as scared of God as he was of them monsters. Didn't know whether he was in jail or hell or walking down the street in New Kensington.

Wasn't nothing we could do wit him. He fought us. Flailing around. Kicking, biting, gagging. Eyes popping out of his head. Help me. Help me. Then you try and help, and the cat has a fit. There's these cloth bands, like bracelets, you know. You slip them over a person's wrists so when the handcuffs go on, his skin don't get tore up. Well, I'm trying to slide em on and the dude's pleading wit me stop, stop, and screaming help all at the same time. Doing my best to help the dude but he's too wild. Couldn't get close without getting hurt. Had to pin him down and knock him out cold before we could get him settled.

Now you know somebody hurting like that needs professional help. What's he gon think waking up chained to a bed in a room with four other dudes chained down who subject to do anything or say anything? Most the time they be so doped up they don't pay one another no mind. But you might get a evil one. A troublemaker. One that teases the others. The smart kind that sees what's making another one crazy and he gets off on torturing and teasing people. Like here come them green monsters, white boy. Here they come and they sure look hungry, and shit like that.

Most of em ain't gon try and kill you or nothing like that but then again some of em is stone crazy. Don't know what they doing. They can hurt theyselves or hurt you, you ain't careful. Puts me in the position of being a guard. Have to get physical sometimes. No choice. That's why I'm here. Keep the nuts in line. Do the dirty work. Protect the nurses. Gets wild sometimes. Stone snake pit. Don't like to do some the things I got to do, but ain't no other way to handle them. They ain't getting no professional help, so we try and do the best we can.

Quiet most the time, though. Dudes is so drugged up they be sleeping they lives away. Gallons of Thorazine. Shoot em up. No problems.

One thing I've noticed since I been working in the hospital. Now I ain't no expert on nuts or nothing but being around them all the time I gets to talk wit em when they ain't nodding. Just like normal people once they calmed down except most the guys come in the Bug Center got more intelligence than the average person. Anyway, when we be rapping, sooner or later God comes up. The Bible or God or Jesus always hooked up with madness. God be punishing or chasing or talking to these guys. God or Jesus. Jesus told me set my mattress on fire. Jesus told me throw shit on the guard. It's like religion is the thing drives men crazy. Religion's hooked up in it one way or another.

Faces change but the beds always be full. One comes and another goes. Probably be my turn one day. Whole lotta guys a little off in the head before they get socked in jail but it's this place too. I mean plenty people just can't take it. If they wasn't crazy when they come through the gate, the joint drives them crazy. It's the same thing happens with a lot of guys who fuck up one way or another in the world. You know. Get theyselves jammed up and wind up doing a light bit. They ain't real crooks. Neophytes. You know what I mean. Got caught in the cookie jar so to speak. Ain't into no life of crime or nothing like that. Just ordinary dumb dudes tried to get away with something and got caught. Well, this is the place of knowledge. By the time a dude gets out of here, most likely he's a stone criminal. Or thinks he is. They got professors and Ph.D.'s in crime giving crime lessons in here. What else dudes got to talk about besides crime? You learn how to go for the big time. Fuck robbing some two-bit gas station, ain't but thirty dollars in the cash register, or breaking into some nigger's house poor as you is. That's for chumps. And you get put away for that bullshit same as they jam you up for robbing a bank. So why not hit Mellon Bank? Or Pittsburgh First National? Or Fort Knox if you got the heart and the smarts? Dig? What I'm saying is a dude comes out the joint worser off than he was when he came in. And it's spozed to be that way, far as I can tell. They saves you a place in the chow line cause they know you're coming back.

What time you have, Bro? Ain't told you nothing about running yet. Must be close to three hours, ain't it? Seems like we just started talking a minute ago. Wall clock says 1:50. I hate even looking at that damn thing. One-fifty is right, though, ain't it? Leaves us fifteen minutes if they give us a whole visit. You can be sure they won't stretch it. Not by a minute. Might cut it short a hour but you don't never get no extra minute.

I remember when it got near time for Tanya to leave. Somewhere inside my chest I was counting every second. Ticking them off one by one. Got so I knew exactly how long we had left. Didn't need to look at no clock. I'd push the clock out my mind. Course, it didn't really go away. Hands kept turning. I knew it was running down, knew it was getting closer and closer to the time for her to go. I played like if I kept my eyes off the clock it would slow down. Like I could be with Tanya another hour and the hand would only move a minute, if I didn't look at it. Like maybe she could be wit me forever if I didn't look. But I always did. I'm telling you, Bro. You gets crazy in here if you ain't careful.

. . .

Robby's silent. Twelve minutes or fifteen or seventeen left. Depends on whose clock counts. My watch has a blue face. The date is displayed in a slot to the right of center. Sixty dashes fence the perimeter of the face. If I observe long enough the minute hand's slow progress will register as it slips from one dash to the next.

No numerals circle the watch face. Inside the fence of dashes a second ring of twelve broader, longer strokes designate the hour. Twelve o'clock is a triangle instead of a slash, the window for the date is three; six, and nine o'clock are marked by slightly fatter dashes. The watch was manufactured by Seiko; it's "Automatic," contains "17 Jewels"—that official information lettered in white within the smallest circle defined by the outer rings. A second hand sweeps the blue face. Its greenish tip, luminous in the dark, orbits once, then again. Starts a third trip before I realize how long I've been staring in silence at the clock on my wrist.

I've learned to expect these silences that punctuate the talks with my brother in the prison visiting room. At first they made me uneasy. Were they a sign that we didn't have as much to say to one another as we'd thought? Would one of these pauses be the beginning of a long, embarrassing silence neither of us would be able to break? The time for visiting was so short. I felt compelled to use it, fill every second. My mind would race looking for a thread, a natural, easy way to resume the flow of talk. In the classroom when I was teaching, these kinds of pauses made me extremely uncomfortable. Had I run out of pertinent information? Had I been unmasked? Could the students see the naked emperor?

Silences troubled me—where was Robby, what was he thinking, why didn't he say something, why didn't I—until I learned to accept the quiet interludes as breathing spaces, necessary reminders of the medium—time—in which we were working. Because when we talked, we did lose track of time. And time was all we had. Time ticked or circled or dryly extinguished itself. Time was the sound of one hand clapping, a moving stillness, a roaring silence always there beneath our voices. When we stopped talking we heard it. We needed to hear it, although it contained no message except the infinite, irreducible hum of its presence.

I learned to anticipate the silences and learned to take my measure, the measure of what my brother and I were attempting to do in the few hours allotted to us in the visiting room. The silence was a reminder of limits. Mine. His. The people we had been, the likelihood or unlikelihood of our ever changing. The silence defined our mortality. Our soft individual pasts, our memories and dreams slowly taking shape, making sense, if they ever do, because they must and will form and reform within the iron silence of time.

In the quiet that swallows even the babel of the visitors' lounge I think of cages, of steel bars and locks and keys, of the thin human skin impermeable as the granite blocks of the prison wall. Against the silence I recall a world I long for in my best moments, in my freest moments, when I go about my business as if walls and limits didn't exist.

I breathe deeply. Raise my eyes from my watch to my brother's face. Robby is not waiting for me to start talking. He's not searching his mind for something to say. Silence does not stretch between us, separating us. It joins us. A common ground, a shared realization that for the moment we've come as far as we can, said what we have to say and

238

maybe . . . maybe there will be more, but there's nothing to say now . . .
just wait now for what may . . . what must come next. . . .

. . .

Mize well get back to the running, man. Mize well start telling you
about it. Got a few minutes till the man's gon grab my ass out here so
mize well get it on. . . .

POSTSCRIPT

O mar, Robby's son, made his first visit to the prison, then another; and it seems as if both Robby and Omar are beginning to understand how much they need each other, what they can do for each other. Father and son. Man to man. Geraldine, Omar's mother, understands also and she is generous and willing again to bring father and son together. That's the good news. Or part of it. Also, Robby completed his degree program and was the main speaker at a graduation ceremony in the prison, a special affair at which the graduates wore caps and gowns, and guests from the outside were allowed to attend. Mom says Robby was eloquent. I knew he'd be. Had the people clapping, rocking in their seats. Like a preacher, she said. And what kept going through her mind over and over as she listened was the phrase, *A mind is a terrible thing to waste.* She was torn by a thousand different emotions, conflicting, overwhelming emotions she didn't have time or space to sort out; but the swelling current of her son's voice, the sound of what she'd always known was inside him, suddenly, brilliantly flowing forth, made her think *A mind is a terrible thing to waste.* That phrase, riffing and twisting counterpoint through the words of Robby's graduation address, helped name what she was feeling.

Words on a page can't capture the effect of Robby's delivery but a copy of his speech will be part of this postscript. The last words of this book should be his. Good news. But then the bad news. A letter I recently received from Robby. Sweetness and light have not descended on the prison. The program that allowed him to work for a degree has been canceled. He was the first and last graduate. This book's done, but today and tomorrow the prison remains what it has been. Robby's still inside.

. . .

I gave considerable thought into giving this speech and came close to declining. To understand why, you must understand the attitude of a great many of my fellow prisoners, which is that the only graduation in prison is parole and that we here are making a farce and a mockery of our conditions.

Also, that to graduate from school in prison is not an honor but a dishonor. So not wanting to be an outcast amongst my peers gave me cause for reservations. However, after considering this, I realized I could not agree with these reasonings nor accept them. I believe to have acquired an education under whatever conditions a very honorable task, and the more extreme the conditions the more honorable the task.

I am serving a life sentence of which I have served seven years plus. Yet I am not here to plead my guilt nor innocence. I mention it only to show that even someone with the time that I possess and as bleak a future as mine can still strive to better his condition by bettering himself through education.

In our society an education has become synonymous with getting a job or getting a better job or some type of material gain. Though this is understandable in our highly competitive world, there is still more to gain. There is the self-satisfaction and self-accomplishment that is equally, if not more rewarding.

And so I give this speech in hopes that my example will help my fellow prisoners to strive for their own self-attainment. I hope that they can look at me and say, "Well, if he can do it with no guarantee that he will ever have the chance to pursue all of his goals, then why can't I?" And if through my example some of society's outcasts will find the will-power to pull their lives back together through education and become productive citizens instead of social burdens, then I will have performed a very worthwhile task. Yet even more worthwhile if through my example others follow and complete the task by showing society that once a man has proven to himself that he can do something productive and can make a life for himself and his family without resorting to crime, then maybe, just maybe, those in power will see that the way to stop the overcrowding and the high recidivism rates we now see is to give to prisoners the education and skills they need in order to become productive citizens. Maybe the Bureau of Corrections will see that they do society an injustice by holding men for two or five or ten years without demanding of these men that they at least learn a vocation before they can be released. But to the contrary, education funds here have been cut back. The Community College program of which I am graduating from here today has been cut off completely, leaving some students stuck with only a few courses to take to receive their Associate Degrees but no way to get them. It is true that Pitt does bring in courses and we have some students here tonight that are Pitt grads, but the cutbacks still hurt. For instance, the degree that I have earned, an A.S. degree in engineering, can't be earned here anymore because of the cutbacks.

I don't have any statistics but I would venture to say that more money is spent in the way of sports and entertainment for the men, and the personnel to run them, than for education. I think that to be a very sad commentary. And so I only hope—no, I pray—that these men here today go back to society and stay there and use their newly acquired skills in a productive way and that through their example our keepers reevaluate the cost of education and the essential need to send out a wiser and better equipped man than the one they received from the courts.

The theme of our program today is "The world shapes and is to be shaped." I find this to be very appropriate. Because the world we were raised in has helped to shape many of the attitudes of us graduates here today. Most of us grew up in the ghettos of Pittsburgh and the surrounding area. There the emphasis was, get the most you can get with the least amount of work. My education helped me to realize, though, that nothing worth having comes without hard work and concrete effort. But being shaped by the world through this "quick get-over" concept and seeing that this concept was folly, it is now time to take our lives and our world into our own hands and shape it for the better. To show our fellow citizens and our children that education is the means by which we can make a world where all men and women can truly be free to dream our own destinies and work hard and learn well and see those dreams become reality.

Before I conclude let me remind my fellow graduates and those

242

who might say, "Why should these criminals be given a free education?" that the cost of this education has been very high indeed. It cost the locking up in a cell fifteen out of twenty-four hours a day. It cost the tears and shame your mothers, wives, and loved ones felt when the judge publicly denounced you and sent you here. It cost the frustrating pain of unnatural separation from our female counterparts. It cost the loss of your dignity as you are treated as a child incapable of self-responsibility. It cost all the Christmases and New Years' and other holidays alone in your cell. It cost all that and more, more than I see fit to bring up here at this podium. But now here this evening we reap the benefits of our efforts. So brothers, accept your diplomas and feel proud and use them to make a better life for yourselves. And show the world that all you needed was a skill and with that skill become a productive member of society and never its burden again.

Thank you.

Hey Bro,

Just got your letter—glad to hear from you. I've been trying to maintain, it's getting real hard to do. School is finished. I got my A.S. degree and three certificates but now I've seemed to have lost a lot of my motivation—I tried to write the road story but I haven't gotten very far. I dunno, I guess everything looks so bleak it's hard to get interested in anything. But anyway, as far as my case is concerned, I put in a habeus corpus in the Federal Court 3rd Circuit. They denied it and I really don't know what else to do. I've run out of ideas. Everything seems against me. I don't mean to sound too pessimistic but things are bleaker than they've ever been. . . .

Inside here they're still tightening things up even more. There's been a note on the bulletin board informing the convicts that the administration is putting out a new rules-and-regulations booklet—and the stories that been going around are that they're going to try some pretty outrageous things—things like six phone calls a year; if you don't have a job you stay locked in your cell except for two-and-a-half-hour evening yard, all kinds of madness—and the joint is busting at the seams with cons and they're sending more every day. Two men to a cell for most of the newcomers, and they don't have enough jobs for the men and then they're cutting back on the school programs. Big time, no rehabilitation, lock em up like animals—then let them out on society crazed and angry. Shit don't make no sense but the people cry for punishment and the politicians abide them—can they really be so blind?

I'm going to start writing the road story again. I really do want it told so I must work if I want rewards. Be cool, Bro.

I SHALL FOREVER PRAY

FOR THE BEST IN PAPERBACKS, LOOK FOR THE

In every corner of the world, on every subject under the sun, Penguin represents quality and variety—the very best in publishing today.

For complete information about books available from Penguin—including Pelicans, Puffins, Peregrines, and Penguin Classics—and how to order them, write to us at the appropriate address below. Please note that for copyright reasons the selection of books varies from country to country.

In the United Kingdom: For a complete list of books available from Penguin in the U.K., please write to *Dept E.P., Penguin Books Ltd, Harmondsworth, Middlesex, UB7 0DA.*

In the United States: For a complete list of books available from Penguin in the U.S., please write to *Dept BA, Penguin,* Box 120, Bergenfield, New Jersey 07621-0120.

In Canada: For a complete list of books available from Penguin in Canada, please write to *Penguin Books Ltd, 2801 John Street, Markham, Ontario L3R 1B4.*

In Australia: For a complete list of books available from Penguin in Australia, please write to the *Marketing Department, Penguin Books Ltd, P.O. Box 257, Ringwood, Victoria 3134.*

In New Zealand: For a complete list of books available from Penguin in New Zealand, please write to the *Marketing Department, Penguin Books (NZ) Ltd, Private Bag, Takapuna, Auckland 9.*

In India: For a complete list of books available from Penguin, please write to *Penguin Overseas Ltd, 706 Eros Apartments, 56 Nehru Place, New Delhi, 110019.*

In Holland: For a complete list of books available from Penguin in Holland, please write to *Penguin Books Nederland B.V., Postbus 195, NL-1380AD Weesp, Netherlands.*

In Germany: For a complete list of books available from Penguin, please write to *Penguin Books Ltd, Friedrichstrasse 10-12, D-6000 Frankfurt Main 1, Federal Republic of Germany.*

In Spain: For a complete list of books available from Penguin in Spain, please write to *Longman, Penguin España, Calle San Nicolas 15, E-28013 Madrid, Spain.*

In Japan: For a complete list of books available from Penguin in Japan, please write to *Longman Penguin Japan Co Ltd, Yamaguchi Building, 2-12-9 Kanda Jimbocho, Chiyoda-Ku, Tokyo 101, Japan.*